PROVENCE

D1420202

I2153643

Landscapes of the Imagination

The Alps by Andrew Beattie
Flanders by André de Vries
The Thames by Mick Sinclair
The Basque Country by Paddy Woodworth
Catalonia by Michael Eaude

Landscapes

PROVENCE

A *Cultural History*

MARTIN GARRETT

Signal Books
Oxford

First published in 2006 by
Signal Books Limited
36 Minster Road
Oxford OX4 1LY
www.signalbooks.co.uk

ISBN 1-904955-23-1 Paper

Cover Design: Baseline Arts
Cover Images: John Heseltine Photograpy; Catriona Davidson; Musée d'Orsay, Paris
Design & Production: Devdan Sen

Photographs:
© Rémy Cantin, pp.x, xxix, 2, 14, 24, 35, 66, 77, 80, 138, 142, 158, 174, 207
© Catriona Davidson, pp.86, 93, 96, 170, 180, 201
© iStockphoto.com/Jan Tyler, p.61, p.210; iStockphoto.com/John Said, p.64;
iStockphoto.com/Fredrik Schjold, p.105; iStockphoto.com/Josep M. Peñalver, p.120;
iStockphoto.com/Luc Gillet, p.154; iStockphoto.com/Virgil Huston, p.160

Printed in India

CONTENTS

Preface

Roughly speaking it was diamond-shaped, pinpointed in the north by Montélimar and in the south by Marseille, and it followed the whole romantic valley of the Rhône... In the west it stretched beyond Nîmes, in the east as far as Apt.

This map of Provence was tattooed across the conveniently substantial chest of Pepe the bull-owner, or so Lawrence Durrell claims in a piece reprinted in *Spirit of Place* (1969). I have adopted much the same definition of Provence as Pepe's: an area that includes places beyond the Rhône that are technically in Languedoc, but traditionally part of Provence—Nîmes, the Pont du Gard, Beaucaire, Aigues-Mortes—and does not include the Côte d'Azur and its hinterland.

This Provence is a rich and varied one, which is why there is no room for the riches of the Riviera. It contains the "edge of the *garrigue*, windy forlorn and rather Brontë" where Durrell once lived; less forlorn orchards, olive-groves and lavender-fields; the Papal Palace in Avignon— the Versailles of its day; and metropolitan Marseille. All this can also be perceived in many different ways: the essentially optimistic Marseille of Marcel Pagnol, for instance, or the more troubled and complicated modern city of Robert Guédiguian. Perceptions can be affected by sunny or sodden memories (the Alpilles hot and cicada-loud or wet and silent in autumn fog), the maps and books you read and the pictures you look at. Maps may be read from bull-owners' chests, followed on site, savoured at home as a souvenir or aide-mémoire, or used more coldly as a necessary reference tool. It is much the same, tattooing aside, with books and paintings. If you have read Zola's account of the Aix-inspired Plassans and then go to Aix, how far do you see the city through his eyes, and how far do you alter Plassans to fit with Aix—or the modern city to fit with that nineteenth-century version? Is it different if you read the book in England or France, Normandy or Provence, French or English? Paintings by Van Gogh and Cézanne condition our sense of Provençal colours, light and forms and may in turn be conditioned by our memories of Provence. It is difficult, too, to see Fontaine de Vaucluse with an "innocent" eye: tourists and the tourist-trade have endlessly relived and reinterpreted what Sir Philip Sidney, in the late sixteenth century, could already call "Petrarch's long-deceased woes".

The true Provence, natives and others have often insisted, does exist, as does the ideal inhabitant. But there are competing versions of the ideal. Is the Provençal talkative or dour by nature, a member of a race apart or perfectly integrated with modern French life—or both? (Cézanne intensively painted his native environment but feared that people who paid too much attention to regional traditions would "embalm" Provence.) Various "true" Provences are to be encountered in this book. They have been experienced or constructed by a great range of people: troubadours and mediaevalists, sun-seekers and nineteenth-century poets in felt hats, Petrarch and Laura, the Marquis de Sade and Virginia Woolf, novel-readers, film-goers, cooks and wine-growers, connoisseurs of Roman ruins and Cézanne and Bouillabaisse.

As usual I have received a great deal of support from Helen, Philip and Ed. I should also like to thank Christine L. Corton, John Edmondson, James Ferguson, Robert Inglesfield and Gillian Rogers for their valuable questions, suggestions and practical help. I am grateful, too, to Yvette Souliers of the Maison de Tartarin in Tarascon, the staff of the Musée de l'Empéri in Salon-de-Provence, and the man from Carpentras whose wine I tasted, and with whom I talked about Petrarch, in the summer of 1998, long before working on this book.

Provençal landscape: "the grace of Italy, the harshness of
Spain; *la grandeur et la mesure*" (Pierre Girieud, 1926).

Introduction

Continuities

If Plutarch's *Life of Marius* is to be believed, local people developed a practical, if rather macabre, approach to recycling after the Romans' great victory near Aix in 102 BC: they fenced their vineyards with the bones of slain Germanic warriors.

Continuity—rearranging bones rather than discarding them—has always been a feature of the history of Provence. The name Provence itself derives from the region's period (temporarily threatened by the invading Teutons) as a *provincia romana*. And that period did not represent a complete break with the way of life of the Ligurians, Celts and Greek colonists who were there before the Romans. Many already lived in towns and were more easily assimilated to Rome than were the more northerly inhabitants of "long-haired Gaul" who were not conquered until sixty years later. Pliny the Elder, in the first century AD, felt that Provence, with its admirable people and ample resources, was more like Italy itself than a mere province.

After the collapse of Roman power Visigoths, Arabs and Franks struggled for control of southern France. But here, where the influence of Rome had been so powerful, people continued to speak a more strongly Latinate language than in other parts of France. Later in the Middle Ages troubadour poetry increased the prestige of the more literary form of the language. Even after Provençal was superseded by northern French in formal and official contexts in the sixteenth century, related dialects survived in everyday use; from the 1850s Frédéric Mistral and the *félibres* drew both on oral tradition and the language of the troubadours in their successful campaign to restore Provençal language and Provençal confidence. (On the language see further pp. xviii-xxiv)

In architecture, too, there has been a good measure of survival and continuity. Roman work both influenced, and was sometimes incorporated in, Romanesque. To go back to bones, this time in a mercifully less literal sense, Gustave Flaubert compared the surviving Roman monuments of Arles to the bones of a skeleton, protruding, here and there, from the earth. Parts of the skeleton are still buried, parts have been exposed for archaeological inspection, but many pieces have had a more eventful history: after centuries as fortresses and shanty-towns, the amphitheatres at Nîmes and Arles resumed their ancient function as places of entertainment—gladiatorial sports then, not completely dissimilar bull-fights and bull-games now as well as opera. The Maison Carrée in Nîmes has served as an imperial temple, Christian church, stable, museum, and by-word for architectural harmony. It remains central to the design and the image of the city, enhanced by its symbiotic relationship with Norman Foster's 1990s Carré d'Art. (See pp.172-3)

On a larger scale, the Rhône has remained a central artery of Provençal commerce, industry and art since prehistoric times, and the distinctive qualities of light on hill and stone which have attracted Cézanne, Van Gogh, and many a less celebrated painter, must surely have had some appeal to much earlier settlers and inhabitants.

Landscape: "infinitely complex chiselling"

In September 1644 John Evelyn and his party came to Aix through a "tract" where "all the heaths or commons are covered with rosemary, lavender, lentisks, and the like sweet shrubs, for many miles together." Travellers also marvelled at the fertility of more cultivated areas. Approaching Marseille, Evelyn noticed vines, olives, oranges, myrtle and pomegranate, as well as the villas or *bastides* "built all of freestone, and in prospect showing as if they were so many heaps of snow dropped out of the clouds amongst those perennial greens." Another seventeenth-century traveller, Mildmay Fane, Earl of Westmorland, found that the same countryside, "deserving the name of gardens rather than of fields, and abounding with golden, russet and purple apples, almost stole away my senses altogether."

Less smiling aspects of the landscape might surprise outsiders: Murray's 1892 *Handbook to the Riviera, from Marseilles to Pisa*, warns, before going on to more practical matters, that

> the Englishman who knows the S. of France only from books—who there finds Provence described as the cradle of Poetry and Romance, the paradise of the Troubadours, a land teeming with oil, wine, silk, and perfumes—has probably formed in his mind a picture of a region beautiful to behold, and charming to inhabit ... [But, for the most part,] Nature has altogether an arid character;—in summer a sky of

copper, an atmosphere loaded with dust, the earth scorched rather than parched by the unmitigated rays of the sun. The hills rise above the surface in masses of bare rock, without any covering of soil. Only on the low grounds, which can be reached by irrigation, does any verdure appear. In summer the aching eye in vain seeks to repose on a patch of green.

To the northerner, says Murray, "neither the bush-like vine nor the mopheaded mulberry... nor the tawny green olive... will at all compensate in a picturesque point of view for forests of oak, ash, and beech."

Provence contains both "perennial greens" and "masses of bare rock"; Jean Giono, in an essay of 1954, stresses how few miles separate mountain moonscapes from fertile plains, Colorado from Corot. There are also marshes, salt-pans, wild stony *garrigue*, and deep creeks or *calanques*. Virginia Woolf, in her diary for 8 April 1925, writes about the fields between Cassis and La Ciotat, like "little angular shelves cut out of the hill, and ruled and ribbed with vines". The "bare rocks and heaths" at L'Estaque move Emile Zola to nostalgic tears but, he fears, will seem merely "arid and desolate" to his correspondent Léon Hennique. The poet Guillaume Apollinaire registers a more extreme bareness while, in February 1915, on military exercises near Nîmes: country "like a skeleton. It's just like a graveyard. Nothing but sharp stones, similar to bones." In less desolate mood as well as more hospitable landscape near Saint-Rémy, Roger Fry appreciated instead, according to Woolf's book about him, "the infinitely complex chiselling of the limestone hills and the intricacy of the squares made by the almond and the olive."

The Rhône and the Durance: "Poor Bunbury"

Freddy Tondeur, in his book on the Camargue and Arles of 1968, maintains that the Rhône was "just as important as the Nile, the Euphrates or the Yangtse in the history of ancient civilization". Certainly it was an important organ of trade and culture, if at times a dangerous one. Downstream travel involved the perils of too much speed, especially at Pont Saint-Esprit, where General Jean-Antoine Marbot and his companions would have drowned on a windy day in the autumn of 1799 had they not, at the last moment, seized boat-hooks and thrust them against the bridge-pier they were about to crash into; the unhelpful boatmen, no true children of the Revolution, had panicked and "fallen to their prayers instead of working." (Marbot was on his way to take command of a division in Italy. He was travelling on the river, with two carriages awkwardly loaded onto the boat, only because his ever more dominant colleague, General Bonaparte, had commandeered all the post-horses while he inspected the fortifications of Lyon.) Going upstream, on the other hand, was slow and difficult work, in places requiring haulage by horse or man.

In the 1840s an English traveller, Selina Bunbury, experienced the dangerous force of the river. In *My First Travels* (1859) she recalls how she separated from her friends in order to visit Arles, intending to rejoin them in Avignon. She boarded the diligence for Avignon in the rain and was somewhat puzzled as to why other passengers kept, amid some agitation, getting off and cutting their journey short. Asked by the conductor if she would keep her place, she replied, "Without doubt; I am going to Avignon" and was hailed, she did not yet know why, as a brave *Anglaise*. She discovered the answer when she realized, as they went along by the Rhône in the dark, that "all that was visible of the six white horses... was just the top of their broad flat backs, rising above the water their feet dispersed." She could hear the deep anxiety in the voices of the driver and conductor. At one point she thought they had finally plunged into the river, but at last there came a cry of joy and they began to climb up out of the water.

They made it through the gates of Avignon. Even here, however, the water was already knee-deep in places. The conductor lifted the dazed and wet Miss Bunbury, "ran across the street, kicked open the door of a house, and dropped me into the passage within it." A woman reluctantly received her, but could provide neither fire nor food. In the morning the building was evacuated as the flood approached. "Where are the hotels?" she asked, and was told "In the waters". There was no hope of finding her friends. Fortunately a young man helped by taking her to a higher part of the town. Eventually she found lodgings at the foot of the Rocher des Doms. Here she was safe from the waters but could obtain provisions and fire-wood only by much flattery and persuasion. Having got the wood, Bunbury could not light the fire with the few matches available.

She called the landlady. In retrospect it was clearly enjoyable to render the Frenchwoman's scornful incredulity, and her own resourceful wheedling, into English with a slight French intonation:

> "What unheard of ignorance! Is it in that manner that you lay the wood? It is my belief you know nothing; no, you know nothing at all."
>
> "Ah! the French are so clever! It is not in our education to learn to make wood fires."
>
> "And yet you travel, you will see all: the English, they say, love to instruct themselves: they spend time and money, and lose their lives on the high roads, because they will instruct themselves. Yet you do not know how to make a fire!"
>
> "But I think I should like to learn. See now, Madame, we have not the advantages of wood fires in England; only dirty coals; and not made, as in France, on an open hearth like this. Ah! if you come to England one day, I should like to make you a coal fire in our grates, just as you would like to show me how you make a wood one."
>
> "Well, if you wish to learn; it is necessary to instruct strangers. Look then, once for all, and be ignorant no more, for when all the world is in the waters..."

In the end the old lady came every day to demonstrate the technique. Things looked up greatly when Bunbury found a market nearby where she bought delicately flavoured lamb and bunches of violets. At last, after a fortnight, the waters receded, leaving much mud and misery. She found her friends at the hotel where they had been marooned, and soon they were travelling on to drier and less landlady-dependent Grenoble.

Such happenings were, the young man who had helped Bunbury assured her, no fault of the Rhône: "It is not our river... that is to blame, but that very ill-natured one, the Durance." Swelled by melting snows in the mountains of Dauphiné, it becomes torrential; "then it meets our river, that is good enough by itself, but when it is charged with these bad neighbours, you see, Mademoiselle, it grows very mischievous." The Durance could indeed, as Murray's *Handbook for the Traveller in France* (1843) warned Miss Bunbury's generation, be a "turbulent and injurious stream". But eventually it was brought largely under control by projects including the building of a side-canal (completed in 1851) and, a century later, damming.

The Mistral and the Cicada: "I hear the symphonist more than I could wish"

The chirp of the cicada dominates Provence in summer, and the howl of the Mistral at other seasons. According to Murray's *Handbook for Travellers in the Riviera* (1891) the Mistral "or piercing N.W. wind... is beneficial in purifying the atmosphere." But it may not feel so beneficial: "it often affects the action of the liver"; Thomas Cook's *Traveller's Handbook for the Riviera and the Pyrenees* (1912) adds that it is "injurious to pulmonary sufferers".

John Ruskin recorded his impressions of the wind in his diary on 20th October 1840. He was travelling between Avignon and Aix and had

> a horrible day for weather: dust like a plague of Egypt, raised by a tremendous north wind which blew up the small stones like hail, and covered not merely the road, but the whole extent of country, with a mist of limestone—the sky darkened, all distant objects invisible for a long time together, the peasants wearing leather masks, with large round hobgoblin glass eyes.

A more local nineteenth-century sage, the entomologist Jean-Henri Fabre, studied the cicada's "strange music-box". Here are some of the less technical results of his investigation:

> When the weather is calm and warm the song of the cicada sub-divides into strophes, each lasting several seconds and separated by brief silences. A new strophe begins quite suddenly. As the abdomen oscillates more and more quickly, the song rapidly reaches its maximum volume; it stays at its peak for several seconds, then gradually weakens and becomes a mere rustle ...Once the abdominal pulsations have ceased silence obtains, lasting variable periods depending on the state of the atmosphere. Then suddenly a new strophe begins: a monotonous repetition of the first. And so on indefinitely.

Cicadas of a sort can now be heard at all seasons: shops in Arles, Les Baux, Saint-Rémy and doubtless many other places sell battery-operated versions with names like "La cigale carillon" or "La cigale qui chante"—shaped as large cicadas and presumably not meant for the southern market since, redolent of summer though the sound may be, natives must surely have heard quite enough of it in season. "I hear the symphonist more than I could wish," as Fabre puts it.

"Their fervid temperament knows no control": Dissident Southerners

Murray's *Handbook to the Riviera, from Marseilles to Pisa* (1892) says that "the character of the people appears influenced by the fiery sun and soil":

> their fervid temperament knows no control or moderation; hasty and headstrong in disposition, they are led by very slight religious or political excitement, on sudden impulses, to the committal of acts of violence unknown in the North. They are rude in manner, coarse in aspect, and harsh in speech, their patois being unintelligible, even to the French themselves... From the loudness of tone and energy of gesture, they appear always as though quarrelling when merely carrying on an ordinary conversation.

The people thus patronized had various ways of asserting their Provençal identity. There were, according to some calculations, more than 350 rebellions (many, of course, small-scale) in Provence between about 1600 and 1715. Many were still to come. Protestantism took and retained a firm hold on many parts of the region in spite of savage repression of the sort visited on the Vaudois villages of the Luberon (see pp.153-5). More recent dissidence has rather different causes, including changes in the ethnic mix of Provence. As well as people of local ancestry there are now many people from North and other parts of Africa; *pieds noirs* and their descendants—white settlers who left Algeria in the 1950s and 1960s; internal immigrants from the rest of France; and a good number from other European countries—workers, retired, second-home owners. Tensions between different groups go some way to explain the strong performance of the extreme-right in some municipal elections—and the strong reaction against these gains. (In 1995 *Front National* candidates won Toulon, Orange and Marignane with 36-37 per cent of the vote. Jean-Marie Le Pen fared well in much of Provence in the first round of the presidential election of 2002.)

The Provençal of literary tradition is usually too exuberant or comical to join rebellions or vote for extremists. He (more often than she) shows his dissidence or his difference from the northerner by loudness of tone and energy of gesture. Alphonse Daudet was one of his main originators. The passionate, gesticulating, fabulating, sun-struck Provençal appears not only in his comic novels and stories but in the more serious *Numa Roumestan* (1881), which concerns the varied fortunes of a politician of southern origin in Paris, inspired in part by the republican leader Léon Gambetta. Daudet saw himself, particularly when young, as full of southern vitality and jest. (His career nearly ended in the Rhône when, in 1863, he poetically saluted, and drunkenly threw his arms round, a bride who was crossing the boat-bridge between Arles and Trinquetaille. She was accompanied by a substantial and unamused wedding-party. A local man, "le Patron Grafet", rescued him and his fellow-revellers just in time, according to Frédéric Mistral's Memoirs.)

For Jean Giono, by contrast, the true southerner is dour and taciturn and very unlike the characters in Daudet: no doubt the stereotypical figure "who brags and plays boules and drinks pastis does exist," but the majority of Provençaux are "much more Latin [in other words Roman], much more human, much more secretive"; people like Daudet's Tartarin de Tarascon (see pp.184-8) simply do not exist. But perhaps the Provençal Quiet Man is almost as much of a myth as the loveable braggart: a distortion of the variety of human nature but as useful for Giono the story-teller as Tartarin was for his creator.

Occitan and the Troubadours

In the Middle Ages southern France spoke a language often called Provençal and known more recently as Occitan (pronounced Oxitan) because it stretched, and in modern versions stretches, far beyond Provence. "Occitan" derives from *Langue d'Oc*, as, of course, does the regional name Languedoc: the language of the land where the word for "yes" was *oc* as distinguished (first by Dante) from the northern French *oïl*, which later became *oui*. It is—in its various dialects—a Romance language like French, Italian, Catalan, Spanish, Portuguese or

Romanian. It stayed closer to Latin than French did because the south, especially Provence, was romanized earlier than the rest of Gaul and remained so longer: Occitan has *amar* for French *aimer*, *saber* for *savoir*, *ora* for *heure*. Occitan survives not only as a language still known by about two million people, and partly known by many more, but in the traces it has left in the way French is traditionally spoken in the Midi.

The great literary achievement of medieval Occitan or Provençal is the poetry of the twelfth- and thirteenth-century troubadours. A popular image persists of the troubadour bouncing and singing through the countryside rather like the minstrels in *Monty Python and the Holy Grail*. Certainly many of them seem to have moved around from court to court, or with a court as it travelled; famous practitioners were much in demand. Contrary to the popular image a number were themselves aristocrats or rulers and their verse was highly sophisticated, intricate and often difficult—qualities which partly explain its attraction for Ezra Pound.

A troubadour or, originally, *trobador*, was one who "found" poems or songs, a lyric poet who would usually compose and sing his own musical accompaniment. (We tend to think of the pieces as poems rather than songs partly because music has survived for only about ten per cent of the poems.) The first known troubadour was Guilhem IX, Duke of Aquitaine and Count of Poitou (died 1126). Other early twelfth-century exponents came from Poitou and Limousin but by mid-century troubadour poems were being written and heard in many of the courts of Languedoc, Provence, Catalonia and northern Italy. Such was the prestige of Occitan that Alfons II of Aragon, partly in support of his political involvement in Provence, himself composed troubadour verse as well as employing and encouraging others to do so. Later Dante thought it the most lyrical of languages and considered using it rather than Tuscan. This rapid diffusion was helped by the poets' use not of local dialects but of a common literary language or *koiné*. (Much the same blend was used in southern administrative documents until the fifteenth century.) And the use of a shared but specialized language encouraged the troubadours' tendency to address each other or to refer to each other's work, praising, parodying, echoing, varying. This kind of literary interest, rather than lovelorn or seductive addresses to an actual lady, is often at the centre of their work; it would be a mistake to take too literally the troubadour Bernart de Ventadorn's proclamation that songs are of little worth if they do not come *d'ins dal cor*, "from within the heart".

About half the surviving lyrics are *cansos* or love poems. (Many others are satirical or political *sirventes*.) They work within the conventions of *fin' amor* or "courtly love", widely seen as what Sarah Kay, in *A Short History of French Literature* (2003), calls "an imaginary corrective to the marriages dictated by dynastic and territorial interest" in aristocratic society. Courtly love is concerned with unfulfillable aspiration and longing, often with *amor de lonh*: "distant love", taken to the extreme in the case of the poet Jaufré Rudel who is supposed to have fallen in love with the Countess of Tripoli before he had even seen her. Kay suggests how invigorating the theme of *fin' amor* can nevertheless be: it is part of "an ongoing debate" whose agenda includes

> To what extent is love sensual or spiritual? Rational or irrational? Socially productive or isolating? Pleasurable or agonising? Morally elevating or degrading? How can one aspire to realise a love that is sustained by aspiration, or seek to overcome the very distance between oneself and the beloved that makes her desirable? Is the lover committed or ironic, delicate or obscene, ecstatic or self-controlled? Is his lady cruel or gracious, monstrous or sublime? In troubadour songs such questioning is not so much answered as amplified.

The most interesting troubadour from Provence itself is Raimbaut (c.1144-73), Count of Aurenga (Orange). He was a champion of *trobar clus*—"closed", hermetic or difficult song: *vers plu greu/fan sorz dels fatz* ("more difficult verses make fools deaf"). As this remark suggests, his work is also noted for its humour and its unusual perspectives. *Escotatz, mas no say que s'es*, begins one poem: "Listen, but I don't know what it is." He "wants to begin" but can find no name for the sort of song he wants to sing. Only some lines further on does it become apparent that this state of uncertainty is connected with a lady's slowness to grant the love she promised.

The mediaeval *Vida* or life of Raimbaut claims he was in love with the Countess of Dia, which is assumed to be Die, north of Provence on the River Drôme. The link between them is generally doubted, but she is worth mentioning as one of the finest of the *trobairitz* or female troubadours, who seem to have been aristocrats who enjoyed a freedom of expression rarely granted to other women. In her four extant *cansos* she explores love and jealousy and talks more directly about sexuality than most troubadours—an intentional contrast, perhaps, with their more abstract and exclusive approach. *Ben volria mon cavallier/tener un ser en mos bratz nut*: "I should like to hold my knight one evening naked in my arms." "When will I have you in my power?" The question, again, will not be answered.

"That detestable corruption of Italian and French"

Soon after his arrival in Uzès in 1661 Jean Racine wrote to La Fontaine about the linguistic vicissitudes experienced on the journey down. In Valence he had asked a serving-woman for a chamber-pot; only when overtaken by his "night necessities" did he discover that she had instead delivered a portable stove. "You can imagine the consequences." Communication was even more difficult in Uzès, where "I swear to you that I have as much need of an interpreter as would a Muscovite in Paris."

People from different regions of France had always had problems deciphering what each other were saying. Perhaps too they had regarded each other's speech as inferior. But writing—or élite literary singing—had been a different matter; the troubadours and their idea of courtly love had great influence on later literature outside the Midi. What had changed by Racine's time was that written Occitan had virtually disappeared. It had rapidly lost status as the French crown took over the regions where it was used. Louis XI gained Provence in 1481 and within a generation or so almost all writing was in French. (Exceptions include the *Obras et rimas prouvenssales* of Louis Bellaud de la Bellaudière (d.1588), poet and fighter in the wars of religion.) The story of the language for the next four hundred years was one of progressive marginalization. Occitan, and southern, Occitan-influenced French, became mainly oral and so subject to greater regional variations and less esteemed by the educated and the powerful. There was no possibility that, even if he had stayed longer than a year in Uzès, Racine would have started composing tragedies in the local language. For him it was not even a single tongue but, he was soon "beginning to realize", a "mixture of Spanish and Italian". Sometimes, he tells La Fontaine, he has recourse to those languages. Many travellers went on making much the same point about what James Boswell, in his journal in December 1765, condemns as "that detestable corruption of Italian and French".

Restoring the Language: the Félibrige

French, in Provence as in other regions, went from strength to strength. National life was centred increasingly on Paris, especially after the Revolution. In the nineteenth century state schooling arrived, teaching French and often dismissing or even punishing the use of local dialects and languages. Mass communications also played an important part in spreading standard French and reducing difference. French is now, of course, the normal, everyday language of most people in Provence, even if some speak with distinctive local accents. But a good number of people today know Occitan or have some acquaintance with it, perhaps knowing traditional songs or expressions and having some sense of how the language works. This situation results in no small part from the activities of the group who took the name *Félibrige* and set out, in the mid-nineteenth-century, to re-establish the high status of what they called Provençal. The group originated in Provence and promoted a version of the Occitan which had survived there, but stimulated similarly vigorous activity in Languedoc and elsewhere in the Midi. Essentially they combined the language as they heard it being spoken, especially in the countryside, with elements of the medieval literary *koiné*. Frédéric Mistral (1830-1914), who emerged as the most important of the *félibres*, produced not only poetry but *Lou Tresor dóu Felibrige* (1878-86), the dictionary which established meanings, spellings and variations and staked the claim of the language once more to be taken seriously.

Joseph Roumanille (1818-91), Mistral's teacher in Avignon and early encourager, was the father of the movement. In the early 1850s Roumanille and Mistral were associated with several other young poets beginning to write in Provençal, most notably Théodore Aubanel (1829-86). In 1854, at the Château de Font-Ségugne near Avignon, seven of the poets formally established the *Félibrige*, which took its name from a reference, in a traditional poem Mistral knew, to *li sèt felibre de la Lèi*, "the seven Doctors of the Law". The best-known writings of the *félibres* include Mistral's long poems beginning with *Mirèio* (1859) and lyrical

"His eyes alight, his cheeks afire with inspiration, proud but smiling kindly ... taking great steps as he paced about composing" (Alphonse Daudet, "Le Poète Mistral").

pieces by Aubanel like "La Venus d'Arle". They sought not only to practise and promulgate the traditional tongue but to spread awareness of, and pride in, Provençal customs and legends and identity. They went to traditional festivals around Provence, promoted them or revived them through their writing, and themselves introduced new processions, fêtes and presentations. Much happened in the open air—in the Provençal sun, at the ancient sites, they celebrated. Aubanel's play *Lou Pan dóu pecat* (*The Bread of Sin*) was performed at Les Alyscamps in Arles, for instance.

The *Félibrige* was not without its divisions. Aubanel's passionately sensual poetry won him the disfavour of the Catholic establishment and, together with his view that Provençal literature was a branch of French literature, it broke his friendship with the more conservative Roumanille. The more general conservatism of the movement was a reason for hostility from many quarters. It is easy to see how its emphasis on purity of language, tradition and race matched later official attitudes in Vichy France. Occitan supporters in general, however, have never been tainted with such associations.

At an earlier stage Emile Zola feared, unnecessarily as it turned out, that the likes of Mistral would split up France. As a champion of things modern and scientific he was suspicious of the *félibre* emphasis on the past. But one of the most provocative attacks on Mistral comes from Jean Giono in a piece first published in 1957. For him Mistral represents a complete misrepresentation of Provence: "a poet of agricultural fairs, a character with a goatee and a big hat, a servant of the throne and the altar, full of bombast, falseness and self-importance". If "my language had been that gibberish (*baragouin*)... I would have learnt Chinese in order to express myself."

"The rational, right and proper food"
Southern France, observes Fynes Moryson in his *Itinerary* (1617),

> by the benefit of the air and sun, yields figs, grapes, citrons, peaches, pomegranates, chestnuts, rich wine, and all delicate fruits, and all the fields are made odoriferous by wild rosemary, myrtles, palm-trees, and many sweet herbs.

There are also melons, garlic (Ford Madox Ford talks about "the good Provençal and his Eden-garlic-garden"), olives, and—sniffed out by pigs or dogs, sold at a high price—black truffles. With fresh fish and meat scented with the "sweet herbs", such fare is, says Elizabeth David in *French Provincial Cooking* (1960), "the rational, right and proper food for human beings to eat". It is "civilised without being over-civilised".

Outsiders have, however, met with some surprises, pleasant and unpleasant: Ford enjoyed "a miraculous platterful of microscopic songsters" in Arles—to the horror of his more ornithologically responsible readers; James Pope-Hennessy endured "that particularly nauseating intestinal dish called *andouillettes*" in a dingy hotel in Apt where "there seemed no question of a menu"; Lady Fortescue (*Perfume from Provence*, 1935) found it necessary to explain to her home audience that courgettes are "things like little round or oval vegetable marrows". *Aïoli* may also be a new experience: the Provençal garlic and olive-oil [*ai* and *oli*] mayonnaise so strong that, Frédéric Mistral told his young friend Paul Mariéton, the Greeks gave it to their soldiers "to give them courage". Other distinctive concoctions include *tapénade* or *tapenado*—from the Provençal *tapèno*, "caper"—made with capers, black olives, tuna, anchovies, thyme, olive oil and garlic, and *anchoïade* or anchovy relish containing thyme and wine vinegar.

The most debated dish, however, is Bouillabaisse (from *bouillir*, "boil", and *baisser*, "lower"—important stages in the rapid cooking of the dish). "There is no authentic bouillabaisse without white wine," Elizabeth David was told; and "it is a heresy of the most deadly kind to add white wine; the best bouillabaisse includes a *langouste* and mussels; *langouste* and mussels are only added in Paris because they haven't the other requisite fish." Dispute rages especially over this question of which fish must and must not be included. W. M. Thackeray's popular "Ballad of Bouillabaisse" expresses the belief that

> This Bouillabaisse a noble dish is—
> A sort of soup, or broth, or brew,
> Or hotchpotch of all sorts of fishes,
> That Greenwich never could outdo.

But George Augustus Sala (*A Journey Due South: Travels in Search of*

Sunshine, 1885) begs leave genially to point out that Thackeray's dish "was more of the nature of a 'matelote', which may be compounded of carp, roach, dace, eels, and crawfish, stewed with fine herbs and red wine, and garnished with mushrooms." Sala gives the more authentic versions of "the famous Provençal *chef* Durand". But even Durand cited two different forms, "that 'à la Marseillaise' and that 'à la Nîmoise'." The Marseille method is as follows: first briefly heat some onion and good oil;

> Then your assortment of sea-fish must be cut in slices, notably your loup [sea-bass], your moraine, your whiting, your rascasse [sea-scorpion] , and your langouste, or cray-fish; but of this last only the tail of him. The slices of fish are then to be placed in the stewpan together with some well chopped parsley and garlic, a slice of lemon, a tomato from which the water and the seeds have been expressed: the whole seasoned with salt, pepper, and a little powdered saffron. The whole mass is then to be sprinkled, and that liberally, with good olive oil, and it is then to be thoroughly "wetted" with a glass of dry white wine and some fish bouillon...

"Double-quick boiling" produces a reduced sauce which is poured onto fine white bread (or, in some recipes, toast rubbed with garlic). The fish-slices are served separately. But in the Nîmes method, according to Durand, "among the fish red mullet, soles, and eels are admitted" and the dish is "served up with a sauce made from the boiled and pounded liver of a fish called a 'baudroie' [angler-fish], mingled with the yolks of three eggs, some good oil, and a glass of Madeira." The sauce is not poured onto bread but served with the fish and "encircled by 'croûtons' of bread fried in butter". There is not much garlic and none of the "almost unpleasantly prominent" Marseillais saffron.

But "genuine bouillabaisse", Sala concludes, whatever the exact ingredients,

> is a fisherman's dish—a rough and ready one, and with a flavour so high, as to require the stomach of a fisherman—or of a horse—to appreciate it thoroughly. The finest bouillabaisse is not to be had at a restaurant. It is best cooked in an iron pot over a furnace in a hole in a rock under the lee of the sail of a speronare [a large Mediterranean

sailed boat]. Most appropriate dinner costume—a red woollen
nightcap or a sou'-wester, a well-knitted jersey, and bucket boots.

For more indoor types, one might add, and for those not endowed
with fishermen's stomachs, there are alternative fish dishes. Fish soup,
which has the advantage of being much cheaper than bouillabaisse, is
served traditionally "avec sa rouille": *rouille*—"rust"—contains garlic,
spices and egg-yolk and is, declares the for ever colourful Roy Campbell,
"the spur and rowel of both one's thirst and one's appetite". Or there is
"that strange Provençal concoction, the oily, creamy cod porridge known
as *brandade de morue*" (Hugh Johnson, *Wine*, 1966).

Provençal meat dishes include *boeuf en daube*, a casserole made
usually with stewing steak, bacon and juniper berries, among other
ingredients. Jean Giono, in a 1950s essay reprinted in the posthumous
collection *Provence* (1993), remembered "the best *boeuf en daube* in the
world". It was to be found at a remote inn on the desolate Plateau
d'Albion, south-east of Mont Ventoux. Here, in the years before the First
World War, a great cauldron was kept going through the winter. It was
never emptied; "day after day they put in beef, hare, wild boar, wild
rabbits, red wine, virgin oil, bacon, bunches of thyme, of laurel, of
nutmeg." The portion, which you served yourself, was three ladlefuls in
a big soup bowl. It cost very little—18 *sous*—and came with as much
bread and wine as you wanted. The farmers and farmworkers who made
up the clientele (there were no villages for miles) needed to be well
fortified. What the innocent reader expects to be one more Provençal
idyll proves to be something more disturbing (although Giono very
likely invented or exaggerated the details, as it was his passionate story-
teller's habit to do). For the customers have come, once the bowls are set
aside, to gamble. In this improbable "*véritable Monaco*" they will stake
not ten francs, not ten thousand, but everything: farms with their barns,
stables, cowsheds and everything in them, cupboards and their contents,
even children's money-boxes, even "the knitting still attached to its
needles". Everything, in fact, but the clothes the family stand up in and
will have to put on the following day when they leave the home that is
no longer theirs. They would do better, one cannot help thinking, to
stick to their *boeuf en daube*.

"Oh, for a beaker full of the warm South": Wine

Wine and the Mediterranean south, where viticulture first developed, have become intimately associated. In "Ode to a Nightingale" (1819) John Keats, exploring various ways to escape from "the weariness, the fever, and the fret", longs for

> a draught of vintage that hath been
> Cooled a long age in the deep-delvèd earth,
> Tasting of Flora and the country green,
> Dance, and Provençal song, and sunburnt mirth!
> Oh, for a beaker full of the warm South.

Vines, like olives, were first planted in Provence, as far as we know, by the Greek founders of Marseille. They also imported great quantities of wine from the Greek colonies of southern Italy, but local growers were well established by Roman imperial times. In later centuries most of the wines of Provence were little known outside their own area, but exports began to increase in the first half of the nineteenth century, when the total size of the vineyards doubled to reach about 90,000 hectares. There was then, however, a long period of decline because of the popularity of rival wines from Languedoc and various outbreaks of disease, culminating in the wasting attack of the louse *Phylloxera vastatrix* which, beginning in the 1860s, spread from the south to the whole of France and beyond.

Today many of the most esteemed wines are red—Keats' "the true, the blushful Hippocrene/With beaded bubbles winking at the brim/And purple-stainèd mouth"—or rosé. The most celebrated rosé is what Roy Campbell in *Light on a Dark Horse* calls "the rosy-brown quarrel-making wine of Tavel (of which one should beware)". For Hugh Johnson in *Wine* (1966) the colour is "leaning towards the onion-skin". While clearly less given to quarrelling than the combative Campbell, Johnson agrees that Tavel is strong. "High-flavoured", it "goes equally well with the herb-smoky grills and the astonishingly thirst-provoking *aioli*" or with *brandade de morue*. Among the white wines are Cassis, sometimes drunk with *bouillabaisse*—not related to the blackcurrant liqueur *crème de cassis*—and the sweet Muscat de Beaumes de Venise, where *beaumes* means caves and *Venise* is from the former papal enclave, the *Comtat Venaissin*.

"A draught of vintage .../Tasting of Flora and the country green,/Dance, and Provençal song, and sunburnt mirth!" (John Keats).

Much the most talked-of wine is red Châteauneuf-du-Pape. The Avignon popes, including Alphonse Daudet's fictional Pope Boniface in "La Mule du Pape", had vineyards and a castle at Châteauneuf. One reason for the quality of the wine (which most of us can afford only to taste rather than to buy) is that it was at Châteauneuf in 1923 that the first *appellation* regulations were drawn up. In order to preserve the purity of the wine, vine-growers led by Baron Le Roy of Château Fortia drew up a charter specifying the area to be cultivated, varieties of grape, minimum alcohol level, timing of the harvest, and many other aspects of production. The whole of France adopted the *appellation contrôlée* system in 1935.

Châteauneuf-du-Pape is at the centre of Roy Campbell's ideal meal, to be consumed with friends after vigorous participation in the bull-related sports of the Camargue (*Taurine Provence*):

> a bottle of Châteauneuf du Pape from whose black column the setting sun strikes one or two Aldebaran-like, crimson, starry sparks; green olives scented with fennel; silver bread; a poutarque [or *boutargue*— black mullet caviar] or two cured by ourselves from our own fishing... and then the gigot of a lamb that all its life never ate anything but rosemary fennel and thyme.

Less exalted drinks include *Myro*, made with *crème de myrtilles* (bilberries) and rosé or red wine; and *pastis*. The highly alcoholic absinthe, containing wormwood and aniseed, was banned in France in 1915. The Pernod company, founded at the end of the eighteenth century, then began to produce a weaker aniseed-flavoured spirit. It became known as *pastis* either from *pastiche* or from the Provençal *pastiser*, "stir". Various other companies (and, less legally, individuals) produced their own brands of the drink, especially popular in the south. Ricard is especially associated with Marseille; Paul Ricard's drink, which contains liquorice as well as aniseed, was licensed in 1938. *Pastis* rapidly established itself as the alcohol southerners were supposed to drink, particularly while playing *pétanque*. A slow drink is the necessary accompaniment of a game where, as the sociologist Laurence Wylie observes, "the members of a team may argue for fifteen minutes about how a shot should be made"; as much as physical skill it is "the wit, the humour, the sarcasm, the insults, the oaths, the logic, the experimental demonstration, and the ability to dramatise a situation [that] give the game its essential interest."

Chapter One
Papal Provence: Avignon

In July 1844, having steamed briskly down the Rhône from Lyon, Charles Dickens observed "the broken bridge of Avignon, and all the city baking in the sun; yet with an under-done-pie-crust, battlemented wall, that never will be brown, though it bake for centuries." He seems to have landed without problems, in spite of the warning issued a year earlier in *Murray's Handbook for Travellers in France* that steamer-passengers "are left in the hands of the porters of Avignon, who are notoriously a brutal set, and whose exactions and insolence ought to be repressed by the police." Soon Dickens was enjoying the streets hung with grapes and blooming with oleander; they were old, narrow streets,

> shaded by awnings stretched from house to house. Bright stuffs and handkerchiefs, curiosities, ancient frames of carved wood, old chairs, ghostly tables, saints, virgins, angels, and staring daubs of portraits, being exposed for sale beneath, it was very quaint and lively. All this was much set off, too, by the glimpses one caught, through a rusty gate standing ajar, of quiet sleepy court-yards, having stately old houses within, as silent as tombs. It was all very like one of the descriptions in the Arabian Nights.

The streets were even—rare praise from Dickens—"tolerably clean". And the following morning, too, there was a "delicious breeze" in the city famed for its irritating windiness. The Baedeker *Handbook to Southern France* (1891) gives the more conventional nineteenth-century account of Avignon: "nearly all its streets are narrow, tortuous, badly paved and dirty, and a stay there is not very pleasant, principally on account of the Mistral; hence the saying: 'Avenio ventosa, cum vento fastidiosa, sine vento venenosa.'" ("Windy Avignon, loathsome when it's windy, poisonous when it's not.")

Bruce, the narrator of *Monsieur, or the Prince of Darkness* (1974), the

first novel in Lawrence Durrell's Avignon Quintet, has personal reasons for seeming to endorse the handbook's sleazy Avignon rather than Dickens' sunny one. When he arrives following the unexpected suicide of his friend Piers,

> its shabby lights and sneaking cats were the same as ever; overturned dustbins, the glitter of fish scales, olive oil, broken glass, a dead scorpion. All the time we had been away... it had stayed pegged here at the confluence of its two green rivers. The past embalmed it, the present could not alter it... It had always waited for us, floating among its tenebrous monuments, the corpulence of its ragged bells, the putrescence of its squares.

Such putrescence has, apparently, its own delights, its indelible associations at least; the city "haunted one although it was rotten, fly-blown with expired dignities, almost deliquescent among its autumn river-damps. There was not a corner of it that we did not love."

The "Babylonian Captivity"

Avignon, as Edward Gibbon puts it, "flourished above seventy years the seat of the Roman pontiff and the metropolis of Christendom". At first the move appeared to be temporary; the papal court was already, like those of other medieval rulers, fairly peripatetic, and Clement V, the former Archbishop of Bordeaux, happened to be in France at the time of his election in 1304. Partly to avoid the papacy falling too completely under the control of King Philippe le Bel of France, Clement moved to Avignon in 1309; it was owned by the King of Naples, who was a papal vassal, and it adjoined the papal territory of the Comtat Venaissin. (Residence in Rome, which was dominated at this time by feuding clans of lawless noblemen, was not a pleasant alternative.) French influence remained strong: the Pope created enough French cardinals to end the Italian majority in the Sacred College, ensuring successive elections of Frenchmen to the papacy. But the King of France could prevail to only a limited extent over some of Clement V's more forceful successors. The most vigorous was Clement VI (reigned 1342-52), who bought the city from his ward, Queen Giovanna I of Naples, for 80,000 gold florins.

Clement VI is supposed to have said that his predecessors "did not know how to be popes." He stood up belligerently for papal rights and powers, his court was luxurious and at times riotous, nepotism and pluralism flourished in the church, and he nearly bankrupted the Curia. But Diana Wood in her useful study of the Pope reminds us of some of Clement's virtues: during the Black Death he supervised nursing care and burial arrangements at his own expense; he is believed to have distributed 30,000 loaves of bread every day; his funeral ceremony in 1352 was simple, in deference to his wish that money should be spent instead on the poor. He was also a man with intellectual and artistic interests. An autograph manuscript which survives in the Vatican Library shows his interest in astronomy, astrology and medicine. Wood further draws attention to Clement's attempt to learn Hebrew, his involvement in a commission which attempted to reform the Julian calendar, his patronage of the music theorist and astrologer Jean de Murs, his enthusiastic book-collecting, his interest in the classics and patronage of the greatest classicist of the age, Francesco Petrarca or Petrarch.

Petrarch's father, a notary, had, like Dante, been exiled from Florence by his political opponents. The family lived in Arezzo and later, drawn like many other Italians to the employment opportunities of the papal court, in southern France. Petrarch was closely involved with the papacy from the 1320s, was granted several benefices, and was twice offered a bishopric by Clement VI. But in spite of the material comforts of his position, he railed tirelessly at the corruptions of Avignon and demanded a return to Rome. In Latin letters, especially those of the *Liber sine nomine*, the point is made through a battery of biblical and classical allusions. This place is worse than Tartarus, the ancient hell. There is no Ariadne to thread the way through this loveless, faithless, labyrinth. Above all this place is Babylon. The Hebrews were captives in Babylon, kept from Jerusalem as the faithful are kept from Rome. Babylon was identified with Babel and its proud, ungodly tower. In the Book of Revelation we meet the Whore of Babylon. And so Avignon is "the modern Babylon, heated, raging, obscene, terrible", where there is, Petrarch intones, "no piety, no charity, no faith, no reverence for God, no fear, no holiness, no justice, nothing of equitableness, nothing trustworthy, nothing human."

Clement VI, however, had no intention of leaving Avignon and neither had his successor Innocent VI who, as if to emphasize the point, built the city ramparts, Dickens' "under-done-pie-crust". Petrarch himself left permanently for Italy in 1353. If an individual was responsible for the popes' eventual return to Rome twenty-five years later it was not him but the purposeful St. Catherine of Siena. She came to Avignon to persuade the vacillating Gregory XI to come home; but, as Gibbon says, her "celestial admonitions were supported by some arguments of temporal policy." Southern France, periodically filled with marauding mercenaries as a by-product of the Hundred Years' War, was no longer the safe haven it once had been, and the Romans both "strenuously invited" him and threatened to elect their own pope if he did not come.

But this was not the end of the story. Gregory died in 1378, a little over a year after his return. Urban VI was elected in Rome but soon fell out with many of his cardinals, who chose a new Avignon pope, Clement VII. The resulting "Great Schism"—a pope in Rome and a rival pope in Avignon—was fully resolved only in 1417. After that papal legates or vice-legates, not popes, were despatched to Avignon, which remained papal property until France finally took possession in 1791. (The most noteworthy building erected in the time of the legates, opposite the Papal Palace, is the former Hôtel des Monnaies or Mint (1619), now the music conservatory. On the facade, by way of reference to the Borghese arms of Pope Paul V and his nephew the Legate, an eagle and a dragon stand flamboyantly on great swathes of fruit, vegetables and vegetation which are suspended from lions' mouths.)

The Palace of the Popes: "an impregnable fortress, a luxurious palace, a horrible prison"

The immense thickness and giddy height of the walls, the enormous strength of the massive towers, the great extent of the building, its gigantic proportions, frowning aspect, and barbarous irregularity, awaken awe and wonder. The recollection of its opposite old uses: an impregnable fortress, a luxurious palace, a horrible prison, a place of torture, the court of the Inquisition: at one and the same time, a house of feasting, fighting, religion and blood: gives to every stone in its huge form a fearful interest, and imparts new meaning to its incongruities.

The impressive size noticed by Dickens and everyone else results from the fact that two palaces, Old and New, have in fact been combined. To oversimplify slightly, the Old Palace, built mainly by Benedict XII (reigned 1334-42), is on the left if you stand facing it and Clement VI's New Palace is on the right. Benedict had been a Cistercian monk and this background is probably reflected in the relative simplicity and austerity of the architecture he commissioned. Clement liked to live on a grander scale, and his massive expansion of the building made him, for Petrarch, "Nimrod, builder of towers"—Nimrod in *Genesis* ruled Babel—but there did need to be room for the vast machinery of church government, the papal court, treasury and archives. And headquarters needed to be well fortified enough to withstand the French king or any other aggressor.

Dickens' perception of incongruity was shared by Prosper Mérimée, for whom the crenellated palace looked more like "the citadel of an Asiatic tyrant" than "the residence of the Vicar of a God of Peace". Certainly the fortress impression remains. Inside, the now mostly bare halls can give little impression of fourteenth-century court splendour. When the palace housed a barracks, between 1822 and 1906 and again during the First World War, a much greater imaginative leap was required. Henry James saw it "left in the befouled and belittered condition which marks the passage of the military after they have broken camp". Soldiers "in one of the big vaulted rooms" (they fuse in memory) were "lying on their wretched beds, in the dim light, in the cold, in the damp, with the bleak, bare walls before them, and their overcoats, spread over them, pulled up to their noses." On an earlier, damper visit, James maintains, "an umbrella was not superfluous in some of the chambers and corridors of the romantic pile."

In the time of the barracks and long before, parts of the palace had been, as Dickens mentions, a prison. In the Tour de Trouillas was lodged the best known prisoner, Cola di Rienzo, the "Last of the Tribunes" of Bulwer-Lytton's once popular novel *Rienzi* (1835) and the early Wagner opera derived mainly from it. But Dickens was more interested in another sort of prisoner, and in the extraordinary, ghoulish guide whom he christened "Goblin":

A little, old, swarthy woman, with a pair of flashing black eyes... came out... with some large keys in her hands, and marshalled us the way that we should go... Such a fierce, little, rapid, sparkling, energetic she-devil I never beheld. She was alight and flaming, all the time. Her action was violent in the extreme. She never spoke, without stopping expressly for the purpose. She stamped her feet, clutched us by the arms, flung herself into attitudes, hammered against walls with her keys, for mere emphasis: now whispered as if the Inquisition were there still: now shrieked as if she were on the rack herself; and had a mysterious, hag-like way with her forefinger, when approaching the remains of some new horror—looking back and walking stealthily, and making horrible grimaces—that might alone have qualified her to walk up and down a sick man's counterpane, to the exclusion of all other figures, through a whole fever.

Goblin, whose ferocity no doubt contributed to that of such other French females as Mme Defarge in *A Tale of Two Cities*, showed the party where the Inquisitors sat in judgement (Clement VI's Salle de la Grande Audience). They went on to the torture chamber with its funnel-shaped roof "made of that shape to stifle the victims' cries". (We now realize that this was the roof of the kitchen, whose funnel had the more wholesome function of releasing smoke and fumes.) Here they were treated to a horribly graphic description of the water torture. To inflict this was, Dickens reflected, strange conduct for God's "chosen servants, true believers in the Sermon on the Mount". Next Goblin displayed the Tour de la Glacière, where in 1791 sixty victims of the Revolution were hurled, dead or alive, into an oubliette and "a quantity of quick-lime was tumbled down upon their bodies." Finally she flung open a trap-door to reveal the black "*oubliettes de l'Inquisition*". But to see the sun shining through the "gaping wounds" in the wall made Dickens feel "a sense of victory and triumph. I felt exalted with the proud delight of living in these [allegedly] degenerate times, to see it."

The Grand Tinel; Pope Clement's Feast
The 48-metre long Grand Tinel or Banqueting Hall, with restored barrel-vault, now displays three Gobelins tapestries in which Alexander triumphs at Babylon, Pope Leo stops Attila before Rome amid much

trumpeting, flag-waving and gesturing, and Louis XIV receives Cardinal Chigi. (The first two are seventeenth-century, the third nineteenth.) Apart from the size of the room there is little to suggest the spectacular feasts held here in Clement VI's time, when the walls were frescoed and the vault, at his command, covered with blue, gold-studded cloth to suggest the vault of heaven.

Some impression of how Clement and his court feasted on great occasions is, however, available. In April 1343 he was entertained lavishly by Cardinals Annibaldo di Ceccano and Pedro Gomez at a palace near Avignon. The occasion was described enthusiastically by an anonymous Florentine witness who clearly felt none of Petrarch's reservations about court life. Nine courses, each sub-divided into three, were served, followed by dessert. After the third course a "castle" was brought in with, in or on it, "a huge stag... a wild boar, roebucks, hares, rabbits, all of which appeared to be alive but had been cooked." The structure was guided by squires and accompanied by gentlemen playing various instruments. After the fourth course a group of the cardinal's clerics and squires announced to the Pope that his host had given him a magnificent white destrier. With surprising restraint, they did not bring the war-horse in, handing over instead a more manageable ring, with huge sapphire and topaz, which the Pope at once put on his finger. It was said, the Florentine eagerly reports, that the destrier was worth 400 gold florins and the ring 150. Others present, from the sixteen cardinals to the twenty-four sergeants-at-arms, were given gifts appropriate to their rank: jewelled rings for the princes of the church, belts of silver worth three florins for the guards. After the fifth course in came a fountain topped by a small tower and column from which flowed five different sorts of wine. Disposed around the fountain were peacocks, pheasants, partridges and cranes, again seemingly alive but clearly edible. There was more music too.

The Pope's new horse may not have been produced, but after the seventh course ten other destriers entered the hall, bearing knights who displayed di Ceccano's arms—a useful reminder as to whom His Holiness should be thanking. An equal number of mounted opponents filed in and proceeded to fight a tourney for an hour. In between other courses there was more combat and more *dolce melodia*. Towards the end, two trees were piloted to Clement's table: one of silver with golden apples, pears, figs, peaches and grapes, the other green and hung with candied fruits of every colour. Afterwards came yet more music, dancing, and a practical joke which the Pope enjoyed from a window: a false bridge deposited a number of innocent priests, monks and others in the river Sorgue as the instruments played on.

Painting the Palace

Many of the rooms in the Papal Palace were originally frescoed. Here and there painted fragments and corners have survived, and the palace also houses some examples from elsewhere in Avignon like the tantalizing traces of a mid-fourteenth-century drinking stag—its antlers a variation on the rapidly sketched fronds which fill the background—from the *livrée* or cardinal's palace of Saint-Ange. More complete decoration is to be seen in some areas, including the work of Matteo Giovannetti, a master of the Sienese school who became official painter to Clement VI. Between 1346 and 1348 Giovannetti covered the small chapel of St. Jean, off the Consistory, with scenes from the lives of the two Saint Johns, the Baptist and the Evangelist. An early exponent of perspective, he made skilled use of the chapel's architecture, especially the window-alcoves. (The lower areas were damaged when the Palace was a barracks: restoration took place in the 1960s.)

On either side of the east window the Baptist and Christ advance towards each other; symbolically the window functions to suggest the light—enlightenment—of their meeting, or perhaps the River Jordan in which the prophet is about to baptize the Messiah. The heavily-bearded John steps forward with an air of certainty. Christ advances more slowly, his hand lifted more gently; he is fully robed while the lower legs of the man of the desert and the Jordan are bare. They look across at each other while some of the figures around them look outwards, perhaps prompting our response to the theologically important moment portrayed. Direction of gaze also seems to be important in the most striking scene concerning John the Evangelist, the Raising of Drusiana. Here one of the spectators, a woman with ginger hair, pale headdress and blue robe, looks serenely towards us while her neighbour, with loose ginger-gold hair, is either looking sideways at her or towards the resurrected Drusiana, who raises her arms and herself at a gesture from the wise, elderly saint.

Above this chapel, off the Grand Tinel, is the Chapel of St. Martial, decorated by Giovannetti and his assistants in 1344-6. The frescoes narrate the legend of the saint who brought Christianity to Clement's home province, the Limousin. If blue, green, red, brown and white are used in the lower chapel, here the blue of heaven—the roof-vault is extensively frescoed—is dominant. (There are also gold stars, light grey buildings, and yellowy-brown hills.) Again there are some interesting individual figures, but the atmosphere is less calmly contemplative than in the lower chapel. There is more interest in the soldiers' realistic armour, in grand architectural backdrops; there are more signs of earthly power, aptly enough since this was the room in which cardinals would cast votes to choose the next Pope (in theory a matter for spiritual consideration, hence the use of a chapel). In one scene St. Peter, fount of papal authority, issues St. Martial with his staff.

Two more private rooms have frescoes by other artists. The Chambre du Pape was decorated by French and Italian painters possibly in the mid-1330s for Benedict XII (but possibly, like so much else, for his successor Clement VI). Here are patterns of curling vines and oak-branches with birds, squirrels and weasels. Empty painted bird-cages are perhaps a playful reference to real birds—nightingales were among the more popular—kept in the room, or simply to the free birds in the frescoes. Animals are more important in the best-known painted room in the palace, the Chambre du Cerf, where the falconer in particular—straight standing in red robe and blue cloak, a falcon on his white-gloved hand, dogs at his heels—has attained almost the iconic significance of the Dame à la Licorne tapestries in Paris: an icon, in this case, of idealized aristocratic leisure in a green romance background.

The Chambre du Cerf, which takes its name from the stag hunted in one of the scenes, was Clement VI's study and bedroom. The frescoes were among the first he commanded, in 1343. The main hunting scenes—the pursuit of the stag by hunters and hounds, of a rabbit by a ferret, fishermen around a well-stocked pool—emerge from a lush and detailed background full of animals, of fruits, of men and boys gathering pomegranates and flushing birds out of trees. Children play by a stream. Birds are everywhere, as in real medieval countryside, which must have been loud with birdsong to a degree now difficult to imagine. It feels an intimate place after all the great halls of the Palace: small enough for the occupant to be simultaneously aware of several different painted scenes, for them to form the visual and sometimes, in ways we cannot know, the imaginative background of life in the room. James Pope-Hennessy sums up the overall effect:

> The scenes are laid in a countryside of poetical and formal beauty—feathery trees with slender trunks and blue-green leaves grow amidst hummocks of flowered grass, while in the background is an undergrowth of close, trim foliage, thickets of wild briar, ferns and white hawthorn. This landscape, carried round all four walls, must have given the illusion of stepping into an enchanted wood. The persons and the animals who inhabit these scenes look tranquilly preoccupied, and seem to be living happily within the dimensions of their painted paradise.

Notre-Dame des Doms

Dickens entered the cathedral during a mass attended by "several old women, a baby, and a very self-possessed dog" which trotted regularly between the altar-rail and the door, "as methodically and calmly, as any old gentleman out of doors". The ex votos in the chapels were another curiosity. "They were all little pictures: each representing some sickness or calamity from which the person placing it there, had escaped, through the interposition of his or her patron saint, or of the Madonna." One crude picture showed

> a lady... having a toe amputated—an operation which a saintly personage had sailed into the room, upon a couch, to superintend... In another case, a lady was in the very act of being run over, immediately outside the city walls, by a sort of pianoforte van. But the Madonna was there again. Whether the supernatural appearance had startled the horse (a bay griffin), or whether it was invisible to him, I don't know; but he was galloping away, ding dong, without the smallest reverence or compunction.

Votive offerings were, Dickens decides, an early compromise between paganism and Christianity. But—he attempts to sound conciliatory after the Protestant fun—"I could wish that all the other compromises were as harmless. Gratitude and Devotion are Christian qualities; and a grateful, humble Christian spirit may dictate the observance."

Now, instead of naive pictures, there are discreet plaques saying "Reconnaissance à Marie Immaculée. Décembre 1905" or simply "Merci à Marie. Avril 1994." But there are traces of an older church: a partly restored statue of the Virgin and Child given by Pope John XXII (reigned 1316-34), glimpses of fresco at the west end (kneeling patrons, traces of a Baptism of Christ with angels, stars on a blue sky). In the Choir there is a twelfth-century episcopal throne in white marble. On its substantial sides are carved a winged lion and a winged ox, the symbolic beasts of the Evangelists Mark and Luke. The lion, visible on the side accessible to visitors, is a creature of dynamic energy, physical or spiritual. With its strong tail curving up between its legs, its wing flowing up with the higher part of the arm-rest, the four legs close together, it seems to be contained with difficulty in the available space. But the lion is not trapped so much as confined temporarily to earthly affairs. Its eyes blaze with fierceness to enemies of the truth. For the moment it has landed here, lending the saint's authority to the human occupant of the throne.

From the cathedral steps and slopes lead higher up the Rocher des Doms, the limestone rock whose Bronze Age hill-fort and early medieval castle preceded the Palace of the Popes. (The powerful position of the early settlement—the dominance of the rock over many miles of surrounding plain—is especially evident when viewed across the Rhône from Villeneuve.) Here gardens were laid out mainly under the Second Empire. Characteristic statues of the period include a rather mannered would-be-sensual Venus. She inhabits the pool by the café, edged by delicate red, light yellow and deeper yellow roses. And of course there are noteworthy views of the Pont d'Avignon and of Villeneuve with (as seen by Ruskin in October 1840) its "noble fortress... a mass which Turner would luxuriate in, poised on heavy rock arches".

"Sur le pont d'Avignon": the Pope's Mule

The traditional song assures us that people dance *on* the bridge at Avignon (the Pont St.-Bénézet) "*tout en rond*"—"all in a ring"—but some commentators insist that they danced *under* it, not balletically treading water but skipping about on the dry land where the bridge crossed the Île de la Barthelasse. It was put up in the late twelfth century, when, according to legend, the shepherd Bénézet was led to the area by an angel. Having moved prodigious quantities of stone, Bénézet completed the bridge, with the aid of his followers, in eight years. It was rebuilt several times (the small surviving chapel of St. Nicolas expanded upwards in the thirteenth century) before the Rhône swept most of it away, leaving the present arches, in the seventeenth century.

Alphonse Daudet, in his comic tale "La Mule du Pape" (*Lettres de mon moulin*, 1869) has no doubt that *on* the bridge is the place to dance. In his fantasy version of papal Avignon: "From noon until night it was processions, pilgrimages, streets strewn with flowers, ... arrivals of cardinals from the Rhône, banners in the wind, galleys decked out with flags, the Pope's soldiers singing in Latin in the squares", the bells ringing. And among the many happy sounds you would hear, from the direction of the bridge, would be the boom of *tambourins*—long Provençal drums. "Because *chez nous* [in Provence] when people are happy we have to dance." And since the streets in those days were too narrow for dancing the *farandole*, people danced on the bridge—"*l'on y dansait*"—day and night. Presumably, however, they could not do it "tout en rond".

This happy place is presided over by the jovial (fictional) Pope Boniface, who grows, and loves to drink, "that fine ruby-coloured wine which since then has been called Châteauneuf des Papes" (or more usually "du Pape"). He also loves his mule, on which he rides every Sunday evening to Châteauneuf to savour the fruit of his vine. He comes back merrily into the city; as he crosses the bridge amid drums and *farandoles* even the mule breaks into "a little skipping amble" while the Pope beats time, scandalizing his cardinals and delighting the people. In fact, Châteauneuf-du-Pape is on the same side of the Rhône as Avignon, but this is not a tale about facts. Its whole basis, Daudet alleges, is an unexplained Provençal proverb about "the Pope's mule, who saved up his kick for seven years." There is also a pun involving "la mule du Pape" as the Pope's slipper, the animal's shoe, and the animal itself.

The papal mule leads a cosseted life until a mischievous and self-advancing youth called Tistet Védène inveigles himself into the Pope's favour. Tistet affects an interest in his beloved mule and is appointed its keeper. Once the mule was served warm sugared wine; now wicked Tistet

"The mighty river sweeping on with strong purpose [is] half-bridged by a quaint old structure, built... under the direction of S. Benezet. ... He heard of the accidents that happened to those who crossed the rapid Rhone in boats, and he considered in his mind that it were well if the prelates and burghers of Avignon would devote their wealth to making a good bridge, instead of squandering it in show and riotous living" (Rev. Sabine Baring-Gould, *In Troubadour-Land*).

and his friends tantalize the creature with the smell before drinking the wine themselves. Under the influence, they pull his tail and ears. Worse, the youth leads the mule up to the pinnacle of the palace, leaving him stranded, panic-stricken and gawped at. Tistet assures the Pope that he got up there of his own accord. Eventually he is brought down with the help of a stretcher and ropes, flailing humiliatingly in mid-air like a beetle at the end of a string.

The mule plots revenge. The revenge mulls for seven years while Tistet goes off and prospers at the court of Naples. He comes back at last and gets himself appointed, still flattering the mule to his master, as papal *premier moutardier*—first mustardeer. (The proverbial *il se croit le premier moutardier du Pape* means roughly "he's too big for his boots".) Next day in the Palace courtyard Tistet prepares to receive his new insignia, the appropriately yellow box-wood spoon and saffron robe. The clergy and soldiers are all assembled for the ceremony. Still the *tambourins* lead the dance "down there, on the Pont d'Avignon". The triumphant Tistet advances, at the climax of his career and of the story. He is now a "magnificent Provençal" with (unusually) blond curls and small golden beard. A great Camargue ibis feather waves on his hood. He makes for the Pope, pausing only to give the mule "two or three friendly little pats on the back." The mule seizes the opportunity to give him such an almighty, long-stored kick "that as far away as Pampérigouste you could see the smoke." Originally Daudet wrote "Pamplona"; no doubt the legendary Pampérigouste is even further away, as well as suggesting, onomatopoeically, Tistet's explosive fate. Amid the "whirlwind of blond smoke... there fluttered an ibis feather—all that remained of the unfortunate Tistet Védène." It is like the extreme, explosive and satisfying endings of some of Roald Dahl's stories; "La Mule du Pape", too, is often popular with children, as much for its gusto, robust exaggeration, and final comic-strip violence as for the neatness of its moral.

The Petit Palais and the Musée Lapidaire

The Place du Palais slopes up towards the Petit Palais, originally a fourteenth-century cardinal's *livrée* and from the 1330s the residence of the Bishop of Avignon. (Benedict XII had demolished its predecessor to make way for the Papal Palace.) Its best-known later occupier and restorer was Cardinal Giulio della Rovere, the future Pope Julius II. The spacious episcopal rooms now display a large collection of medieval and Renaissance paintings including a couple of Botticellis. As in many such collections there is much fine work, much gold and many Madonnas—a problem only because they are gathered in such numbers. More extraordinary, but almost never mentioned in the guidebooks, are the delicate mid-fourteenth-century frescoes in the first room. They come from a house near Avignon and show scenes, some badly damaged, of hunting (dogs, their keeper, a huntsman with horn and spear), a castle, ladies at a fountain (two let the water run through their fingers), courtly figures dancing in woodland. Two lovers, their hair bound with fillets, the woman in a red dress, are locked in an embrace, about to kiss beneath the trees. A bird flies over, another looks on. It is like a fourteenth-century romance, if more teasingly enigmatic than most since we do not know the story.

The first few rooms also have some interesting sculpture, including the tomb of Cardinal Jean de Lagrange (1388-9) from the church of St. Martial. Before the revolutionaries' hammers hit it, it was fifteen metres high. (Usefully an eighteenth-century drawing of the intact structure has survived.) Separate figures now fill Room 2 and the *transi*—the skeletal reminder of mortality—has a wall to itself.

Stone of an earlier time is kept in the Musée Lapidaire in the former Jesuit chapel off Rue de la République. Marble sculpture and the pale stone of the chapel harmonize to give a powerful ensemble effect. Many of the exhibits are from ancient Provence: busts, fragments and inscriptions from Avignon, the damaged but sparkling head of a diademed woman of the first century AD from the theatre in Arles, the head of a young Tiberius from the theatre at Vaison-la-Romaine. Probably the best-known piece is the "Tarasque of Noves", a monster made some time between the third century BC and first century AD and partly resembling a lion, a wolf or a crocodile but not much like any real creature. Its fierce claws grip two human heads and an arm protrudes from its jaws. (One may think of monsters like Grendel in *Beowulf.* For the Tarasque of Tarascon see pp.181-4.) Probably the Tarasque has, apart from giving human fears "a local habitation and a name", a significance in the pre-Roman cult of the severed head. More reassuringly practical activity features in a second-century AD relief, from Cabrières d'Aigues, of two bearded men hauling a boat carrying barrels along the River Durance. A third man, also bearded and with hair segmented in distinctive Gaulish style, steers from the back of the boat.

The Musée Calvet

The museum grew from the original collection of the Avignon physician and professor of medicine Esprit Calvet (1728-1810); there is a bust, together with one of Esprit Requien (1788-1851), the naturalist whose library and specimens provided the foundation for the Musée Requien next door. Since 1833 the Calvet has occupied the mid-eighteenth-century Hôtel de Villeneuve-Martignan. Long, light rooms surround a courtyard with plane trees.

Apart from neoclassical statues (ancient work is in the Musée Lapidaire), this is mainly a collection of paintings. There is a good range of pieces by the local seventeenth-century painters Pierre and Nicolas Mignard, including Nicolas' Nativity and Louis XIV in armour. Once attributed to Pierre was the scene in which Alexander the Great sweeps towards Thalestris, Queen of the Amazons, with Baroque theatrical aplomb—yet courteously too. Thalestris, who wants to have a son by him, looks a mixture of modest and composedly happy while the Amazon who is removing her breastplate looks a little more baleful (being an Amazon queen is not usually about encouraging men to have sex with you); a turbaned figure at right looks merrily and lewdly out at the viewer, one long finger to his lip, as if daring us not to respond to the situation with appropriate mythological dignity and distance.

A later dynasty of originally local painters was the Vernet family. At the Calvet there are seascapes and landscapes by Joseph (1714-89) and a tribute by his grandson Horace (1789-1863), *Joseph Vernet, bound to a mast, studies storm effects*. Sailors struggle to control the boat amid large waves, the steersman loses his hat, and passengers pray desperately. Meanwhile the painter maintains his enthusiasm at the prow, eyes alight as the lightning flashes, red cloak billowing, one hand raised in gesture of inspiration, the other clasping a sheaf of paper. Another, no less romantic painting by Horace Vernet shows Mazeppa, the Pole, tied to the back of a wild horse in Byron's poem. As horse and sufferer go through a great forest they are followed by the flashing-eyed wolves whose "long gallop... can tire/The hound's deep hate, and hunter's fire." The same artist's smaller "Mazeppa among the Horses", in another room, takes the story forward to the point where the horse collapses and dies from exhaustion, leaving the despairing hero "Link'd to the dead and stiffening wretch." For a moment other horses wheel around them before galloping on. Eventually, in the nick of time, he will be rescued by Cossack peasants.

Other painters represented here include Hubert Robert, Corot and Daumier. There are some good Largillière portraits and some early views of Avignon. A small collection of twentieth-century art, including some Picasso and Modigliani, is part of the Musée Angladon, where there are also several rooms of mostly eighteenth-century furniture and painting.

The Avignon Festival

The festival began in the summer of 1947 as a week of performances (later two weeks and then a month) led by the great actor and director Jean Vilar (1912-71). He played Shakespeare's Richard II—the first known French production—in the Cour d'Honneur of the Papal Palace. From their wide, open wooden stage in Avignon, Vilar and his company challenged what they saw as the conventional, unadventurous and Paris-centred French theatre of the time. The festival atmosphere, the open-air setting, and Vilar's bold style, helped him inject into theatre that "Dionysian" or carnival element that he felt was missing: Apollo, the pure intellect, "can do no more for our theatre."

Vilar was able to take back to Paris what he was practising in Avignon when, between 1951 and 1963, he directed the Théâtre National Populaire at the Palais de Chaillot. At the same time, and until his death in 1971, he continued to direct the festival, with productions regularly moving between Paris and Avignon. The Maison Jean Vilar, in a former bishop's palace in Avignon (near Place de l'Horloge in Rue de Mons) has a wonderfully rich collection of documentary, sound and video material on Vilar's career and other theatrical topics.

From 1966 the festival was open not only to theatre but to other performing arts. Maurice Béjart and Merce Cunningham came, among other noted choreographers and dancers. Jean-Luc Godard's *Les Chinoises* was shown in 1967. The festival went on expanding. Fewer than 5,000 people came in 1947; 120,000 in 1970; at least 1500,000 in more recent years. A vigorous fringe festival, "Le Off", started in 1969. Many different venues around the town were opened up, among them the former chapel of the fraternity of Pénitents Blancs (hooded white figures are still to be seen at either side of the facade), the surviving parts of the mainly fifteenth-century Celestine monastery, and the 1840s municipal theatre or opera-house in Place de l'Horloge. (At the entrance large statues of Molière and Corneille look out, dignified and perhaps rather sleepy, across the festival crowds.) There are also abundant street-happenings. In the Cour d'Honneur, post-Vilar highlights included the stylized, balletic, oriental-influenced Shakespeare productions by Ariane Mnouchkine's Théâtre du Soleil in 1982 and 1984.

One of the festival's most extraordinary productions took place, in 1985, not in the city but in the Callet quarry at Boulbon, a few miles to the south. This was the premiere of *The Mahabharata*, Jean-Claude Carrière's version of the Sanskrit epic, directed by Peter Brook. Irving Wardle, reviewing the production for *The Times* on 7 July, described how "Brook's spectators undergo a pilgrimage—a long walk up a dusty hillside" and are then rewarded with the magnificent sight of "an amphitheatre facing a blasted cliff-side, with a lofty upper pathway for the actors, and a desert floor divided by a canal. Surrounded by the most sophisticated of lighting rigs, the show is rooted in the basic elements of the universe—water, stone, and fire." It is a setting well suited to Brook's economical style:

> For his battles, you can trace the flight of the mimed arrows, and visualize the horses from the sight of chariot drivers whipping a single heavy wheel over the desert. As before in his work, the immediate impact produces amazement and pleasure: the long-term effect is the imprint of images of tenderness, triumph and death that lodge in the memory for ever.

Villeneuve-lès-Avignon

Villeneuve, across the Rhône from Avignon, came into the possession of the kings of France in 1271; the French end of the Pont Saint-Bénézet was defended by the tall tower named after King Philippe le Bel, who began it in 1293. (The tower is all that is now left of a larger fortification.) Papal Avignon, however, strongly influenced the development of its neighbour. John XXII's nephew, Arnaud de Via, built the collegiate church of Notre Dame in the 1330s, and gave it, said Prosper Mérimée when he inspected it in 1834, "the same military character distinctive of the buildings of Avignon: high defensive walls, huge towers, solid, heavy construction". And a number of cardinals built their palaces or *livrées* here, where there was more land available.

The palace of the saintly Cardinal Pierre de Luxembourg, who died in 1387, is now the art museum named after him; it contains one notable painting, Enguerrand Quaranton or Quarton's 1453 *Coronation of the Virgin*. The painter's identity was unknown until 1895, when a detailed contract between him and Canon Jean de Montagnac came to light. The identical—as specified—Father and Son, with the Holy Ghost as dove between them, crown the Virgin. The colours, particularly the red robes of the Godhead, have remained remarkably lustrous. Mérimée felt that Father and Son wonderfully combined beauty and majesty, but liked the head of the Virgin less—it is too big and square, "the type that was fashionable in about 1500, for there are fashions in faces, as well as in clothes." Angels and the Elect marvel and worship on each side. Below are the cities of Rome and Jerusalem, and beneath them the Last Judgement proceeds. There is some grisly detail of the sufferings of the damned. Pain is inflicted by devils who include one like a green lizard beside the usual more goat-like specimens.

In 1356 Pope Innocent VI undertook the conversion of his former residence (when he was Cardinal Aubert) into the Chartreuse du Val de Bénédiction, a huge Carthusian monastery. Innocent, who died in 1362, was buried in the monastery church; his effigy in white marble is covered by three towering (restored) tabernacles in Pernes limestone. In 1834 Mérimée found the tomb in the possession of a poor wine-grower. (At the Revolution the Chartreuse and its land had been sold off in lots.) Innocent was surrounded by barrels, logs and enormous ladders; it was hard to see how "these thin columns and foliage, so light, so elegant" had not already been broken. But there they remained: "nothing more slender, nothing more graceful". The alabaster statues which had decorated the base had been sold, the base was now being used as a cupboard, and the effigy was "fort mutilée", but still this magnificent monument offered "one of the finest examples of Gothic decoration of the fourteenth century". It survived mainly because Mérimée took an interest.

Other survivors at the Chartreuse include, in what was once the chapel of Innocent's *livrée*, tempera paintings of scenes from the lives of Christ and John the Baptist by Matteo Giovannetti or his workshop. Although much damage was done to the fabric of the buildings during and after the Revolution, arguably the spirit of the monastery has remained intact. This is especially true of the Small Cloister, with its gravel paths, cypresses, and various plants, including pale purple irises in late spring. A notice reminds us that the Carthusian ideal cloister prefigures the Heavenly Jerusalem.

After the Revolution Villeneuve more generally fell on hard times. Nathaniel Hawthorne, after a hot walk across the suspension-bridge from Avignon in June 1859, found it "the stoniest, roughest old town that can be imagined... I passed through its scrambling streets (paved even more vilely than those of Avignon, and strewn with loose stones besides) without imagining that princes of the church had once made their abodes here." Henry James, with much greater experience of such places, is more favourably disposed towards this "picturesque, half-deserted little town". He takes most interest in the Fort St.-André, the strong-bastioned fourteenth-century castle which stands over Villeneuve on the rocky hill of Mont Andaon. True, the interiors of such castles have "a wearisome family likeness", but:

> these dense gate-towers of Philippe le Bel struck me... as peculiarly wicked and grim... They contain ever so many devilish little dungeons, lighted by the narrowest slit in the prodigious wall, where it comes over one with a good deal of vividness and still more horror that wretched human beings ever lay there rotting in the dark.

James knows that "every dark hole at Villeneuve is called a dungeon... There were plenty of black holes in the Middle Ages that were not dungeons, but household receptacles of various kinds; and many a tear dropped in pity for the groaning captive has really been addressed to the spirits of the larder and the faggot-nook." Even so, he cannot help thinking about the mentality of people who seem not to have been disturbed by such familiar ideas as "the blackness of a 'living tomb'." But perhaps, "as I have heard it maintained... everyone in the Middle Ages did go mad—every one was mad."

A cure for madness might be found in the gardens of the ruined abbey of St. André, enclosed by the fort. The lower gardens are full of roses and wisteria. There is a good view of Avignon with the Alpilles and the Luberon beyond it, from the terrace, which is supported by massive vaulting—one of the features of the abbey which survived the Revolution. Higher up there are olives, palms, pines, the odd prickly pear, and the restored Romanesque chapel of St. Casarie, who is said to have died in a cave nearby in 587.

Chapter Two

Petrarch's Provence

Carpentras

Avignon was so crowded and uncomfortable in the years immediately after the papal court arrived that Petrarch's father sent the family to live in Carpentras, the capital of the Comtat Venaissin. Petrarch and his brother Gherardo were taught their rhetoric and grammar here by the Tuscan scholar Convenevole da Prato, and here Petrarch began his intense engagement with the work of classical authors and particularly Cicero. In 1316, when he was twelve, his father despatched him to study at the University of Montpellier, but more than forty years later, writing to his schoolfellow Guido Sette, he was still grateful for "those serene and tranquil years" when, far from the turmoil of human affairs, he was fed the first milk of learning,

A few buildings from Petrarch's time at Carpentras have survived. Among them is the thirteenth-century castle keep. During Petrarch's lifetime strong defensive city walls were built, of which only the Porte d'Orange remains. Bishop Malachie d'Inguimbert was responsible, in the mid-eighteenth century, for some of the more notable later buildings: the Chapelle Notre-Dame de Santé and the Hôtel-Dieu (in whose chapel is his tomb). Such was d'Inguimbert's fame locally that N. Piot, a versifying member of the Vaucluse Athenaeum, declared that "His generous hands have left, in Vaucluse,/The poor, without needs, the ignorant, without excuse." The surviving synagogue, founded in 1367 and the oldest in France, was also rebuilt at this period.

The cathedral of St. Siffrein was mostly rebuilt in the early fifteenth century. Some, including Elsie Whitlock Rose (*Cathedrals and Cloisters of Southern France*, 1906) have found the result disappointing:

Nothing more meagre nor dreary can be conceived than the façade with its three, poor, characterless portals... The principal charm of the interior is negative; its dim misty light, by concealing a mass of

Mont Ventoux, where Petrarch endured "toil and repentance and torn clothes and scratches from the rocks and briars" on the path to enlightenment.

tasteless decorations and the poverty and bareness of the whole architectural scheme, gives to the generous height and size of the room an atmosphere of subdued and mysterious spaciousness.

The south door merits the faint praise that its "few carved details... are so simple and chaste that they do not inevitably suggest poverty of conception." Altogether, Rose believes, Provençal Gothic, which here replaced Romanesque, "is a style so foreign to the genius of the province that it could produce only feeble and attenuated examples of the art. Compared with its northern prototypes, it is surprisingly tentative; and awkward, unaccustomed hands seem to have built it after most primitive conceptions." But for Marcel Brion in the 1950s the cathedral is simply "a bold, animated, Gothic church."

Petrarch must have been familiar with the Roman triumphal arch at Carpentras. It was built in the early first century AD and at some point in the Middle Ages was moved from the street to become an entrance to the bishop's palace, later the Palais de Justice. Two reliefs show chained prisoners—the usual assertion of Roman power combined, perhaps, with some ethnographic interest. On the more decayed east side are two figures who, James Bromwich explains, are wearing "Greek costume, and are from the east, perhaps Syria." On the more impressive west side are an easterner in tunic, cloak and Phrygian cap and a more conspicuously "Barbarian" German in a thick cloak. A chained German might have different meanings for different groups and individuals: a warning against dangerous non-Romans, a reassurance that they could be defeated, or an emblem of old nobility—like the proud tribesmen of Tacitus' *Germania*—unbowed in spite of the chains.

In May 1933 Virginia Woolf encountered a different kind of captive in Carpentras. She and her husband Leonard were *en route* for Italy in their new car when she characterized in her diary

a little servant girl with honest eyes, hair brushed in a flop, and one rather black tooth. I felt that life would crush her out inevitably. Perhaps 18 not more; yet on the wheel, without hope; poor, not weak but mastered—yet not enough mastered but to desire furiously travel, for a moment, a car... Oh how I envy you—able to travel. You like Carpentras? But the wind blows ever so hard... The odd little honest face, with the black tooth, will stay on at Carpentras I suppose: will marry? will become one of those stout black women who sit in the door knitting? No: I foretell for her some tragedy; because she had enough mind to envy us the Lanchester.

Mont Ventoux

The mountain is 6,273 feet or 1,909 metres high. Until 1973 cars were raced up the road to the summit and in some years it forms part of the Tour de France; in July 1967, in terrible heat, the world champion British cyclist Tom Simpson died two miles from the top.

Petrarch tells his former confessor, Father Dionigi da Borgo San Sepolcro, that he and his brother Gherardo climbed Mont Ventoux on 26 April 1336. They left Malaucène before day-break. At an early stage of the climb they met an old shepherd who tried to dissuade them: in his youth he had made the ascent and (in Morris Bishop's translation from the *Familiar Letters*) "had got nothing from it but toil and repentance and torn clothes and scratches from the rocks and briars." But "young men's minds are naturally incredulous of good counsellors" and up they went, leaving their extra baggage with the shepherd. Gherardo "chose the shortest and steepest course, directly up the ridges" while Petrarch preferred an easier and more winding route which several times, to his frustration and his brother's mirth, led him downwards. At this point in the letter he begins to attach explicit allegorical significance to the climb—less to the surprise of Father Dionigi, no doubt, than to those modern readers hoping simply to find Petrarch as accomplished a mountaineer as a poet. (Just possibly the whole ascent is fictional.) His failure to progress up the mountain is like "spiritual straying". Earthly pleasures hold him back. "But after much wandering," he tells himself, "you will either have to climb upward eventually, with labours long shirked, to the heights of the blessed life, or lie sluggishly in the valley of your sins."

Having thus exhorted himself, he reached the summit. He admired the vast view to the Alps and the sea; he sighed for his native Italy. He also looked back over the decade since his and Gherardo's return from their studies in Bologna: "I was happy at my progress, I wept for my imperfections, and I took pity on the common inconstancy of human actions." As the sun began to go down he surveyed the view again and decided to take out his portable *Confessions* of St. Augustine, a gift from Father Dionigi. The book opened, he says, at "Men go to admire the high mountains and the great flood of the seas and the wide-rolling rivers and the ring of Ocean and the movements of the stars; and they abandon themselves!" Chastened, he reproved himself for admiring worldly things and descended the mountain in silence, chewing over the quotation, meditating on "the vanity of men's purposes". On such occasions Petrarch is, as Nicholas Mann says (*Petrarch*, 1984), modern in his self-awareness "yet medieval in his self-abasement".

Scholars have concluded that this letter was not put into its final form until 1353. By then the straight-climbing Gherardo had reached spiritual heights as a Carthusian monk. "Seventeen years later," as Mann says, "a day's excursion had become a programme for life."

Fontaine-de-Vaucluse: Discoursing with Love

In spring the resurgent river Sorgue emerges, spectacularly foaming, at the foot of a 230-metre high cliff (a "huge forehead of bare stone", Henry James calls it) at Fontaine-de-Vaucluse. There is an annual flow of 630 million cubic metres; in the most active periods the water arrives at a rate of 90 cubic metres per second. John Addington Symonds was excited by the next stage in the progress of the "many-flashing, eddying" Sorgue, "lashed by millwheels, broken by weirs, divided in its course, channelled and dyked, yet flowing irresistibly and undefiled. Blue, purple, greened by moss and water-weeds, silvered by snow-white pebbles, on its pure smooth bed the river runs like elemental diamond, so clear and fresh."

Petrarch came to live by the waters, away from Avignon and the corruption and intrigue against which he so often inveighed, for several extended periods between 1337 and his final move to Italy in 1353. Here he embarked on his Latin epic about Scipio Africanus, *Africa*. Here, too, he sought to calm the youthful "ardour" of his love for Laura, the woman whom, he tells us, he first saw in the church of the Cordeliers in Avignon in 1327 and who died in 1348 (probably a victim of the Black Death). Conceivably she is pure invention but more likely she corresponds to, or is developed from, a real Laure de Noves who married—the main reason the poet's love is unrequited—Hugues de Sade. (Later cynics have been pleased to note that the Marquis de Sade was descended from the object of Petrarch's idealized love. The Marquis himself claimed she appeared to him in dreams.) The relationship with Laura—the cycle of hope, rebuff, renewed hope, eventual move towards recognition of the larger divine love—is the main subject of the *rime sparse* ("scattered verses") which he worked and reworked over a lifetime. Although in the finished *Canzoniere* there is an eventual move to subsume human love in divine, it was the "icy fire" or sweet pain of unrequited passion which influenced later European poetry most deeply.

Petrarch's house at Vaucluse was on the left bank of the Sorgue. On its traditional site is now the Musée Iconographique et Bibliographique de Pétrarque et de Laure, which displays a good selection of Petrarchan illustrations and editions. He had two gardens, one, subject to flooding, near the source, and the other, nearer the house and more cultivated, on an island in the river. Among the trees he grew was laurel—a reference both to Laura and to the laurels of poetry. He led, he was at pains to tell his correspondents and posterity, a simple life at Vaucluse, dedicated to study, thought and composition. Often on moonlit summer nights, more poetically, he would wander alone in the fields and the hills. Sometimes he went to the source, daring to enter the great cavern which was "frightening to enter [even] by day and with other people". In the Latin letters such wandering in nature is usually presented as part of the focused, reflective life of the scholar in the country. In the Italian poems it often functions differently. In a metrical epistle to his friend Giacomo Colonna he seeks solitude but sees the face of the beloved everywhere in the forest; she rises from the waters, appears in the clouds, issues from the rocks. And in "Solo e pensoso..." (*Canzoniere* 10) he paces "the most deserted fields" he can find, fleeing any sign of the fellow humans who can see his inward burning; it seems that only the mountains, banks, rivers and woods truly understand what his life is like, and no path is too "harsh or wild" for Love to accompany him, "*ragionando* [discoursing, talking] *con meco, ed io con lui.*"

Across the river, above the village, was the castle of Petrarch's friend Philippe de Cabassoles, Bishop of Cavaillon. (There had been an "oppidum" or hill settlement here as early as the seventh century BC.) Visiting the crumbling remains involves scrambling up some equally crumbling paths but affords a fine view and an escape from the crowds. The approach to the "Fontaine" is lined with souvenir stalls; fortunately, however, one is no longer offered, as in Henry James' day, "a brush dipped in tar to write your name withal on the rocks".

James was so struck by "the vast sad cliff... still and solid forever, while the liquid element rages and roars at its base" that he had "no difficulty in understanding the celebrity of Vaucluse. I understood it, but I will not say I understood Petrarch." He tended to find the poems "factitious and literary". In the mildly humorous *Voyage à Vaucluse* (1811) by Victor Augier of Orange, Petrarch speaks more straightforwardly. His laurelled shade emerges from the column erected seven years earlier on the five-hundredth anniversary of his birth and buttonholes two young men in verse: *Restez, messieurs, je suis l'amant de Laure...* At one point he sighs "as if to say", rather more directly than his real poems, "Ah! if only Laura had wanted to!..." But, James continues, "the poet and his lady are, of course, the stock in trade of the little village, which has had for several generations the privilege of attracting young couples engaged in their wedding-tour, and other votaries of the tender passion."

Robert Browning and Elizabeth Barrett Browning followed in this tradition, with little of James' scepticism about Petrarch or "the tender passion". In October 1846 they were on their way to Pisa, having left England a week after their marriage—initially secret because of the bride's father's implacable hostility to any of his children marrying. In Paris they had met their mutual friend the art historian Anna Jameson who, with her young niece Gerardine, was also on the way to Italy. Jameson was taken with Barrett Browning's courage and resilience and by Browning's devotion and "his poetical fancies and antics, with every now and then the profoundest seriousness and tenderness interrupting the brilliant current of his imagination." But, as she wrote to her friend Lady Byron, the poet's widow, she was so worried about the wife's health and what she saw as the husband's complete, poetical impracticality, that she felt it essential to go with them to Pisa—saving Barrett Browning's life in the process, she believed. The party laboured on by road to Lyon and then descended the Rhône to Avignon "in a dirty confined steam boat, the rain pouring in torrents". By the time they arrived "our poor invalid" was much exhausted but hoping to be able to go to Vaucluse with the others. In *Memoirs of the Life of Anna Jameson* (1878) Gerardine Macpherson remembered this "poetical pilgrimage":

at the very source of the "chiare, fresche e dolci acque" [the waters of *Canzoniere* 126] , Mr Browning took his wife up in his arms, and, carrying her across through the shallow curling waters, seated her on a rock that rose throne-like in the middle of the stream. Thus love and poetry took a new possession of the spot immortalized by Petrarch's loving fancy.

The day before, Anna Jameson had assured Lady Byron—whose married experience tended to suggest that poets were dangerously unreliable characters—that the "mutual deportment" of the pair "has been marked by the most graceful propriety." In October there was not much water, but it is good to hear that propriety did not prevent true lovers getting at least a little wet.

L'Isle sur la Sorgue: "delicious streams"

On 28 August 1789 the agricultural reformer Arthur Young had a remarkably busy day in Avignon, sightseeing, interviewing "some gentlemen understanding in agriculture", and arguing with locals about what he saw as their country's complete unpreparedness for war with England. After all this, eager to get on to Fontaine-de-Vaucluse, he travelled through the heat of high summer to L'Isle, where he was surprised and delighted when

> on coming to the verge of it I found fine plantations of elms, with delicious streams, bubbling over pebbles on either side; well dressed people were enjoying the evening at a spot, I had conceived to be only a mountain village. It was a sort of fairy scene to me. Now, thought I, how detestable to leave this fine wood and water, and enter a nasty, beggarly, walled, hot, stinking town; one of the contrasts most offensive to my feelings. What an agreeable surprise, to find the inn without [outside] the town; in the midst of the scenery I had admired! and more, a good and civil inn. I walked on the banks of this classic stream for an hour, with the moon gazing on the waters, that will run for ever in mellifluous poetry: retired to sup on the most exquisite trout and craw fish in the world.

If he was sufficiently refreshed to look around the town before proceeding to Fontaine-de-Vaucluse (whose Petrarch had made the Sorgue a "classic stream") Young could have inspected Notre-Dame-des-Anges. James Lees-Milne did in September 1976; he noted in his diary the "church lined with seventeenth-century Baroquery, and fine picture frames of that century... containing dingy, poor religious canvases." James Bentley (*Provence and the Côte d'Azur*, 1992) responded better to the lavish Baroquery: "Angels and gilded clouds, and cherubs and gilded swags deliriously swirl."

The poet René Char (1907-88) was born at Les Névons, a large house in L'Isle, spent much of his life in the area, and included a poem addressed to the Sorgue in *Fureur et mystère* (1948). During his early Surrealist period he was visited by Paul Eluard and André Breton and co-wrote the poems of *Ralentir travaux* (1930) with them. One piece was written, according to a manuscript note, during an evening car-journey from L'Isle to Avignon. Car travel itself was still fairly surreal for most people in the French provinces; the poem, with Breton's "heart on the blackboard" and Char's stones which follow their own "bitter-sweet shadow", is more so.

Salon-de-Provence

The strong castle which dominates Salon-de-Provence was begun in the tenth century by the Archbishops of Arles, whose overlords were the Holy Roman Emperors—this is the origin of the name Château de l'Empéri—and from 1481 the kings of France. Much of the present building is thirteenth-century, but in the early sixteenth century Archbishop Jean Ferrier made it into a more comfortable and palatial environment. The château was deemed suitable to receive royal visitors to Provence. In October 1564 arrived a group varied and important enough to fulfil a historical novelist's wildest fantasies: a queen, king and two future kings of France—Catherine de' Medici, her sons Charles IX and the future Henri III, and Henri of Navarre who became, many adventures later, Henri IV.

The future was much on Catherine's mind; her sons were in their early teens and political and religious factions were vying to control them and France, and she used the opportunity to consult the learned doctor and astrologer Michel de Nostredame or Nostradamus, who lived in Salon between 1547 and his death in 1566. His house, in Rue

Nostradamus near L'Empéri, informatively if rather solemnly narrates his life and ideas in a series of audio-visual tableaux. The sequence begins as a very young Michel, thoughtfully holding an apple, listens as his wise grandfather, Jean de Saint-Rémy, tells him about life and death, religion and the Cabala: *Regarde bien, Michel...* The medical side of his genius is commemorated at the castle itself, where in 2003, the five-hundredth anniversary of his birth, a garden of his "simples" was laid out. The plants include olive, iris, oregano, fennel, peppermint, and varieties of cabbage and thistle.

According to some sources, Nostradamus confirmed to the anxious mother an earlier prognostication that her son Henri would be succeeded as king by Henri of Navarre. To make absolutely sure, the mage had closely examined the naked Navarre; study of his moles apparently confirmed his royal destiny. (Catherine therefore decided, we are told, that her daughter Marguerite must marry Navarre.) Presumably Nostradamus did not tell the queen anything about just how terrible the coming period was to be: renewed wars of religion, the St. Bartholomew's Day Massacre authorized by Charles IX, the assassinations of the two Henris and many others.

War is a main subject of the Musée de l'Empéri, which fills some thirty rooms of the castle. Two boys from Marseille, the brothers Raoul and Jean Brunon (born in 1892 and 1895), began collecting militaria in the early years of the twentieth century. Eventually the collection was acquired by the Army Museum in Paris, and given a permanent home in the Empéri, in 1967. The first room on the right after the entrance hall looks at its beginnings. The brothers owned a great variety of lead soldiers, including, from their own period, members of "Compagnies Cyclistes"—some shooting from the partial cover of their machines, resting their rifles on the cross-bars, one with a dismantled bicycle on his back, others cycling or pushing with what now seems the innocent aplomb of a pre-Somme world. There are Alpine infantry with skis and alpenstocks, infantry of the line led by sword-waving officers, and the cavalry—cuirassiers, hussars, dragoons—whose names and whose horses thunder through nineteenth-century history and fiction. From an earlier period Joan of Arc with her standard rides out followed by knights and foot soldiers, an opportunity for the production of model lances, spears, halberds, bills, swords, cross-bows and trumpets. In 1908 an uncle gave the first larger objects, including an 1866 rifle and a Bavarian helmet of 1870.

Even at the front after 1914 the Brunons gathered material. Their tunics are shown: Raoul's from the 14th Battalion of Chasseurs Alpins, Jean's from the 57th Artillery Regiment. Raoul was killed in action in 1917, but Jean went on collecting, dedicating the results to his brother's memory, for the following fifty years and more. (He died in 1982; his son Raoul was the first curator of the museum.) He focused particularly on the French army between Louis XIV and the end of the First World War. The downstairs display on the royal armies of 1700-92 seems to conduct us, whatever the real bloodshed involved in eighteenth-century warfare, away from the stark reality of Raoul's death. Here are swords with beautiful basket-hilts, fine firearms, tricorns, cavalry officers' broad-topped boots.

Even further from the actuality of battle is the selection of magnificent, outrageous, remotely classically-inspired shining brass helmets from the nineteenth century. There are other sorts of exotic headwear—chapskas and shakos—and everywhere there are plumes of red or white feathers, red or black horsehair. Apparently First Empire plumes could reach 55 cm, while 30 cm was normal under the Ancien Régime. Red, golden and silvery epaulettes of varying widths are also on display.

There are waxwork figures of many proud male warriors and also of two of their useful female supporters, the uniformed *cantinières* (both Second Empire, but in the line of their earlier colleague who helps Fabrice del Dongo in Chapter III of Stendhal's *La Chartreuse de Parme*). An artillery *cantinière* stands at the ready with her plumed bonnet, apron, knife, cask and canteen. The other woman is Eugénie Larquet, who served with the 1st Regiment of Grenadiers of the Imperial Guard and was married to one of them. They represent, of course, a rare opportunity for women to make their presence felt in this museum.

Upstairs come the main sections on the army of the First Republic and First Empire. There are uniforms, weapons, documents, paintings. An extraordinary "glaive de l'Ecole de Mars" of 1794 takes the eye—a short, broad sword with golden fittings and unuseably stylized guard. It was designed for the military academy, with characteristic neoclassical fervour, by Jacques-Louis David. Napoleon's Egyptian campaign is featured: there are plates from the huge *Description de l'Egypte* (1809) produced by the expedition's scholars and artists. An infantryman of 1796-1800 stands on the sand before a large blow-up of the *Description* frontispiece with its fantasy panorama of Nile monuments.

Napoleon's other campaigns are covered with the aid of proclamations and pistols and commemorative medals, uniforms, yet more sabres and shakos, a bearskin reserved for élite units. There is a propaganda-warehouse-load of bronze and gold imperial eagles on badges, helmets and papers. Later periods are covered with almost equal thoroughness. Finally, in a thirteenth-century room to the left of the entrance hall (which itself was once the chapel), there is a spectacular array of firearms: matchlocks, flintlocks, special high-quality weapons for the Imperial Guard, eighteenth and nineteenth-century naval blunderbusses.

Orange: "the most beautiful wall"

Louis XIV declared, with the definiteness which befits an absolute monarch, that the theatre at Orange was "the most beautiful wall in the kingdom". The great *scaenae frons* or façade makes it the best preserved Roman theatre in Europe, and gives it a markedly less open, less Greek look than such more ruined specimens as the one at Arles. Some have found it rather oppressive: for John Addington Symonds it is a "colossal, towering, amorphous precipice" ("Old Towns of Provence"). He goes on to imagine the "Roman knights and deputies, arisen from the dead, with faces hard and stern as the warriors carved on Trajan's frieze" taking their places in the Orchestra; and "after proclamation made, the mortmain of imperial Rome... laid upon the comforts, liberties, and little gracefulnesses of modern life."

Probably this familiar notion of stony Romans results not only from their own toughness and habit of proclaiming it, but from the sheer amount of stone which has survived with their mark upon it. But what Symonds saw was more blankly stony than what we see—the twice life-size imperial statue above the central stage entrance was not put back in place until 1951. In its present state it represents Augustus; the legs and torso were found at the theatre but the head and arms were added by the archaeologist Jules Formigé. Originally, there were many more statues and columns and everything was faced in shining marble.

Against this varied background a considerable variety of spectacles and events took place: plays, mime, dancing, religious rituals and processions, acrobatics, choral singing. "Faces hard and stern" were no doubt in a minority.

In the Middle Ages the theatre was put to other uses. Its great wall was a useful bulwark. Houses gradually filled the interior; Murray's *Handbook* of 1843 comments on the recent removal of "miserable hovels" whose inhabitants had extended them by "burrowing like moles... in the thickness of the walls, regardless of the risk of undermining them." But eventually restoration progressed far enough for summer performances to begin again in 1869. Sarah Bernhardt played here, Darius Milhaud's *Suite provençale* (1936) was written originally to accompany Valmy-Baisse's *Bertrand de Born*, and the Chorégies festival continues to perform music, mainly opera, each summer.

The town museum, just across the road from the theatre, includes further memorials of Roman Orange, most importantly the series of fragmentary marble tablets, discovered in Orange in 1949, which have enabled scholars to reconstruct local land-surveys or *cadastres*. The impact of the triumphal arch is more immediate. John Ruskin, in 1840, found it "the most picturesque Roman ruin I ever met with, sadly smashed but what was left exquisitely rich and delicate." The arch (in "a tertiary limestone abounding in fossils", notes Murray) was probably put up in the 20s BC and restored in 26-27 AD. It may commemorate particular Roman victories or it may assert Roman dominance more generally. On the top storey of the north and south fronts there are reliefs of Roman cavalry and infantry fighting both Gauls and Germans; Ruskin, when he came back to Orange in 1850, thought these "far finer than I supposed Romans could do; no ideal form nor much grace but thorough hard fighting; rich confusion of forms, and vigorous ornamental arrangement of them." On the first attic, on either side of the pediment, are scenes of naval confusion—scattered prows, rams, rigging. It used to be believed that these represented the ships of Antony and Cleopatra decisively defeated at Actium a few years before the arch went up, but the reliefs are now generally thought to date from the later restoration. Possibly they refer to fighting on the Rhine, in the borderlands of eastern Gaul. Further down, above the two side arches, are various spoils of war—swords, shields, trumpets, standards and the like—and on the sides are less well preserved military trophies, Barbarian prisoners, and tritons. Ruskin, however, was more impressed by the "naturalism of the purest kind" he found in the vegetal ornament of the central architrave and "a superb writhing roll of flowing leafage" on the inner side of the pilasters.

The attic storeys of the arch survived, presumably, because they were found useful when it was turned into a fortress in the early Middle Ages. The main literary monuments to medieval Orange, or at least to a general notion of its existence, are the twelfth-century *chansons de geste* of the Guillaume d'Orange cycle—tales, often playful as well as heroic, of the adventures of this legendary leader. (See p. 173) In *La Prise d'Orange* the disguised hero and two of his followers have entered the palace in the Saracen-controlled city. They are discovered but hole up in a tower, slaying any number of attacking Saracens and, for good measure, Turks, Persians and Bedouin too. Eventually they are captured but saved from a ghastly fate by a mixture of valour, the help of the Saracen queen Orable, and a useful underground passage through which reinforcements reach them. They take Orange. Orable is baptized, adopts the name Guibourc, and marries Guillaume, who for thirty years will use the city as his base for further fights.

William (Guillaume) of Orange is, of course, a name that refers to at least three markedly different figures: the warrior in the *chanson*, the sixteenth-century Dutch patriot leader also called William the Silent, and his descendant who, as King William III, ruled Britain. The improbable Dutch connection came about when William the Silent inherited the principality of Orange in 1544. Coincidentally the town, like the Dutch United Provinces he fought to establish, was mainly Protestant. "Orange rejoices in its closeness to the truth as held by Calvin, Avignon in the meretricious teachings of Rome," declared Mildmay Fane, Earl of Westmorland in the seventeenth century. In the 1620s William's son Maurice built a fortress on the Colline St-Eutrope, site of the pre-Roman settlement. Most of the fortress was destroyed under Louis XIV, inveterate enemy of the Netherlands, in the early 1660s, and Orange officially passed to France in 1713 after several further periods of occupation. Its fame was mostly for antiquities until, in 1995, it controversially elected an extreme right-wing Front National mayor, Jacques Bompard.

Vaison-la-Romaine

In Petrarch's time and long afterwards the once flourishing Roman town of Vasio was mostly either in ruins or invisible, buried in the alluvial sand of the river Ouvèze or used as foundations for later buildings. The spectacular exception was the single-arch Roman bridge which still spans the river. Much of the pre-Roman *oppidum* of the Vocontii was covered by the castle that the Counts of Toulouse built on the rock overlooking the town in the late twelfth century (much altered in the fifteenth and sixteenth centuries). The medieval church of Notre-Dame-de-Nazareth, which had cathedral status until the fifteenth century, was on Roman foundations.

Elsie Whitlock Rose visited Notre-Dame in the early years of the twentieth century. In *Cathedrals and Cloisters of the South of France* she registers mixed feelings about the "picturesque irregularity" of the exterior: the plain side-walls "have a quaint and pleasing harmony of line", but "the west front is so featureless that it hardly deserves the title of façade... The central apse is rectangular and heavy, the little southern apse is short and round, and that of the north is tall and thin as a pepper-box."

The interior is "of fine and strong antique simplicity" and the late twelfth-century cloister "small and simple in its rather heavy grace." There was little else to see in Vaison which was, in Rose's day, "but a little country-town, served by the stage-coach." Nothing much seemed to be left of its ancient glories "except the remains of an Amphitheatre [actually a theatre] on the Puymin Hill." But in 1907, only a year after Rose's book was published, excavation began in earnest. Although the forum and the principal temples are buried somewhere beneath later buildings, considerable remains were found in both the Puymin and La Villasse quarters, including several large houses with peristyle (colonnaded) courtyards or gardens, a theatre, shops, and streets.

Among the main focuses of the Puymin site are the so-called Praetorium, a grand house with traces of garden and summer dining-rooms and, by the street, communal latrines; the House of the Messii (named after the family mentioned in inscriptions) with pool, garden and some large paved rooms; and the theatre, the subject of now controversial reconstruction. Abbé Joseph Sautel dug at Vaison between 1907 and his death in 1955. In 1911-12 he concentrated on the theatre remains and in 1932 brought in Jules Formigé to transform the rubble into something more recognizable. While acknowledging Sautel's tireless work to recover ancient Vasio, later archaeologists are somewhat frustrated at the extensiveness of restoration and the amount of concrete used. Much of the site is fixed in its imperial Roman heyday, making it more difficult to look at earlier phases.

Some buildings remained to be investigated, using more modern techniques, by Christian Goudineau and Yves de Kisch. At Puymin the House of the Peacock, a villa excavated by Kisch, yielded five stylistically varied second-century AD mosaics. In one of them the eponymous peacock is surrounded by other birds and, in a spandrel, what James Bromwich (*The Roman Remains of Southern France*) calls "an original splendid mythical beast: a panther with a twisting snake's tail ending in flower petals!"

The mosaics are displayed in the Musée Théo-Desplans, also on the Puymin site. Most of the finds from Vaison are here, the best-known of which are the imperial statues in white marble from the ruins of the theatre, where they would once have adorned the stage-wall. Claudius wears a crown of oak-leaves both, as Bromwich points out, in honour of Jupiter and Juno and "as saviour of his people". Domitian—killer of a fair number of his people but here the respected emperor and general— wears a breastplate with reliefs of Medusa, Pallas Athena and the Victories. Hadrian asserts his philhellenism; the nakedness recalls Greek heroes and the beard Greek rulers. It is tempting to make much of the contrast between the naked emperor and the well-covered statue of his wife, Sabina—he looks assertive, she rather mournful—although the contrast is really more between two conventional representations than between two people. Bromwich describes her and the situation which may make us want to read more than is actually there:

> Stately calm is embodied in the pose and the well-draped material: the true aristocratic lady. The only excess is the plaited hair heaped in two diadems above her brow. The marriage was not happy. Sabina appears to have lacked sparkle and was married to a multi-talented intellectual, art-lover and traveller. Her friends were removed from court and she had no children, possibly not unconnected with Hadrian's attraction to young men.

The other well-known statue in the museum is a silver bust of a less mighty-looking character, perhaps the owner of the house in La Villasse where Sautel discovered it. "It is a homely bourgeois face," thinks Paul MacKendrick (*Roman France*, 1972). The museum has a good collection of the objects among which the man of the silver bust lived: ceramics, jewellery, weapons, hairpins.

Grignan

The château of Grignan is set among the mountains and woods of Le Tricastin but has often been compared to the great châteaux of the Loire Valley. Its present imposingly classical appearance is the result of mid-sixteenth and late-seventeenth century building campaigns and careful twentieth-century restoration.

The château is known particularly for its association with Marie de Rabutin-Chantal, Marquise de Sévigné (1626-96) and her letters. Of her known 1120 letters 764 were sent to her daughter Françoise, Comtesse de Grignan (1646-1705). She had married François de Castellane-Adhémar, Comte de Grignan, in 1669 and first gone south with him in 1671, when the flood of correspondence begins. Sévigné, a widow since her mid-twenties, visited Grignan in 1672-3, 1690-1, and from 1694 until her death in 1696. Françoise also came to Paris for several extended periods.

There is little by way of detailed description of Grignan in Mme de Sévigné's surviving letters. But there is much about the relationships of those who lived or visited there. Her relationship with her daughter was sometimes strained: the mother worried about the cost of the Grignans' luxurious lifestyle, her daughter's fragile health, her pregnancies and how—in Sévigné's opinion—she might try to delay them by, for instance, sleeping apart from the Count. There was a fundamental difference in nature between the witty, energetic, outgoing mother and the much more reserved daughter in whom she was so passionately, perhaps obsessively, interested. Very few of Mme de Grignan's letters are extant to tell her side of the story, but it is clear that they achieved a mostly amicable *modus vivendi*.

Somewhat to her mother's surprise, Mme de Grignan seems fairly successfully to have fulfilled her duties as wife of the royal Lieutenant General. The Count's job was no sinecure, or at least he did not treat it as one. He acted not only in the military sphere—taking Orange for the king in 1673, for example—but, in effect, as substitute for the absentee Governor of Provence. It fell to him to entertain a succession of royal guests, laying on parades and receptions in Aix, Marseille and elsewhere. And at Grignan he offered grand feasts to his visitors. His mother-in-law was concerned that "*cette magnificence est bien ruineuse*", but could see its appeal: at Grignan, she wrote to a friend in July 1694, she has come to a place so different from the everyday world that it seems like "*un château enchanté*", for here one sees "neither poverty, nor hunger, nor illness... One would think one was in a different world entirely." Such hyperbole is not calculated to appeal to critics of the *ancien régime*.

In the enchanted castle the quality of the food was suitably perfect, she told her cousin Philippe-Emmanuel de Coulanges in September 1694: partridges fed on thyme and marjoram, plump quails whose meat falls away from the bone, turtledoves, fine melons, figs and muscat grapes. Even if they wanted, *par quelque bizarre fantaisie*, a poor-quality melon, they would be obliged to order it from Paris. The figs are sweet, the muscat grapes like crunchable amber and sufficient, if you eat too many, "to turn your head... because it's as if you were sipping the most exquisite [local] Saint-Laurent wine."

Aristocrats were expected to live well and to run up debts unashamedly. The Grignans did, however, begin to retrench somewhat, wintering at Grignan for the first time in 1690-1. Sévigné, there with them in February 1695, presented the extreme cold to Coulanges with the same literary verve that she had presented the food. Keen to demonstrate to friends in Paris that living in Provence is not always a matter of ambling "through meadows, with parasols... in the shade of orange-trees", she declares that "it is a hundred times colder here than in Paris. We are exposed to all the winds"; "no longer can our perished fingers ply our pens" and, in any case, the ink has frozen over. Yet of course, unstoppable as ever, she manages to write. "We breathe nothing but snow" and the mountains are *charmantes dans leur excès d'horreur.* But if the Mistral was fierce, the Grignans' most serious financial problems were at least over. They had swallowed their pride and arranged for their son and heir, Sévigné's grandson, to marry the daughter of a very rich tax-farmer. The once unthinkable *mésalliance* between one of the "oldest" families in France and a bourgeoise took place in the collegiate church of Saint-Sauveur, attached to the château of Grignan, on 2 January 1695.

Mme de Sévigné died in April the following year and was buried, in her blue brocade gown, in the family vault of the same church. During the Revolution, allegedly because lead coffins could be melted down for patriotic purposes, the vault was opened. The local magistrate who was involved was apparently interested in Mme de Sévigné, and his curiosity impelled him to remove the upper part of her skull and send it to Paris for phrenological study. What happened to it no-one knows. Ten years later, in somewhat less chaotic times, the Abbé Martinel, curé at Saint-Sauveur, began his long campaign to persuade people that no such desecration had occurred. He organized an elaborate ceremony in the church in her honour. He demanded a public enquiry into what had happened, and he and others persuaded themselves that she had died of smallpox and been buried in a wooden coffin in a separate, unviolated vault. But this was wishful thinking, as was verified in 1870 when the Grignan vault was opened by the curé of the time and two local dignitaries. (One of them, Léopold Faure, had bought the château ruins.)

In the château today Mme de Sévigné's restored apartment can be visited: her bedroom with portraits of family members and d'Aubusson tapestries, her *cabinet* papered in green striped satinette, the mountain views. In the town square stands her bronze mid-nineteenth-century statue, with quill and paper, wide skirt, and *hurlupé* hair—the short-curled "tousled" look fashionable in the 1670s. Her letters, mainly because they seem so much more spontaneous and personally revealing than the more formally polished communications of most of her contemporaries, continue to be widely read.

Chapter Three

Van Gogh's Provence
Part One: Arles

The Greek settlement of Theline was established on a hill overlooking the Rhône in the sixth century BC. It was dependent on or subject to Massalia (Marseille) but profitably sided with Caesar against it, and Pompey, in the mid-first century BC. The town, by this time called Arelate and famous for its shipwrights, was able to build Caesar twelve ships in thirty days. He remembered this prompt assistance well enough not only to record it in his *Civil Wars* but to raise Arelate to the status of a Roman *colonia*, settle veterans of the Sixth Legion there, and give it much of the territory of the vanquished Massaliotes. Abundant Roman remains testify to its importance as a port and provincial centre.

Arles suffered from Barbarian raids in the third century AD but enjoyed new prosperity in the fourth. Constantine the Great had a palace here during his time based in Gaul—"the most innocent and virtuous period of his life", Gibbon believes, and one when "the provinces were protected by his presence from the inroads of the barbarians, who either dreaded or experienced his active valour." Today the palace has gone but there are sizeable remains of the public baths probably built at Constantine's command.

In the late antique period the city, like most of Provence, was battered as Ostrogoths, Visigoths, Franks and Arabs fought for control. It re-emerged as a stable and powerful place only in the twelfth century; the cathedral and cloister of St.-Trophime were built at this time. Arles became rather less significant, however, after it became subject to the Counts of Provence in 1239. Not until the nineteenth century did it really become well known again outside Provence. It then, as a still fairly thriving town with splendid physical reminders of its much more thriving past, became a *locus classicus* of the *Félibrige* movement led by Frédéric Mistral. But for the *félibres* and for northern visitors the glory of

Costumed Arlésiennes: "It's what is called the Graeco-Roman look" (Gustave Flaubert); "both monastic and aphrodisiac" (Edmond Goncourt).

Arles was not purely archaeological. The women of Arles had something of a cult following even before Mistral helped to fix and to popularize their distinctive costume. The northerners often extended their delight in southern sun and well-preserved antiquities into (usually male) fantasies about (usually female) modern inhabitants. Flaubert, full of joy at his first extended absence from Normandy and the parental hearth, observed that

> the Arlésiennes... are pretty... It's what is called the Graeco-Roman look; their figures are strong yet slim like columns of marble. Round their exquisite profiles they wrap a broad band of red velvet which goes up over the head, is fastened at the neck, and so sets off the black colour of their hair and complements the brightness of their skin.

Dumas *père* also claimed to notice Greek elements but wanted to go further east, attributing to the women "black velvet eyes, such as I have seen only among the Indians or the Arabs." And Edmond Goncourt, in his diary entry for 4 October 1885, came closer to explicit comment on the effect on the male viewer of these "nuns of love", with their costume "which has something both monastic and aphrodisiac about it."

Van Gogh's Arles: "to express, with red and green, the terrible passions of humanity"

Vincent van Gogh arrived in Arles after a fifteen-hour train journey from Paris on 20 February 1888. He came in search less of exotic women and ancient monuments than of intense light and some equivalent of the "floating world" of Japanese art.

Van Gogh arrived in heavy snow, unusual in Arles, which provided the subject of some of his first paintings here. But in late March and early April he painted, in his usual rapid but controlled way, a series of orchards in blossom—apricot, peach, cherry, pear, plum. By the summer he had produced a considerable body of work; by the time he left Arles the following spring he had completed about two hundred paintings and more than a hundred drawings. Various aspects of the town and its surroundings are included, although the emphasis is always more on combinations and associations of colours than on topography. *View of Arles with Irises in the Foreground* (now in the Rijksmuseum Vincent van

Gogh in Amsterdam) concentrates on the May meadows full of buttercups and, in front of them, violet irises in a ditch. He also painted or drew cornfields and harvesting; coal barges on the Rhône; public gardens by the river; *Arlésiennes* in costume; a peasant from the Camargue; a "green vineyard" and the same very red vineyard later in the autumn; his friend Roulin, who dealt with post at the railway station. In August he painted sunflowers "with the high spirits of a Marseillais eating bouillabaisse."

Van Gogh lived first in the Hôtel Carrel and then, between May and September 1888, at the Café de la Gare, 30 Place Lamartine. (The building was destroyed by Allied bombing in 1944.) This functioned as a "night-café", where customers—some of them people who could not afford a bed for the night—could stay until morning. Van Gogh painted the big room with tables and chairs at the edge, bottles and used glasses, the billiard table and its shadow. The *patron* in white coat stands by a chair. There are a few, mostly slumped, customers, a man and a woman more awake in a corner, bright lamps radiating yellow light. We see mirrors rather than windows. He told his brother Theo that he had "sought to express, with red and green, the terrible passions of humanity." He wanted to show the café as "a place where one can ruin oneself, go mad, commit crimes," to show the power of evil in this *assommoir* (literally, a place where you knock yourself out with a cosh, brain yourself) and yet "with an appearance of Japanese gaiety and the good nature of [Alphonse Daudet's] Tartarin." The contrast will be achieved by the colours: pink and red and "soft Louis XV and Veronese green contrasting with harsh yellow-greens and blue-greens. All this in the atmosphere of a devil's furnace of pale sulphur." In another café painting, also done in September, the colours are more celebratory, and the effects both of van Gogh's loneliness in Arles and of his intensely religious background less evident. Here too it is after dark but the scene is outside, on and in front of the terrace of the café in Place du Forum. Couples sit beneath the illuminated yellow awning. Further out there are smudges and flecks of stars in the deep blue sky.

In September van Gogh moved into the "Yellow House" at 2 Place Lamartine. This building too was destroyed in 1944 but survives in van Gogh's versions of it in oil and watercolour, both in Amsterdam. Established in his own studio and planning eagerly for other painters to join him there to create a "Studio of the South", he enjoyed representing the house and neighbouring buildings, yellow in "the sulphur-coloured sunshine" by the yellow pavement and roads. But the only artist who came, after much delay, in October, was Paul Gauguin. There has been much debate about exactly what went wrong with the two painters' relationship, leading famously to van Gogh's cutting off part of his own ear, chasing Gauguin down the street with it, and presenting it to a prostitute, on 23 December. Their differences as painters, rivalry or suppressed rivalry, and van Gogh's intense and unrealistic expectations of the relationship obviously played a part. Anaemia, epilepsy and depressingly rainy weather have also been blamed. But clearly the quarrel precipitated rather than caused van Gogh's breakdown.

Gauguin soon left for Paris. Van Gogh was committed to hospital, the Hôtel-Dieu, until 7 January 1889, went on painting, but suffered further attacks and was taken in again, highly disturbed, on 7 February. He had thought that he was being poisoned. Ten days later he was well enough to go back to the Yellow House but the neighbours, always suspicious of this eccentric and sometimes wild outsider, were not happy to see him. Thirty people signed a petition asking the mayor to remove him; he drank and bothered women, the petition said. The police returned him to the Hôtel-Dieu. After an initial period of confinement he was allowed to go out, but chose to stay there until, on 8 May, he left Arles for the mental hospital in St-Rémy.

At the Espace Van Gogh the hospital gardens he knew have been reconstructed and the Hôtel-Dieu itself restored. There is a conspicuous lack of original van Goghs in Provence, since no-one bought the work locally and he sent almost all of it to Theo in recognition of his frequent gifts of money, paints and canvas. The Fondation Vincent Van Gogh opposite the arena, however, presents responses and homage from artists including Francis Bacon and David Hockney.

The Arena

The amphitheatre of Arelate, constructed from "enormous blocks of stone dressed with entirely Roman precision", as Prosper Mérimée says, dates from a time when the city was expanding in the late first century AD. It was a time too—one of general Roman prosperity—when there was a particular enthusiasm for such massive permanent venues for combat between gladiators, or between gladiators and wild animals, and for some less violent sports; it is roughly contemporary with the Colosseum and with the amphitheatres at Verona and Nîmes. There was space for up to 20,000 spectators.

The huge high-sided ellipse made an excellent early medieval fortress. Three of its watch-towers survive, providing good views of the arena, the Rhône and the roofs of Arles. Later the space was gradually filled with houses. The quality of the housing, which looks fairly acceptable in the often-reproduced seventeenth-century engraving of the amphitheatre, seems to have declined steadily. Murray's *Handbook for the Traveller in France* (1843) remembers with a shudder how, until quite recently, the amphitheatre had been filled with and surrounded by

> an accumulation of mean hovels, occupied by the poorest and worst part of the population of the town, to the number of 2000, part of whom burrowed under the vaults, or nestled in its recesses, reminding one of the fungi and parasites springing up over the trunk of some venerable monarch of the forest.

Clearing away these accretions in the 1820s had practical as well as archaeological advantages, except perhaps for the unfortunates trying to live in the "mean hovels". It meant that the arena could be returned to its original purpose as a place of public entertainment. The first bull-fights here, in 1830, celebrated the French capture of Algiers. Since then it has been heavily used for *corridas*, for other taurine sports like the *Course à la cocarde*, where competitors armed with metal combs or *crochets* must remove a cockade from the base of the bull's horns, and for opera.

Augustus Hare (*South-Eastern France*, 1890) describes how in the *Course* "numbers of young men" play with the bulls, "excite them with cries, entice them with handkerchiefs and, when the bulls make a rush, vault over the barriers into safety with marvellous agility. Any very hair-breadth escape is vehemently applauded by the spectators." But sometimes the spectators are themselves the focus of attention. Rev. Sabine Baring-Gould (*In Troubadour-Land: a Ramble in Provence and Languedoc*, 1891) went to see some tauromachy at the Arena and found

himself particularly interested, like the other nineteenth-century male visitors mentioned above, in the Arlésiennes:

> Between each *course* all the spectators promenaded under the galleries and on the terrace at the top of the amphitheatre, the women in gala dress of white lace bodices, black mantle, and dark silk skirts; and a very fine sight they were; it was worth the forty centimes I paid for admission to see the majestic women pace along and sweep the little men from their path as they careered round and round the amphitheatre, with cold, stern faces, full of pride of ancestry and conscious beauty.

The Theatre: "sisters of Mireille"
The Roman theatre was built within about twenty years of the arrival of the first legionary veterans, in the mid-20s BC. It was about the same size as the better preserved equivalent in Orange and could hold an audience of about ten thousand. It now looks so much less substantial

than Orange because much of the stone, including most of the great *scaenae frons* or stage-wall which is so prominent there, was quarried in the early Middle Ages. A priest named Cyril had his foot crushed when one of the marble blocks was dislodged, says the life of St. Hilarius. Lovers of ancient buildings have accorded him little sympathy. What remained of the theatre was fortified in the ninth century; one tower survives. Later in the Middle Ages, as the fortifications decayed, the site became covered by houses, gardens and a church. Excavation began fitfully in the seventeenth century and was completed in more scientific fashion in the nineteenth. Two columns from the *scaena* are still standing, next to the bases of others; in the absence of the wall, oleanders and dark pines form a backdrop. It is rather like a Greek theatre without the hill. As well as the columns, patterned *orchestra* and tiers of seats, there are areas of ungrouped fragments of pillars, bases and other worked stone: carved acanthus leaves, rosettes, some dimly discernible figures, with the grass growing around them.

Various elements of decoration have also been found and are now mostly in the Musée de l'Arles Antique. The altar of Apollo, to whom theatres were dedicated, shows the god between his laurel-trees leaning, as often, on his lyre. The flaying of Marsyas, who dared to pit his pipes against the god's lyre, is also represented: a warning, perhaps, to hubristic performers or their votaries. The higher aspirations of the theatre and the community may also be implied—Apollonian rather than Dionysiac. Traditionally, as *Hall's Dictionary of Subjects and Symbols in Art* puts it, "the cool sound of strings was felt to have a spiritually uplifting quality, while the coarse sound of the reed pipe stirred the passions."

The first significant find, in 1651, was the so-called Vénus d'Arles. This statue was the subject of scholarly debate later in the century, when some maintained that she was actually Diana (inconveniently deprived of her bow or other attributes). By this time, however, the subject of debate was far away since "at length the wiser magistrates of the town agreed to send it as a present to their august monarch ... and if you have a mind to see an inanimate woman who has made such a noise in the world, you will find her at Versailles" (Philip Thicknesse, *A Year's Journey in France and Part of Spain*, 1777). Subsequently she went to the Louvre and is still there; the Musée de l'Arles Antique has a cast. This famously absent piece of local heritage became something of an icon for the nineteenth-century Provençal revivalists—an instance of the cultural distinction of Provence and the way the north had appropriated it. The fact that the Venus was found at the Theatre contributed to its place in local affections. In September 1877 Théodore Aubanel delivered his "Venus d'Arle" there in front, says the journal *Lou Provençau*, of a wondering, tearful multitude. It was a much-remembered moonlit night and other Provençal poets had already stirred the audience. "All the *félibres*" had joined Félix Gras in the refrain of his "famous poem of King Pierre".

Encouraged by such earlier outpourings of Provençal feeling, Frédéric Mistral decided to hold here the *Festo Vierginenco*, or Fête Virginale, of 1904. At the *Festo*, Jules Charles-Roux reports in *Le Costume en Provence* (1907), some "370 *chato* [girls] put on their Provençal costume for the first time, and came to promise they would never abandon it." Mistral himself presided: photographs show the elderly poet posed graciously, broad hat on head or in hand. To each girl he handed a diploma—an offering to these "sisters of Mireille" or *sorre de Mirèio*. The paper also shows a Provençale at her toilette, butterflies, a cicada, olive-branches, and the two columns of the theatre on a starry night. As the recipients filed past, the girls from Maillane sang Mistral's specially composed cantata, saluting the charms of the *chato* of each town and village represented and in the last verse referring to his Mireille as an exemplary coif-wearer. Then Mireille herself, in words at least, arrived: Marius Jouveau's flattering, indeed fairly blasphemous poem "Mirèio à Frederi Mistral" was spoken by two young Arlésiennes bearing sprays of *saladelle* (statice or sea-lavender). The master is praised for having had the "idée élevée" which "makes us truly take communion with the race as in a sacrament"; Mireille addresses him as "High Priest".

Photographs of the stage and seats overspilling with people, parasols massed before the stage, the girls from the Camargue on horses amid great blocks of fallen ancient masonry, suggest that Mistral was right to use the theatre rather than the arena. In spite of all the speechifying and diploma-delivering, it was a fairly intimate occasion, part rally, part speech-day with proud parents watching their daughters in their Sunday best. An event involving mature men and specially dressed-up teenage girls may make us somewhat uneasy today, but at the time, of course, the great majority of organizers and participants saw it all much more innocently.

Place du Forum and the Cryptoportiques

Two Corinthian columns and part of a pediment, built into the wall of the Hôtel du Nord in Place du Forum, are all that is left above ground of the Roman Forum. They may come from either a gateway or the façade of a temple. Near this trace of Roman greatness was erected in 1909 a statue of Frédéric Mistral, the man regarded as best expressing the city's sense of resurgently Provençal identity. The present statue is a replica made in 1945 to replace the original, which was lost in 1942. The poet stands with stick, hat, and coat draped over his arm. Above a dedication from Provence smiles one of the ubiquitous carved Arlésiennes. There was much pomp and speech-making at the statue's unveiling; Mistral's own private response to this figure (so obviously waiting for a train), was less reverent: "all that's missing is his suitcase."

Because the Forum was built into the side of a hill, it needed shoring up with a large substructure. The Cryptoportiques (or Cryptoporticus) consist of a U-shape of vaulted subterranean arcades of about the 20s BC (later extended). The most popular theory about their use apart from supporting the Forum is that they were a granary or some other kind of storehouse. But it may be difficult for visitors, descending the several flights of stairs down from the former Jesuit chapel to these dimly-lit tunnels with their sound of dripping water, to imagine this as anything as prosaically useful as a store. Particularly if you manage to come here alone, or nearly alone, you half-expect to meet a Roman, half-think you are one. Some ritual should unfold here: calmly hieratic, you may feel in the near-silence, or something a little more nightmarish once other visitors' voices begin to echo while they themselves are often out of sight.

Les Alyscamps

Some of the sarcophagi which line the long walk through the ancient and medieval cemetery of Les Alyscamps—or the Champs-Elysées, the Elysian Fields—are inscribed and patterned, but most have entered a dignified, harmonious anonymity. The lack of sculptural detail, the length of the walk, and the dust, pine-cones, leaves or leaf-mould which at different times of year deaden the footfall, are all conducive to contemplation. There is an extraordinary variety of trees. (Van Gogh and Gauguin painted the poplars.) The tombs are empty, their heavy lids seem now unnecessary. Paul-Jean Toulet (1867-1920) pays tribute to the atmosphere in his short poem "En Arles". Here, in such peace, doves can be expected to be quiet and love to be spoken low: "*Et que se taisent les colombes:/Parle tout bas, si c'est d'amour,/Au bord des tombes.*"

After so much open-air simplicity it can be strange, at first, to enter the dim interior of the comparatively well preserved church of St. Honorat, and see carved helmets and shields and great round piers, and hear your steps on a stone floor or the echo of a child's cry. But once, when this was one among many churches and chapels, the cemetery must have been a fairly active place. Certainly it was much more extensive than now, and a pilgrimage centre of some importance in the early Middle Ages. St. Trophimus, an early saint subsequently buried here, is supposed to have prayed successfully for Christ to come and bless the site; He returned annually to say mass. Some legends made Les Alyscamps the resting-place of Charlemagne's paladins, or of other heroes slain in conflict with the Saracens. Less shadowy figures were definitely buried at St. Honorat, including in 429 St. Honoratus, bishop of Arles, himself. At the funeral, according to the Latin discourse by his relative and successor St. Hilarius, everyone wanted to kiss the holy man's body or at least his bier; "at first it lay vested with a great display of faith; afterwards, on its way to the grave, with a greater display of faith it was almost stripped naked."

Most corpses, of course, arrived more quietly. Many, according to tradition, were floated down the Rhône in boats from towns and villages further north. The family or friends of the deceased would put the burial fee in the boat with them and the monks of St. Honorat would stop the boats and bury the bodies.

As more bodies arrived, whether by water or by land, the necropolis expanded to a considerable size. (Its fame was widespread too. Dante mentions the tombs at Arles in *Inferno* Canto IX, comparing and then contrasting them with the hotter and more crowded versions in which the heresiarchs are confined.) Even when Philip Thicknesse came (*A Year's Journey Through France and Part of Spain*, 1777), there were still many sarcophagi, if in less than good order. You had to thread your way, apparently, between an infinite number of Pagan and Christian monuments, lying thick upon the surface in the utmost disorder and confusion, insomuch, that one would think the Day of Judgment was arrived and the dead were risen. Neither Stepney church-yard, nor any one in or near a great city, shows so many headstones as this spot does stone coffins of an immense size, hewn out of one piece; the covers of most of which had been broken or removed sufficiently to search for such things as were buried with the dead.

And a good number of the sarcophagi, broken or whole, were already elsewhere. Some had been used for building material. Many had been donated by the city to august visitors including King Charles IX, who lost a boatload of sarcophagi (and some porphyry pillars from Notre-Dame-de-la-Major, near the arena) in the Rhône.

The problem got worse as Arles declined in importance. Sabine Baring-Gould is not entirely exaggerating when, in *In Troubadour-Land* (1891), he says that "so [economically] depressed did Arles become some time ago, that its only lively trade was in old coffins." Since "the curators of the museums of Paris, Marseilles, Avignon, Aix, etc, thirsted after sarcophagi, the mournful [Arlésiens] went to their necropolis, dug up as many as were wanted, and forwarded coffins to those who had made requisition for them." Others went to less caring homes:

> In every farmyard the pigs eat out of old sarcophagi. The fountains spout into them, the bacon is cured in them. The farrier dips his hot iron into a sarcophagus. In the churches the altars are made of them. The foundations of the houses are laid in them. The very air seems to be pervaded by the dust of the dead, and this dust lies heavy on the spirit and energies of the inhabitants.

The near-final blow for Les Alyscamps itself had been the coming of the railway to Arles. A marshalling yard was built over much of the site and made what was left, for a time, much noisier. (Today's houses and workshops are more discreet.) But the one avenue has survived, and the Musée de l'Arles Antique, building on the work of earlier local collectors and museums, possesses a spectacular selection of the sarcophagi, only rarely now the preserve of princes or pigs.

The Musée de l'Arles Antique

The great triangle of Henri Ciriani's strikingly modern, spacious museum was completed in 1995. (Ciriani also designed the Historial de la Grande Guerre at Péronne in Picardy.) There are no room divisions: load-bearing concrete columns allow the use of one vast museum space. Deep blue enamelled glass makes the exterior less forbidding than it might be, and from the light interior there are views of grasses, trees and the river.

One of the most attractive features of the museum is its beautiful reconstructions, in two or three dimensions, of the ancient city: of fourth-century Arelate, for instance, with its amphitheatre, theatre, forum, circus and straight main streets, its walls and gates, necropolises—one became Les Alyscamps—and surrounding farm-land and marshes. There are also separate models of the Forum, Cryptoportiques and bridge—six stone arches at either end and then a flexible arrangement including drawbridges and anchored boats—and so on. To help suggest the size of the mid-first-century AD Circus, the remains of which have been excavated near the museum, even the model is unusually large; the original was 101 metres wide and 450 long and could hold 20,000 spectators. Also shown are some of the oak and pine piles which supported the structure on its marshy site. The granite obelisk from the Circus was eventually installed in what is now Place de la République in 1676.

The museum covers, in considerable detail, pre-Roman Arles and every possible aspect of the Roman city from its art and religion to its lead pipes. A few objects stand out: a colossal marble head of Augustus fished out of the sea off Fos in 1987; from the decoration of the theatre, a fine white marble bust of Aphrodite with elegant hairstyle and a look of Greek abstraction—a first-century BC copy of a fourth-century BC Greek original. There is a large collection of funerary inscriptions and sarcophagi from Les Alyscamps and elsewhere. A detailed hunting scene on a third-century white marble sarcophagus from Les Alyscamps shows horsemen, slaves and dogs bringing down stags, and hunters on foot with dogs attacking boar. Much action is deployed in the space available. The hunters appear fairly calm while the slaves work hard, one holding the ropes of a trap, another seizing a stag by the snout and neck and bracing himself against it with his foot. A superb series of mosaics comes mostly from the villas of Trinquetaille, just across the Rhône. Among the subjects treated are Europa on the bull Jupiter, Orpheus charming the animals, and the god Aion (or Aeon) holding the wheel of the Zodiac.

Even more evidence of the ancient importance of Arles, especially as a port, will reach the museum over the next few years. Particularly since the mid-1990s archaeologists have found many objects on the bed of the Rhône at Arles, mostly from the first century AD and often in good condition. In one month of 2004 alone, finds included 350 amphoras (160 of them complete), 600 other pieces of pottery, bronze cups, two wooden anchors and one of iron, as well as probable traces of a quay. One of the most unusual discoveries so far is a seven-metre oar.

Saint-Trophime: "so cruel, so monstrous, like a Chinese nightmare"
The early cathedral on this site was dedicated to St. Stephen. It was rebuilt in the eleventh and twelfth century and the remains of St. Trophimus were transferred here from Les Alyscamps. The new church became Saint-Trophime in 1152 and its decorated west portal was completed in about 1190. The structure of the portal is thought to be derived from the Roman triumphal arches of Provence, and some of the detail from the area's abundant Roman sarcophagi. Elsie Whitlock Rose, in *Cathedrals and Cloisters of the South of France* (1906), gives a usefully clear explanation of the upper parts of the portal:

> In design it is simple, in execution incomparably rich. The principal theme of the Last Judgement has Christ seated on a throne as a central figure, and about him are the symbols of the Four Evangelists [man, lion, eagle and ox]. This is the treatment of the tympanum. Underneath, Patriarchs, Saints, Just, and Condemned form the beautiful frieze. The Apostles are seated; and to their left is an angel guarding the gates of Paradise against two Bishops and a crowd of laymen who have yet to fully expiate their sins in Purgatory. Behind them, naked, with their feet in the flames, are those condemned to everlasting Hell; and still beyond is a lower depth where souls are already half-consumed in hideous fires. On the Apostles' extreme right is the beginning of our human history, the Temptation of Adam and Eve; and marching toward the holy men, on this same side, is the long procession of those Redeemed from Adam's fall, clothed in

righteousness. An angel goes before them, and hands a small child—a ransomed soul—to Abraham, Isaac, and Jacob. The end panels treat the last phases of the dominant theme; —a mammoth angel [Michael] in the one weighs the souls of the dead; and an equally awe-inspiring devil in the other is preparing to cast two of the Lost into a sea of fire.

To Rose's description of the frieze one might add that the "Just" or saved are not only clothed in righteousness but voluntarily linked by love, whereas the damned are naked and chained together. The first group moves right, towards the centre, Christ and salvation. The second group also moves, or is propelled, to the right—away from Christ and salvation. The sharp flames help to give a rippling, unstoppable effect. One of the damned, poignantly, looks back.

Beneath the saved, the damned, and the twelve apostles at centre, come nativity scenes: the Magi, the Massacre of the Innocents; the Annunciation just left of the door, the nativity itself on the right. In the recesses on either side of the entrance are large figures of saints. St. Trophimus, one hand raised in blessing and the other holding his crozier, has a mitre placed on his head by angels. St. Peter carries his usual keys. On the right is the stoning of St. Stephen; his soul is lifted up to Heaven. There is also a great variety of lions. It is the sort of façade you can look at for a long time—even, perhaps, if you accept Alan Borg's verdict in an entry for *The Dictionary of Art* (1996) that the sculpture "despite its virtuosity... has a mechanised and mass-produced appearance, which suggests that it was carved very rapidly." Van Gogh reacted more intensely: the portal was beautiful but also "so cruel, so monstrous, like a Chinese nightmare".

The large interior of Saint-Trophime was restored in the 1870s to a semblance of its medieval self. For Rose, in spite of some remaining "excrescences", "a fine, exquisite loftiness, a faultless balance of proportion, are in this severe interior." The cloister, however, has generally excited more interest. The north and east wings are late twelfth-century Romanesque, the others fourteenth-century Gothic. On the corner pillars the saints include, again, the cathedral patrons Trophimus and Stephen: the one serene in benediction, the other perhaps slightly resigned but still secure, well grounded. (His savage stoning to death features, again, in the next panel.) The Romanesque capitals are carved with such biblical scenes as the Flight into Egypt, while the Gothic wings concentrate on the life of Trophimus (south) and legends like St. Martha's (west).

In Michael de Larrabeiti's *The Provençal Tales* (1988) a shepherd explains "why two sides of the cloister of St. Trophime are miracles of art and why the other two are not." Apparently it was no dry matter of Romanesque versus Gothic. The Archbishop of Arles has hired the great Master Sculptor to work on the new church. The churchman, mindful of the glory that will accrue to him if the work is perfect, will pay anything, let the Master do anything, to advance the project. With his authority the Master wanders the streets of Arles searching for suitable models for the figures on the cloister capitals:

> When he found what he wanted the archers who accompanied him would seize the person chosen and take them back to the cloisters, ignoring their protestations. The Master was ruthless in his art. He had no pity, dressing his models, men and women, in the roughest of clothes or stripping them naked to study their muscles or their bones. Often he made them pose for hours without rest or food, cursing them if they dared move without his express command...He was like a man possessed, and began to produce his sculpture so rapidly that many said the rumours were true, that he was indeed a magician.

When the Archbishop sees the first capital he is tremendously impressed but pretends not to be, suggesting to the Master that, fine though the figures are, a little more life could be infused. The sculptor has a solution, as the mason Faldo discovers: he does indeed have magic powers and uses them to incorporate his models in his sculptures—the ultimate way of making them "lifelike". A petty thief becomes Judas; "in his eye, the light of cunning was seized in flight and stilled forever." The Master maintains to Faldo that he takes worthless lives and makes them beautiful and immortal.

Faldo informs the Archbishop of his discovery but he will not listen to anything which spoils his dream of glory: what Faldo saw was a result of fatigue or "a trial of your devotion". And so the work on the east and north cloister continues. Eventually—it will stop him talking again, for one thing—the Master decides to use Faldo for his Lazarus at the north-west corner. But the mason, before he is conjured into marble, utters a mighty curse: "May you lose all your powers... both natural and magic. May you be spurned by those who admired you... And may you always know what you have lost, and may your heart always be empty so that you suffer as your victims suffer. With this curse I curse you." And so it happens. When the Master moves on to the west side he has lost his ability and his spells no longer work on his models. The Archbishop takes away his gold and his fine house—"What is half a cloister to me?"—and, when he has still achieved nothing after a month, condemns him to the galleys. The Archbishop will not have his perfect cloister, but keeps what he has: he is furious when his Deacon suggests that he should find a magician who can free the people trapped in the stone. In fact he wants to find one who can do the same for the rest of the cloister and the church.

The Musée Réattu and the Museon Arlaten

The Musée Réattu was, in the opinion of Van Gogh, an atrocious "hoax" or "humbug". Jacques Réattu (1760-1833) had lived here in what was once a Grand Priory of the Knights of Malta, begun in the fifteenth century. The museum shows many of his paintings of classical and religious scenes. Somewhat more distinctive are his grisailles for a proposed 1790s sequence in honour of the patriotic martyrs of Marseille: pieces on such thoroughly Revolutionary topics as "The Tree of Liberty defended by Strength and Prudence against the attacks of Royalism, [Religious] Fanaticism, Atheism and Ignorance". The most interesting art at the Réattu, however, is in the twentieth-century section. There are paintings by Dufy, Vlaminck, Léger, late drawings by Picasso, and sculptures by Osip Zadkine (1890-1967) including an odalisque and a proposed monument to the van Gogh brothers. There is also an important photographic collection.

The Museon Arlaten, in the sixteenth-century Hôtel de Laval-Castellane, has a stronger place in local tradition. It is a shrine to Frédéric Mistral, who created it and spent his 1904 Nobel prize-money on it. It also continues to uphold his intention of preserving Provençal culture. He put the same sustained effort into gathering, labelling and organizing exhibits as he did into the composition of long poems or his Provençal dictionary. His will still rules; this is a museum of his time as much as ours, with its handwritten labels and rather dimly-lit rooms. Visitors are greeted by costumed Arlésiennes, as stipulated by the master. (This strikes some people as living tradition, others as mere quaintness.) Costumes are also among the exhibits, with musical instruments, *santons* (nativity figurines), pottery, prints of local scenes and events, tableaux of traditional farm-life, and some Mistral memorabilia. A large poster advertises the "fiftieth anniversary of *Mireille*. Jubilee of F. Mistral", a great three-day event in Arles in May 1909: a torch-lit musical procession, the inauguration of the new museum premises, a dance (*farandole*) competition, Camarguais horse-races, illuminations and concert in the Place Lamartine, a production of Gounod's Mistral-based opera *Mireille* in the Arena—and doings with bulls there the following day—and a concert and "fête vénitienne" on the canal.

Older festivals and legends are also covered. There is a splendid range of processional, model, and pictured "tarasques", versions of the monster associated particularly with Tarascon. Most have spikes on their backs. Some have lions' heads. The main processional specimen has some rather snail-like features (the toilet-roll-style horns look like antennae) but would appear fiercer in movement. Finally in the courtyard the remains of a Roman temple and paved area have been excavated.

Montmajour

For much of its history the hill of Montmajour, near Arles, was surrounded by marshes. Wandering wild boar, says Abbé J.-M. Trichaud in his enthusiastic 1854 monograph on the abbey ruins, used to come here to feed on thyme, aspic and rosemary. The remoteness and fertility of the near-island appealed not only to discerning pigs but to people seeking a refuge from the secular world or the Saracen wars. Gradually a small community of anchorites grew up, and legend declares that in the sixth century King Childebert was so impressed by their hospitality— they served him wild fruit and cool, limpid water—that he built the first church here.

Other stories have Childebert recognizing the purity of the anchorites' faith as well as their water. This, besides, is one among several foundation myths. Later the monks associated themselves with St. Trophimus and showed his throne or confessional to visitors. Another tale has Charlemagne (742-814) founding the chapel of Sainte-Croix

after defeating the Saracens nearby; his paladins are buried at Montmajour, as at so many other places. But in fact the first church of St. Pierre seems to have been built (into the south flank of the hill) in the tenth or early eleventh century. The much larger church of Notre-Dame and the small chapel of Sainte-Croix date mostly from the mid-twelfth century, and the robust 26-metre-high tower or keep from 1369. The fortification was undertaken by the Benedictines as a sensible precaution after the siege of Arles by Bertrand du Guesclin in 1368. The less military cloister also survives, carved eclectically with New Testament scenes, monkeys, bears, salamanders, a head of Tantalus, a knight fighting a lion, and a fierce man-eating monster or Tarasque.

Pilgrims came across the marshes in large numbers to venerate the fragment of the true cross which, the monks claimed, had been given by Constantine the Great—another important connection to go with Trophimus and Charlemagne. There was both a need, and the money, for extensive monastic buildings. Most of these, however, including the library and kitchen, collapsed in 1703 or were destroyed by the fire of 1726. The remains of their 1720s-30s replacements have survived. The new quarters were, apparently, fairly luxurious. Jean-Maurice Roquette, in his guide to the abbey (1993), cites a 1780s manuscript account of the spacious terraces, monks' rooms with iron balconies and marble chimneypieces, a splendid library, "superbes salons" for guests, and abundant fish served with exquisite wines. But in 1786 this civilized existence was abruptly ended by events far from Montmajour. The last abbot, the Cardinal-Prince de Rohan, was forced to resign following his involvement in the "necklace affair"—a complicated scandal in which the prelate was fooled into believing that Queen Marie-Antoinette had made secret assignations with him and sold him a priceless piece of jewellery. Louis XVI suppressed the monastery; a few monks stayed on site but were soon removed by the Revolution, in the course of which Montmajour was sold in various lots. These had gradually to be bought back before restoration could begin in the 1830s. There had been some quarrying; the painter Jacques Réattu, however, had bought and saved the tower.

A fair amount of restoration had been completed by the time Vincent van Gogh first came upon this "ruined abbey on a hill covered with holly, pines, and grey olives" in March 1888. He returned several times from May onwards and produced a powerful series of drawings in pencil, reed pen and black and brown ink, mostly not of the abbey but of its views across the plain of the Crau or to Arles. "In these vast plains," says Ronald Pickvance (*Van Gogh in Arles*, 1984), partly paraphrasing a letter to Theo, "van Gogh felt infinity and recovered his native Dutch landscape tradition, the tradition of Rembrandt, Salomon Koninck, and Jacob van Ruisdael." At Montmajour itself the attractions were more southern. In July he was there with his friend from Arles, Second Lieutenant Milliet (subject of a portrait; a fidgety sitter); they "explored the old garden and stole some excellent figs." Here, he told Theo, were

high reeds, vines, ivy, fig-trees, olive-trees, pomegranates with full flowers of the most vivid orange, hundred-year-old cypresses, ash trees, and willows, rock oaks, half-demolished staircases, ogive windows in ruins, blocks of white rock covered with lichen, and fragments of crumbling walls scattered here and there amid the greenery.

Chapter Four
Van Gogh's Provence
Part Two: The Alpilles

The London Alpine Club, says Alphonse Daudet in *Tartarin sur les Alpes* (1885), is renowned "jusqu'aux Indes". There is this difference between it and the Club Alpin of Tarascon: "the *Tarasconnais*, instead of leaving their country to conquer foreign peaks, have contented themselves with what was to hand, or rather to foot, on their doorstep." They go not to the Alps but to the "Alpines"—more often called the Alpilles:

> that chain of little mountains scented with thyme and lavender, harmless and not very high (150 to 200 metres above sea-level), which provide the roads of Provence with an undulating blue horizon and which local imagination has endowed with such fabulous and characteristic names as "le Mont-Terrible", "World's End", "The Giants' Peak", etc.

On Sunday mornings, claims Daudet, you can see the members going off to these mountains, gaitered, pick in hand, bag and tent on back, for climbs amid what the local press exaggerates into terrifying abysses, gulfs and gorges. Tartarin, although he is President of the club and will eventually find himself forced to ascend the Alps, rarely takes part in these expeditions. He prefers reading out the newspaper's "tragic accounts" with "much rolling of eyes and intonation fit to make the ladies pale".

The Alpilles, it is true, are not enormous. But their appearance and structure—the pale limestone moulded into jagged, irregular crags—belie the lack of height. In rain or fog they can be quite forbidding. If they are an easy target for Daudet's comic distortion, they also lend themselves to van Gogh's more intense rearrangements or realizations. In *Olive Trees with the Alpilles in the Background* the mountains (Mont

Les Antiques: the mausoleum or cenotaph and arch at the edge of Roman Glanum.

Gaussier and the Montagne des Deux Trous) ripple in deep and even deeper purple and the grey-blue sky shows through the "two holes". In *Mountains at Saint-Rémy* van Gogh looks at the mountains from a different angle and further away; the Alpilles here are yellow, green, purple. The yellow shapes in the foreground are more liquid and mobile while the deep colour is reserved mainly for the more static—but it looks like a temporary stasis—Montagne des Deux Trous.

Saint-Paul-de-Mausole: "light turning into conflagration"

Van Gogh saw the Alpilles most often from the asylum of Saint-Paul-de-Mausole, where he voluntarily interned himself on 8 May 1889. This site between Saint-Rémy and the mountains has long been associated with healing—possibly since ancient times when pilgrims came to the sacred spring at the city of Glanum, probably since the early Middle Ages. There was a church here by 962; the surviving church is mostly twelfth-century apart from the eighteenth-century façade and is adjoined by a small cloister. This leads on to the former asylum, where patients with mental and other problems were tended by Franciscan Observantine monks in the seventeenth and eighteenth centuries. After the selling-off of ecclesiastical property during the Revolution the asylum was run by lay staff, later in collaboration with two orders of nuns. The institution van Gogh entered had been formally established in 1855. Since 1995 the Maison de Santé Saint-Paul-de-Mausole has been associated with Valetudo, an organization named after the goddess of health worshipped at Glanum. Art is one of the therapies practised, and some paintings by current patients are on sale. Van Gogh himself fantasized about using the corridors and empty rooms to exhibit paintings.

The treatment available at Saint-Paul in 1889 was fairly unsophisticated. It consisted mainly of hydrotherapy: regular long baths. This often calmed the patients, but did little to effect long-term cure. Boredom was the norm, not the Gothic "melancholy of death" perceived in the sleepy grounds and "suffocating" buildings by Paul Mariéton (*La Terre provençale*) a year earlier: van Gogh wrote to his brother Theo on 25 May 1889 about "these unfortunates who, having absolutely nothing to do (not a book, nothing to occupy them but games of boules and draughts) have no other daily distraction but to cram themselves with chickpeas, beans and lentils" in regular quantities at regular times. It is an inoffensive and a cheap way to fill your day, particularly since "digesting such stuff presents certain difficulties." On rainy days the inmates gather in a room "like a third-class waiting-room in some stagnant village" where the would-be passengers look the part with their hats, glasses, sticks and travelling clothes. It is almost as if they were at the seaside. (More evidently disturbed patients were confined to another part of the building.)

Van Gogh, however, had an inestimable advantage over the other bean-eaters and would-be railway-passengers: he was allowed, except during his periodic crises, to go on painting. This was one of the privileges afforded to him as someone who had entered of his own free will and was evidently not, most of the time, conventionally "mad": Dr. Peyron at Saint-Paul, among others, diagnosed epilepsy. He was given not only a bedroom but a second room for use as a studio, from which he could see the cornfield and large wall which figure in a number of the paintings. There are some reproductions, as well as reconstructions of the rooms, at Saint-Paul today. Mariéton complained at "such misery and darkness" so near the "poésie lumineuse" of the landscape; van Gogh, however, engaged with the surrounding brightness. Melissa McQuillan (*Van Gogh*, 1989) points out that in the Saint-Rémy paintings especially he sought "luminosity"; he moved on to "a subtler range and mixture of hues... as if light as colour had ceded to light as charged atmospheric illumination."

For the first few weeks he worked in his studio and the asylum garden, producing paintings and drawings at his usual remarkable speed. From June he was also allowed to go into the countryside with an attendant. Later, work would be interrupted by his attacks and convalescence. The first attack since Arles came on when he was painting on a windy day in July, leaving him depressed and frustrated at being forbidden to paint for about a month. In December during an attack he tried to poison himself, as on other occasions, by eating paints. A third crisis came soon after a visit to Arles on 19 January 1890 and a fourth while he was actually in Arles on 22 February. This time van Gogh was ill—often, reported Peyron, "despondent and suspicious"—until April. His own theory about this collapse was that it had been caused by his reaction to the enthusiastic article about his work by Albert Aurier, published in *Le Mercure de France* on 1 January: he feared, he said, that punishment would somehow follow praise. Some have felt that the problem had more to do with suppressed feelings of exclusion following the birth of a son, at the end of January, to Theo and his wife Jo (an event he claimed, at least, to welcome wholeheartedly). By the end of April van Gogh was desperate to leave the asylum, which had clearly not been able to cure his condition—although Peyron surprisingly wrote "guérison", "cure", in the "Observations" column of his register. On 16 May he left for a brief visit to Theo and his family in Paris, a final move to Auvers-sur-Oise, and suicide at the end of July.

In spite of the breakdowns, van Gogh achieved a great deal at Saint-Paul. Producing an average of one work per day, he painted the asylum garden, the corridors and vestibule (ochre, red, brown), rich blue irises, quarries, wheat fields, the Alpilles, white almond-blossom against a blue sky as a welcome to his baby nephew, the church of Saint-Paul with autumn trees and field, and imaginative re-workings of prints by Rembrandt, Delacroix, Millet and Daumier. He painted fifteen pictures of olive-groves, including one where what he calls the leaves' "violet shadows on the sunny sand" have an extraordinary pulsing effect. He worked on two versions of his "pale, blond yellow" wheat field with a reaper who figures death, he told Theo, but "a death where there is nothing sad; it happens in full light with a sun which floods everything with a fine gold light." The cypress, too, was traditionally associated with death but one would not gather this from most of the paintings:

> its lines and proportions are as beautiful as an Egyptian obelisk. And the green is of so refined a quality. It is the splash of *black* in a sunny landscape, but it is one of the most interesting black notes, the most difficult to get exactly right that I can imagine. Well you must see them against the blue, or, to put it better, *in* the blue.

Some of van Gogh's most famous cypresses occur in "Starry Night" (Museum of Modern Art, New York), one of his most popular and most interpreted paintings. Ronald Pickvance notes that "suggested sources range from the Bible (Genesis or Revelations) to Whitman and Longfellow, from Zola and Daudet to Dickens and Carlyle." In a sense this is a view over Saint-Rémy with houses and Alpilles, but the pointed, aspiring bell-tower of the church is completely unlike the real one, and what is happening in the sky seems too vast or too apocalyptic to be tied to a locality. This is perhaps the painting which can be most readily aligned with Aurier's ecstatic early account of van Gogh's dazzling skies of "sapphires and turquoises", skies "like flows of fused metals and crystals" sometimes irradiated by "terrible solar discs"; a strange nature, both real and somehow supernatural, which involves "form becoming nightmare, colour becoming flames, lava, and gems, light turning into conflagration, life, hot fever."

Aurier's visionary rhetoric applies less well to the portraits which van Gogh sometimes said were his most important area of endeavour. At Saint-Paul there were fewer opportunities for portraiture than in Arles. But François Trabuc, the chief orderly, sat for him as did Trabuc's wife Jeanne. Van Gogh was interested by his look of "contemplative calm" in spite or because of the fact that he had witnessed much death and suffering—he had worked in a hospital in Marseille during two outbreaks of cholera. Writing to Theo, van Gogh went on searching for the essence—physical appearance expressing inner quality—of Trabuc. He has a rather military air and "small keen black eyes"; he would look like a bird of prey were it not for his evident intelligence and kindness.

The same interest is arguably evident in the self-portraits he painted in September 1889, just before his Trabucs. In the first, the haggard face in pale greens and yellows "emerges, unearthly, from the surrounding darkness" (Ronald Pickvance). It is easy to see this as an image of the artist's situation or state of mind: precarious composure as he recovers from his most recent collapse, perhaps renewed commitment to his art— he shows himself here with smock, brushes and palette. The extraordinarily different images projected in van Gogh's various self-portraits should caution us, however, against too simply psychological a reading: they are controlled experiments as much as personal statements or mood-barometers. Even the second Saint-Paul version (at the Musée d'Orsay in Paris), begun immediately after the first, is strikingly different: the background and the coat are light blue and the expression in the blue eyes may be read as reserved, perhaps a little suspicious, sad but resolute, more inward-looking—or as the painter put it himself to Theo, "vague and veiled". Even in his last months at Auvers he was still searching for ways to represent "our impassioned expressions".

Les Antiques

Saint-Paul-de-Mausole takes its name from an ancient monument a few hundred metres away, the mausoleum on what has long been known as the Plateau des Antiques. The mausoleum, now in fact believed to be a cenotaph—a memorial rather than a burial-place—stood just outside the entrance to the Gallo-Greek and Gallo-Roman city of Glanum and quite close to the Via Domitia, the main road from Narbonne to Arles. With the triumphal arch which marked the entrance to the city, the cenotaph remained largely intact while the rest of Glanum was worn away, quarried and gradually covered by alluvial deposits from the Alpilles.

The mausoleum, probably built in about 30-20 BC, honours members of a Gallic family who appear—they took the name Julius—to have been rewarded for loyal military service with a grant of Roman citizenship from Julius Caesar. Sextus, Marcus and Lucius Julius commemorate their father Caius and their grandfather. Identifying the two statues was once a popular local pastime. Mary Darmesteter, writing about a trip to Provence for *The Contemporary Review* in 1892, claims to have been told that they were Julius and Caesar, the similarly divided general Caius and Marius, or "the great Caius Marius and the Prophetess Martha, the sister of Lazarus... They were, as you may say, a pair of friends."

The base celebrates, by mythological analogy, the family's heroic achievements. The relief on the south face shows Meleager hunting the Calydonian boar with the help of the mounted Castor and Pollux. The struggle is fierce: Meleager's wounded colleagues are to be seen at left and at right an axe spills over from the main frame. Desperate battle also figures on the west side, a scene from *The Iliad* in which Menelaus defends Patroclus' body from the Trojans. To the north unidentified horsemen fight; this time a sword and the front-quarters of a horse spill over. To the east, according to most interpreters, the noble ancestor unseats a mounted Amazon, a figure of Victory puts a hand on his shoulder and, on the left, Fame delivers to his family news of his success and perhaps the grant of citizenship.

The general emphasis on battle around the base contrasts with the serenity of ordered arches, columns and effigies above: a four-sided arched structure, a frieze of tritons and other legendary creatures, the funerary inscription, and then a circular *tholos* whose Corinthian columns surround the two figures in togas. Physically and metaphorically the ancestors are lifted high above the contingent, if glory-gaining, world of conflict.

The arch at Les Antiques (c. 20AD) has lost its attic storey and is generally in worse condition than its neighbour. But enough remains to suggest something about the attitudes of Romans and Gauls in the post-conquest period. The east side shows chained Gaulish captives, one bound to a "trophy"—a heap of weapons. On the west side are more chained prisoners; a female figure sitting on a second heap is either another of the defeated or, more likely, the victorious goddess Roma. Most interestingly, a free Gaul or Gallo-Roman wearing his traditional cloak or *sagum* is shown beside one of the prisoners. There may, as has sometimes been suggested, be some implied sympathy for the vanquished, or it may simply be that Rome needs to be shown defeating strong, worthy adversaries. If there is sympathy, it is purely retrospective. In the present, Rome offers a choice: you can be like the cloaked figure—dress traditionally rather than engage in traditional armed resistance—or you can be bound with the defeated. Glanum has chosen the first option, it is implied.

The abundance available to the cooperative is suggested by the fruits and flowers on the frieze of the archivolt. Nearly nine centuries later, Paul Mariéton delighted in the actual vegetation nearby. For him the site was Greek rather than Roman, with its asphodels and "small Attic flowers" and its air "balsamically perfumed" by aromatic herbs.

Glanum

The site of the city, excavated mainly from the 1940s onward by Henri Rolland, slopes gradually up a defile through the Alpilles, the Vallon de Notre Dame de Laval. Stone for building was available in plenty; a small late-Roman quarry has left its traces just before the site entrance and there are larger quarries nearby. Near the Mas de la Pyramide the so-called Pyramid, a pillar of stone over 20 metres tall, indicates the depth dug down from the original surface level. The other, perhaps the main, reason for settling here was the presence of a spring. From early times it was regarded as sacred and, probably, associated with healing.

Neolithic and Bronze Age people lived here, and by the seventh century BC there was a Celto-Ligurian settlement which traded, after

600, with the new Greek colony of Massalia (Marseille). In later centuries Glanum (or Glanon) itself developed along Greek lines. (Two models in the entrance building helpfully reconstruct the Gallo-Greek city of 150-50 BC and the Gallo-Roman version of 50 BC-AD 270.) The most clearly visible Gallo-Greek remains are at the south end of the site. A second-century BC staircase leads down to the sacred spring-head, still a numinous place, cool even in a hot Provençal summer. Beside this destination of ancient pilgrimages were shrines to Hercules and later— no doubt replacing or complementing earlier equivalents—to the Roman goddess of health, Valetudo. The town's principal Greek building was the once-tiered *bouleuterion* or council-house. The presence of so many olive-trees near the site, especially in the grassy area between it and Saint-Paul-de-Mausole, is another reminder of the Greeks—as well as the sign of a flourishing local industry today.

Not surprisingly, somewhat more is left of Roman Glanum, mostly at the middle and north end of the site. The main public buildings included the basilica and, next to it, with prominent apse and still substantial walls, the curia. Part of the façade of one of the twin temples of the imperial cult was reconstructed in 1992. Its white pillars provide a useful landmark for visitors trying to understand this rich and sometimes confusing site. There are traces too of the public baths, most visibly the cold pool. Towards the north end are the remains of some large private residences, among them the House of the Antes, a Hellenistic and Roman peristyle house with courtyard.

Glanum is one of the most attractive of archaeological ensembles. It is surrounded by trees and inhabited by cicadas, lizards, butterflies, damselflies. And the Alpilles are always there in the near distance, low enough for trees and greenery, steep enough for large stretches of bare pale rock. Mont Gaussier is the dominant hill, to be seen too from the streets of Saint-Rémy. Further left is the "Montagne des Deux Trous" which van Gogh painted, its dark holes clearly visible above the undulating olive-trees.

Saint-Rémy-de-Provence
When there was first talk of excavating at Glanum, the poet Mistral worried that any objects found on site would end up in Paris, as had the Venus of Arles; better they should remain buried, like the legendary local

treasure guarded by the Cabro d'Or, the golden goat. (The story was probably inspired by occasional finds of coins and other objects during the period of Glanum's entombment.) In the event, fortunately, attitudes to the dispersal of finds had changed by the time excavation actually took place, and most of what was unearthed went down the hill to Saint-Rémy, the town which began to supersede Glanum as early as the third century AD. (The later name comes from a connection with the abbey of St Rémy in Reims.) The museum in the Hôtel de Sade contains statues and statuettes, reliefs, inscriptions, lamps, jewels and ex-voto altars from the site.

The sculpture includes the figured four-headed capitals from the portico near the sanctuary. They depict Apollo crowned with laurel, Dionysos, Hermes with small wings attached to his hair, Africa crowned with elephant-skin, and a damaged Pan whose horns and goats' ears are still visible. The classical and the Celtic are interestingly blended: the gods and mythological figures are often Greek, and to have capitals at all is classical, but the figures have a Celtic air, imparted mainly by their ringed, staring eyes. Celtic religion clearly remained a presence in the Gallo-Greek city as perhaps in the Roman: there is a lintel with recesses for human skulls like those from Roquepertuse and Entremont, and a squatting figure with torcs, bracelet and exposed genitals may once have rested his arms on severed heads.

At the twin temples of the Roman imperial cult two more simply classical pieces were discovered: heads generally supposed to represent Augustus' sister Octavia and his wife Livia. The first, as A. Trevor Hodge says in *Ancient Greek France* (1998), "has a round, open, almost chubby face", the second "a longer aristocratic face with high cheek-bones". This is the way the two were traditionally portrayed, perhaps even the way they looked: the noble, put-upon Octavia and the intelligent, purposeful Livia or, in more extreme versions, the hapless, rejected Octavia of Shakespeare's *Antony and Cleopatra* and the ruthless Livia of Graves' *I Claudius*.

The Hôtel de Sade itself, built in the fifteenth and sixteenth centuries, is one of a number of fine former aristocratic residences in the old town. Nearby is the finest, the Hôtel Mistral de Mondragon, the sixteenth-century building which, with its seventeenth-century neighbour, houses a museum of local history, geography and tradition, the Musée des Alpilles. Here the façade blends classical, well-proportioned elegance of architecture and somewhat more vigorous and grotesque elements in the decoration—faces framed by extreme hair, horned masks or skulls and the heads of fierce, noble lions with manes flying. The building runs along one side of Place Favier, a smoothly paved, gently sloping square with horse chestnuts and a small fountain, an area, as James Pope-Hennessy says in *Aspects of Provence* (1952), "more like a room than an open space". Place Péllissier, a somewhat larger square but still compact, has stout plane-trees, a small fountain derived from that of the Four Dolphins at Aix-en-Provence, and the town hall in a former seventeenth-century convent.

Also in the old town is the Hôtel Estrine, which is occupied by the Centre d'Art Présence Van Gogh. In the absence of the paintings themselves (many of them are in Amsterdam) the ground-floor of the gallery shows an audio-visual presentation on the artist, high-quality reproductions of some of the work done at Saint-Paul, and relevant extracts from the letters. A 1956 bronze by Osip Zadkine shows van Gogh drawing with visionary concentration. Upstairs are both temporary exhibitions and selections from the permanent collection of modern painting. Elsewhere in the town are various other galleries. The partly twelfth- and thirteenth-century Chapelle Notre-Dame-de-Pitié houses religious and other works by Mario Prassinos (1916-85). The large Musée Jouenne shows landscapes and townscapes—the popular, fairly realistic works of Michel Jouenne—which will appeal to a very different taste.

Les Baux: "bastions and buttresses and coigns of vantage"

The rock of Les Baux (from Provençal *baou*—"rock" or "escarpment") has been inhabited since Neolithic times. Both human and natural agency are strongly apparent in the pocked, holed, battered, fissured ruins of the buildings begun by the Counts of Les Baux in the tenth century and subsequently much reduced, rebuilt, blown up and quarried. (The light-coloured stone can be dazzlingly, painfully white in summer sun, when the whole hill-top seems as much Middle Eastern as Provençal.) Underfoot now are bare rock, loose stones and sandy soil.

Between the twelfth and the fourteenth centuries particularly, the rulers of Les Baux dominated and sometimes terrorized the surrounding area. They fought long wars with the Counts of Barcelona for control of Provence. Occasionally conflict reached Les Baux itself, as when Roger de Duras laid siege to it in 1355. The castle now displays a reconstruction of one of Roger's weapons—a four-ton ballista in dark wood—and such other medieval siege-aids as a massive trebuchet and a battering-ram. Some more organized demolition followed a rebellion of the once fiercely independent Baux against the kingdom of France in 1483. Restoration and rebuilding followed after 1528, under the aegis of the then owner, Constable de Montmorency. There are remains of the once elegant, porticoed Hôpital Quinquéran, founded in 1583 by the governor's wife, Jeanne de Quinquéran. She also built the so-called Pavillon de la reine Jeanne, in the Vallon de la Fontaine.

But Les Baux looks predominantly medieval, not Renaissance, because of the new demolition campaign of the early 1630s. The town, mainly Protestant, was involved in the rebellion led by Louis XIII's dissident brother Gaston, Duke of Orléans. Royal troops attacked the citadel from the convenient Plateau of Costapera, and once the rebels were defeated the dismantling, on Cardinal Richelieu's instructions, began. Further damage was sustained during the Revolution. In the nineteenth century quarrying continued and parts of the site became houses or store-rooms.

What remained by the 1870s impressed John Addington Symonds ("Old Towns in Provence") as "a naked mountain of yellow sandstone, worn away by nature into bastions and buttresses and coigns of vantage, sculptured by ancient art into palaces and chapels, battlements and dungeons". Art and nature are "confounded in one ruin", for, Symonds insists:

> blocks of masonry lie cheek by jowl with masses of the rough-hewn rock... the doors and windows of old pleasure-rooms are hung with ivy and wild fig for tapestry... High overhead, suspended in mid-air hang chambers—lady's bower or poet's singing-room—now inaccessible, the haunt of hawks and swallows.

As well as birds, he writes, there are two hundred poor inhabitants. They too witness to the glory that has gone, "foddering their wretched goats at carved piscina and ugly sideboards, erecting mud-beplastered hovels in

the halls of feudal princes." This is not the well preserved medieval town described in Murray's guide. It is more like "a decayed old cheese... The living only inhabit the tombs of the dead." A small community continued to live in the village of Les Baux. Near the entrance building of the château is a small twentieth-century graveyard. Here a memorial shows that even such a place lost nine men in 1914-18, two of them, Marius and Célestin Autran, members of the same family. A memorial board in the village church adds a tenth victim.

Now, of course, the locals are more likely to fodder tourists than wretched goats. One food tourists have thrived on is the bloody history of the Lords of Les Baux. Symonds seems to relish this more than the troubadour associations of bowers and singing-rooms. (The most notorious villain based at Les Baux was the murderous Raymond de Turenne, "Scourge of Provence" at the end of the fourteenth century, who was said to enjoy forcing his enemies to jump to their deaths from the towers of the citadel.) Sir Theodore Cook, too, experiences, on his Edwardian readers' behalf, the pleasing frisson of historical violence: at

Les Baux "you feel as if a blood-stained band of medieval cut-throats were lurking behind every crag, or slowly retreating, as you mount, to lure you on to final, irremediable fate."

For years already, Rose Macaulay observes in *Pleasure of Ruins* (1953), "from the walls of Victorian drawing-rooms discreet pale water-colours [had] looked down, entitled in flowing scripts, 'A Robbers' Eyrie in Provence', and painted by great-aunts." (The shade of irony distinguishes Macaulay's account, and her generation, from Cook's or Symonds'.) And much visited Les Baux has, she says, "grown vulgar". Nevertheless "it still makes its flamboyant dramatic effect"; it still has Macaulay figuring "a fantastic Doré scene of infernal nightmare", a place "sprawling over its high escarpment with the crazed air of an extinct moon."

Chapter Five
Roy Campbell's Provence:
The Camargue

"The Four Winds dry their wooden shoes": Martigues

At the beginning of the 1920s the South African poet Roy Campbell (1901-57) worked on an Italian boat which operated mainly on the Marseille-Naples route. On one occasion the crew were shipping eels at Martigues—"Christmas eels" for Genoa and Rome, Campbell tells us in *Broken Record* (1934). The eels from the local fishing boats

> were poured into our spherical net, bounced on to the weighing machine, shot into the hold, tallied and paid for on the spot. It is the most bewildering work. One's eyes become utterly flummoxed by the myriad slithering, whirling, revolving, dashing and swirling mountains of lubricated and electrified macaroni.

He claims that the ship's mate met a horrible fate when he slipped and fell into the hold, drowning amid eels and slime. According to Campbell's later account in *Light on a Dark Horse* (1951), "Moro's end rather put me off eels for the time being, so I went and helped with the grape-harvest."

The poet soon took up other maritime activities. Martigues, "an amphibious, crustacean-looking town" whose canals link the Etang de Berre and the Golfe de Fos, was full of fishermen and sailors. One of their recreations, and a way of winning some extra cash, was the ferocious sport of water-jousting. Campbell was always eager to proclaim both his physical prowess—a pointed contrast with the Bloomsbury effeteness he detested—and his complete integration with the natives. He was accepted as a member of his local team, La Joyeuse Lance Martégale. Mounted on platforms at the stern of charging motor-boats (oared boats after speed restrictions came into effect in 1933) contestants

The Camargue: "in its natural state a vast, salt-caked and sandy desert, sparsely clothed with coarse grasses... and marsh samphire, and broken by lagoons" (Marcel Brion, *Provence*).

armed with lances would attempt to knock each other into the water. Once he took particular delight in fighting "a verminous socialist"; socialists were among the more frequent objects of his ire, together with Jews, Calvinists, the literary establishment, tourists, psychoanalysts and the being he satirically christened MacSpaunday—MacNeice, Spender, Auden and Day-Lewis.

Roy Campbell achieved at least some of the feats he said he did. Moro the mate may or (with luck) may not have perished as described. Certainly Campbell fabricated or at least embroidered some of the stories he told in his autobiographical writings. He was inventive, he drank freely, and he wanted to live up to an image of himself; his daughter Anna, while stoutly defending him from others' disapproval, confesses in her memoir *Poetic Justice* (1986) that "what irritated me most was that this very gentle man should spend so much time and energy trying to prove that he was tough." The comment is inspired by the incident when, as a young child, she rescued him from a fight by biting his adversary in the calf.

Campbell was vulnerable as well as tough and had fled back to Martigues from England in 1928 in the wake of his wife Mary's affair with Vita Sackville-West. This, and Sackville-West's involvement also with Virginia Woolf, did much to fuel his Bloomsbury-hating. The affair soon ended and Mary Campbell, at first reluctantly, rejoined her husband. Gradually harmony was re-established. Anna Campbell Lyle remembers it as a mostly carefree, settled time for her and her elder sister Tess. From 1929 the family rented "a small house shaded by giant umbrella pines, at a place called Tour de Vallier, some kilometres from Martigues. In front of this house was a broad terrace with a low wall and beneath this terrace stretched two fields of olive trees that shivered into silver in the Mistral." Her father, in *Light on a Dark Horse*, explains that the landlady allowed him to chop up two enormous trees, which had nearly stopped producing olives, for fuel. He again enjoys remembering his practical skills, directed this time to domestic ends:

> The wood of the olive root has different grain from any other sort of wood. It has to be struck with great force repeatedly in the same place with wedges and it comes off suddenly in rugged chunks as big as one's head. It burns slowly like coal, and has a rather acrid smell, but it is

beautiful wood. From it I carved the figures of Our Lady and the Infant Christ with St Joseph, and the other figures of the traditional Provençal crib for my children's Christmas.

From the small house or "cabanon", Anna Campbell Lyle tells us,

a meandering path led down through the woods to the Etang de Berre, not a lake at all but a miniature sea... In our day, before it was polluted by factory wastes, it teemed with marine life. There were ink-blue, rust, or sage-green sea-urchins, seaweed of every colour imaginable, shoals of darting fish, and one small solitary fish with the brilliant hues of a kingfisher.

Martigues and the Etang have changed indeed, mainly with the growth of the oil industry. The town has been called "the Provençal Venice" but, Jean Giono caustically observes, "it has nothing in common with its glorious godmother except that it smells of petroleum, like Riva degli Schiavoni when the wind blows from Mestre." Its earlier appearance survives in some of the paintings at the Musée Ziem, a collection of Provençal and other artists including the nineteenth-century Félix Ziem, and in some of Campbell's poems. He and his family moved on to Spain in 1933. Here his political and religious views became more evidently extreme. His strong support for General Franco (later atoned for, in the eyes of many, by his service in the British army in the Second World War) earned him much opprobrium and resulted in some less successful poetry. Martigues, where

Around the quays, kicked off in twos
The Four Winds dry their wooden shoes

provided memories of a simpler time.

The Plaine de la Crau: "goblins of light"
The geographer Strabo (c.64 BC-after 121 AD) considered the origins of the stony plain now called the Crau. (We now know that the stones were deposited by the River Durance during the last Ice Age.) Perhaps, thought Strabo, as translated by Horace Leonard Jones, the Mistral was involved:

"the Black North, a violent and chilly wind, descends upon this plain with exceptional severity" and it is said "that by the blasts the people are dashed from their vehicles and stripped of both weapons and clothing." Perhaps, while it is about it, the wind rolls the stones into place. Strabo cites Aristotle on the way stones vomited up by earthquakes roll together. He also cites Poseidonius, who reckons, rather, that a former lake has solidified. Either theory is plausible, Strabo thinks, but the poetical account given in Aeschylus' *Prometheus Unbound* (a play surviving only as a few fragments, including the one Strabo gives) has remained better known.

Prometheus is telling Heracles how to get from the Caucasus to the Hesperides. He explains that when he comes to "the undaunted host of the Ligurians" his weapons will fail him and it will be no use looking for stones to throw because the ground thereabouts is very soft. Zeus, however, will obligingly supply "a cloud with a snow-like shower of round stones" which will cover the soil. With these Heracles will be able to pelt the Ligurians and push them aside. The dramatist had sensibly removed "what was difficult to account for", with regard to the "Stony Plain", to the realm of myth.

The plain still seemed a place of mythic power to Roy Campbell who, he says in *Broken Record*, once crossed it in a taxi:

> Here I saw for the first time the amazing mirage of the Crau, far more extraordinary than anything I had seen in the Kalahari or the Karroo. The huge red hangars at Istres appeared to be whirling in the air. The distant ranges of the Alpilles were expanding and contracting like a concertina. Fierce white water seemed to be streaming at us. Trees ranked themselves above the horizon. Everything was vibrating in this dance of the goblins of light.

The Camargue: "the verges of the earth"

The Provençal story *La Bèstio dóu Vacarés* (1926), by Joseph d'Arbaud (1874-1950), is set among the marshy islands and woodland around the Etang de Vaccarès, deep in the Camargue. Here a fifteenth-century *gardian* or herdsman encounters what at first seems to be a "beast" but proves to be a Pan-like demigod of old, surviving precariously in these remote parts where he is still able to control thousands of animals with his music. The *gardian*, fascinated in spite of himself, is moved at first to fear and then to deep compassion. But, knowing that he will be branded heretic or insane, he can tell no-one but posterity what he has seen.

Necessity drives the "beast" into a land which strikes some as flat and unwelcoming: the haunt perhaps of flamingoes, white horses and otters but certainly of mosquitoes. From the safety of a château "high up on the westward slopes of the Alpilles", the first-person narrator of Lawrence Durrell's *Monsieur* (1974) can see "the distant flats of the tedious Camargue with its lime-green ribbon of shallow sea". Philippe, in Maurice Barrès' *Le Jardin de Bérénice* (1891) finds the area around Les Saintes-Maries-de-la-Mer—partly, it is true, because Bérénice has just married someone else—a windswept wasteland with no place for the life of the individual; the only objects which stand out are "a few clumps of black cypresses... in the middle of a leprous mass of moss and sticks." (Following various drainage schemes and the introduction of large-scale rice-growing in the 1960s much of the Camargue is now much less of a wilderness.)

For many, however, the distinctive landscape and life of the Rhône delta have proved inspiriting. Even the insects can be made poetic. In "Summer Morning", a poem by Marius Jouveau (1878-1949), a *gardian* rides out from his *cabane* at sunrise, leaving everything silent except for the sounds made by a reddish-brown horsefly. It does its flying and its buzzing with the aid of some splendidly onomatopoeic Provençal words: *voulastrejant* along, it *vounvouno* against the window. And the world Jouveau's *gardian* goes into is one of creatures—bulls and white horses— whose romantic potential is more immediately apparent than the fly's. In Provence the most famous champion of the *gardians* came from a rather unlikely background: the ancestors of the poet and novelist Marquis Folco de Baroncelli-Javon (1869-1943) had moved from Florence to Avignon in the fifteenth century and he lived there in what is now the Palais du Roure. But in 1895 he left this comfortable life for that of a Camargue *manadier* or rancher. *Lou Marquès*, as he was known, worked tirelessly to maintain and revive local traditions; he was a friend and collaborator of Frédéric Mistral. (The life of the *manadier* and the *gardian* is documented, with other local traditions, at the Musée Camarguais near Albaron and the Musée Baroncelli in Saintes-Maries.).

Joseph d'Arbaud, once a poet and law student in Aix, followed his distant kinsman Baroncelli's example, breeding bulls in the Camargue until ill-health forced him back to the city. In d'Arbaud's Provençal poem "Rêverie d'un gardian" the old cowboy, sitting now with his purring cat, remembers how once he would ride out in the clear light of windy morning to round up bulls, drive them into a town or village, and gallop *imbrandable*—invincible—into the arena, applauded by the girls on the balconies. Roy Campbell renders the more riotous side of such occasions in *Taurine Provence* (1932): "shots are fired into the sky; kettle-drums are beaten; whips crack; petards are let off, as the herd come thundering down the main street."

In "Horses on the Camargue" Campbell focuses on the animals rather than the people, though he uses the horses partly as a metaphor for the kind of freedom he aspires towards. At the beginning of the poem the Camargue is a place Durrell or Barrès would recognize: "the grey wastes of dread,/The haunt of shattered gulls" and silence. But the horses replace the grey with snowy white, the deathly silence with "a sudden harmony of hooves". Aptly in a place where there is so much land and so much water—and so much wind over both—the horses are often described as, or compared to, creatures of the sea; "white horses", of course, can mean breaking waves. They race "spray-curled, like waves before the wind". Their "Master's trident" is both Neptune's attribute and the *gardian*'s indispensable prod. They "only haunt the verges of the earth/And only on the sea's salt herbage feed."

Campbell's poem ends with the Romantic assertion that

Still out of hardship bred,
Spirits of power and beauty and delight
Have ever on such frugal pastures fed
And loved to course with tempests through the night.

The "grey wastes" bring bracing hardship, no longer "dread".

Les Saintes-Maries-de-la-Mer: "the blue whiteness of the Milky Way"

From the roof of the church at Saintes-Maries you can watch flamingoes flying overhead and look out at the Camargue, the Mediterranean, and the seaside resort which has developed in this once desolate place. The building, "less a church than a brutal fortress" felt Maurice Barrès, needed its observation-posts and needed to be like a fortress, since its position made it highly vulnerable to attack by pirates. In 869 Arab raiders made off with the visiting archbishop of Arles and demanded a large ransom for his return. Unluckily he died in captivity, but his astute kidnappers placed the body, in full episcopal regalia, on a throne, paid it polite attentions and somehow left with the ransom before the Christians noticed the deception.

The military bulk of the twelfth-century and later pilgrimage-church also became a sign of militant faith. Legend deposited a group of saints including Mary Magdalene, Martha, Lazarus, Mary Salome and Mary Clopas or Cleophas, on the coast near Saintes-Maries; they had miraculously survived a journey from Palestine in the sailless and rudderless small boat in which their enemies had cast them off. The saints fanned out in various directions to bring the Gospel to Provence; Maries Salome and Clopas remained in the place which later took their name. Their cult was promoted by King René, who ordered the church to be searched for their relics in 1448. These were duly found, encased in reliquaries and subsequently displayed in the chapel of St. Michel above the choir. (Barrès disapproved of this "chambre Louis XV" with its white and gold woodwork and wretched ex-votos, utterly inappropriate as the chapel of the "*graves saintes Maries*".) They are ritually lowered from the chapel, to be touched by the pilgrims, each 25 May and again in late October. The less precious but also venerated statues of the Maries in their boat, usually kept above a side-altar in the nave, are then carried in procession back to the beach where they are supposed to have landed and then on into the sea. But it is mainly because of Sarah, the black servant who traditionally accompanied the Maries, that the pilgrimage is so well known today. Sarah became patroness of gypsies and since at least the mid-nineteenth century they have come to Saintes-Maries in great numbers and from some distance. In 1852 *L'Illustration* enthusiastically reported the presence of a whole "population nomade" with its covered wagons, donkeys and horses; the streets were full of "fragrant Arlésiennes" and everywhere were mendicant hermits and people selling religious images, sweets, oranges, and candles. Sarah's highly-adorned statue processes from the crypt to the sea each 24 May.

It was the sea itself which most affected Vincent van Gogh when he came here from Arles for five days in June 1888. It was his first sight of the Mediterranean, which was, he told his brother Theo, coloured as changeably as mackerel: by turns, as the light varied, green, violet, blue, tinged with pink or grey. A walk along the deserted shore one night provoked a more visionary response to the deep blue sky and

clouds of a blue deeper than the fundamental blue of intense cobalt, and some others of a clearer blue, like the blue whiteness of the Milky Way. In the blue depth the stars sparkled, turned green, yellow, white, pink... like precious stones... opal... emeralds, lapis lazuli, rubies, sapphires. The sea [was] very deep ultramarine—the shore of a purplish and reddish-brown colour... with bushes on the dunes... Prussian blue bushes.

Saint-Gilles

St. Aegidius, whose name managed to mutate into Gilles, was a semi-legendary hermit who lived probably in the seventh to eighth centuries. He came, claims a tenth-century Latin life, from Athens to the mouth of the Rhône. According to the later rhymed *Vie de Saint Gile*, it was a tough area, full of wild beasts including bears, lions, deer, boar, *Olifans e bestes cornues* ("elephants and horned animals"), "vipers and tigers and tortoises", "serpents of many kinds" and centaurs. The author of the poem, Guillaume de Berneville, appears to have lived in distant Normandy or even England; he supplies the beasts appropriate to medieval hermits and heroes wherever they live.

But Gilles, who puts his trust in God, is unafraid. Like many saints, in fact, he has a good relationship with wildlife. King Flavius (or Flovent) is out hunting one day when one of his archers shoots an arrow at a doe. The hermit is pierced instead of the deer, which turns out to have been keeping him alive in the wilderness by feeding him her milk. In spite of his wounds he talks to and greatly impresses the king and accompanying bishop. Flovent wants to give the holy man presents and treasure, but instead Gilles asks him to use his money and plate and some of his land to establish a monastery and provide it with as many monks as possible. They will pray night and day for the king and the people. The king enthusiastically agrees to hand over "lands and woods, vineyards and

meadows". He will build the sort of fully-equipped monastery later monks and pilgrims will expect: church, dorter, chapterhouse, a good cellar, refectory, and other fine looking buildings. Inside will be magnificent vestments, books, hangings, carpets, censers, lamps, crosses, candlesticks. The foundation is also well endowed with lands.

Guillaume de Berneville's monastery is not, like his fauna, fantastical. Around the shrine of St. Gilles a rich and powerful institution had grown up by the twelfth century. Since most of the buildings were destroyed or badly damaged in either the sixteenth-century Wars of Religion or the Revolution, it is difficult to imagine the size and splendour of the medieval establishment. Gilles' tomb was an immensely popular place of pilgrimage. Because of the injuries he sustained in place of the doe, he became patron saint of the physically impaired, and later of lepers. And because the doe fed him and he protected her he became patron of nursing mothers. Saint-Gilles was also conveniently placed on the main southern route to and from the even more popular shrine of Santiago de Compostela; this route came to be known as the "Via Aegidiana". Numbers were swelled, too, by pilgrims, merchants and crusaders *en route* for the Middle East.

The abbey, which was subject to the mother-house at Cluny but allowed considerable autonomy, attracted gifts and privileges from such important patrons as Pope Clement IV (reigned 1265-8). He was originally, as Guy Foulque, from Saint-Gilles; traditionally he was born at the "Maison romane", which now houses a local museum. The Counts of Toulouse were also, sometimes, generous patrons. Monastic wealth, however, was always a temptation to rulers less idealized than King Flavius, and rivalry between secular and ecclesiastical powers was a constant of medieval society. Raymond IV of Toulouse actually took back some of the gifts he had given and was forced to restore them only at the Council of Nîmes in 1096 when, in the presence of Pope Urban II, he set his spiritual and secular house in order before departing for the First Crusade. (It was during this visit to France that Urban dedicated the new abbey-church of St. Gilles, although most of the building seems not to have begun until 1116.) Raymond's sons and successors, Counts Bertrand and Alphonse-Jourdain, in turn seized the abbey, were excommunicated, and eventually submitted to papal authority.

Raymond VI's tussle with the papacy was more complicated. Like his forebears he had a tendency to persecute the monks of St. Gilles. But he was also, more worryingly for the church authorities, well disposed towards the Cathars or Albigensians; their heresies included an opposition to churches, the sacraments administered in them, and the relics (for instance St. Gilles') venerated there. In 1207 Innocent III sent his legate, Pierre de Castelnau, to denounce the count and renew the sentence of excommunication already passed on him. "From this day forward," went the traditional formulation Castelnau delivered, "you are the enemy of God and of men. Your subjects are released from all oaths of fealty to you. Whoever deposes you will be right to do it. Whoever kills you will be blessed." But it was not Raymond who died; soon after leaving the court, in January 1208, the legate was murdered by one of the count's squires—probably acting on his own initiative, although out of loyalty to his master.

There is an obvious parallel with the killing of Thomas Becket nearly forty years earlier. Like Henry II of England after that incident, Raymond VI was forced to submit to the church in very public fashion.

On 12 June 1209 he presented himself at the door of the abbey of St. Gilles. Naked apart from his *braies* (linen trousers), he had a cord round his neck and carried a lighted candle, the symbol of repentance. He kneeled before the legate Milon and swore allegiance to the pope and his legates. Milon then drew Raymond into the church by the cord; as he walked, he was whipped with rods. In the crowded church the legate sermonized the count at length; among the fairly convincing charges against him were that he had favoured heretics, was suspected of Castelnau's murder, had imprisoned the bishop of Vaison and his clergy and destroyed his palace, and had used churches as fortresses. Finally the malefactor passed through the crypt, near Castelnau's tomb. The Albigensian crusade would now begin in earnest, although in spite of his submission Raymond was soon fighting on the other side, against the papal crusaders.

By the time Raymond repented in front of the church it was almost certainly graced with its surviving façade. The central tympanum was replaced in the seventeenth century but otherwise the sculptures date from the twelfth century—whether early or late is disputed; some earlier scholars argued that they influenced the mid-century figures of the Royal Portal at Chartres. At St. Gilles the tympana portray, from left to right, the Virgin and Child, Christ in Majesty, and the Crucifixion. The frieze beneath narrates the Passion of Christ from the Entry into Jerusalem to his risen appearance to the Holy Women. Twelve much larger Apostles are grouped by the main portal. It has been suggested that this orthodox subject matter may have been intended as an anti-Cathar declaration. Whitney S. Stoddard argues, in *Art and Architecture in Medieval France* (1972), that the unusual prominence afforded the Crucifixion and Last Supper is aimed at an earlier (possibly 1120s) heretical group whose leader, Pierre de Bruys, did not believe in the efficacy of the Mass. "To emphasize his feelings, he and his colleagues stole the wooden crosses from Saint-Gilles, and on Good Friday they roasted meat in front of the abbey on a fire made of the crosses. A few days later the Church replied, and Peter and his companions were burned as heretics on the same spot."

The St. Gilles figures were inspired chiefly by classical sculpture, perhaps mainly on sarcophagi. Sacheverell Sitwell in *Monks, Nuns and Monasteries* (1965) calls the style "ultra-Roman Romanesque":

But, then, [St. Gilles] is in Provence , where so many classical remains are above the ground... Even the clothes worn by the figures on the fronts of both churches [St. Gilles and St. Trophime in Arles] hang down in long folds and are like fringed togas. The new emergence is in the crouching animals below the apostles' feet. This is the beginning of another and fresh art, while the processions of small figures are of sarcophagus monotony and as dull as that.

That the façade, whether dull or fresh, has survived at all is extraordinary. Most of the monastic buildings were burned down by victorious Protestants in 1562. Sixty years later, amid a new outbreak of fighting, what was still standing or had been rebuilt was being used as a fortress. As Louis XIII's army approached, the Protestant Duc de Rohan decided to blow the whole place up rather than let it fall into Catholic hands. The bell-tower and other parts of the church had been detonated when, fortunately for posterity, the royal forces arrived.

Aigues-Mortes: "a bright, quiet melancholy"

"Suddenly it appears, the towered and embattled mass, lying so low that the crest of its defences seems to rise straight out of the ground." Henry James, coming across the vast surrounding flats by train, registered the wholeness and compactness of Aigues-Mortes. King Louis IX of France (St. Louis) developed the town in the 1240s as the only Mediterranean port in his domains; the grid-pattern, with ramparts completed by his son Philippe III later in the century, was designed to make the remote site easier to defend. Louis set off from here on the Seventh Crusade in 1248 and, with fewer supporters, on the Eighth in 1270. (The first expedition stayed in the Middle East for six years. Early in the second, Louis died at Tunis.) But after these famous interludes the port began to decline in importance. The harbour silted up and trade was eventually lost to Sète in the seventeenth century. Closer to Aigues, Le Grau-du-Roi prospered as a fishing-port and more recently as a seaside resort. The salt-pans—a dominant feature of the wide views from the towers and ramparts—supplied the town's surviving industry.

"The sand, the salt, the dull sea-view, surround it with a bright, quiet melancholy," James felt. A particular subject for sadness might be the Tour de Constance. St. Louis built it both to defend his new town and as a residence which he used briefly in 1248 and 1270, but its main later role was as a prison; James notes its "extraordinary girth and solidity". Knights Templar were held here after the sudden dissolution of their order in 1307 by Louis' grandson Philippe Le Bel. Between 1686 and 1768 over two hundred Protestant women, mostly from the Cévennes, were consigned to the tower. (Men were more often sent to the galleys.) In the tradition of the Camisard rebels of the early eighteenth century, most of them steadfastly refused to abjure the faith. Many died here. In *La Tour de Constance* (1970) the novelist André Chamson (1900-83), who was married to a descendant of one of the internees, and himself descended from Camisards, tells the women's story. They were shut up in their "high circular room, their raised tomb about twenty feet in diameter, nearly always enveloped in shade", subject to freezing or torrid wind, streaming with damp. They were racked with coughs, attacked by fleas, bugs and scorpions, twisted with rheumatism, prone to fevers. (James, shown round by the custodian's wife, found her "yellow with the traces of fever and ague", as might have been expected "in a town whose name denotes dead waters".) Usually death was the only release.

France celebrates Bastille Day on 14 July, but for Chamson the real, if unjustly forgotten Bastille was at Aigues-Mortes. In no other prison has "so much innocence and purity been kept in irons." The tower is named after Constance, wife of Raymond V of Toulouse, who built the original structure in the twelfth century, but the name is particularly appropriate to those who showed, as Chamson says, the power of "the constancy of a woman's heart and the firmness of a human soul".

Such constancy is well illustrated—in fact as well as in the novel—by Marie Durand, who was incarcerated in 1730. Her father and fiancé were also arrested, the former released as an old man in 1743, the latter released and banished in 1750. Throughout her thirty-eight years in the tower she was an inspiration to the other women, and tradition has it that it was she who inscribed *register*—a dialectal version of *resister*—on the coping of the tower's central well. Eventually the Protestants began to be less fiercely persecuted and, in April 1768, Durand was released, soon to be followed by the few other remaining prisoners. Chamson describes her disorientation on entering at last a world which seems immense, as if God has suddenly altered the units of measurement. She

"The constancy of a woman's heart and the firmness of a human soul" (André Chamson): La Tour de Constance, prison of Marie Durand.

returned to her dilapidated house and was granted a pension by fellow-believers in Amsterdam; she shared it with a neighbour released from the galleys. She died in 1776, her place assured in the pantheon of Protestant south-western resisters. Chamson (born in Nîmes) was steeped in Cévenol and Camisard history from childhood; true to that past, he himself served in the Resistance as well as going on to celebrate Durand's more passive fortitude.

Chapter Six

King René's Provence: Aix

Entremont and Aquae Sextiae

At Entremont, just north of Aix-en-Provence, have been found the remains of a Celto-Ligurian *oppidum* or fortified hill settlement. The Saluvii tribe built the huts of the upper town in about 190 BC and the larger lower town, with houses in a grid-pattern and strong stone fortifications, in about 150-140. Finds from the site are displayed at the Musée Granet in Aix. (See pp.114-15)

Entremont needed defending: it was prominently involved in several violent encounters with its neighbours and, more dangerously, their Roman backers. Massalia called in Roman assistance against the Saluvii in 125 BC. Ballista-bolts and spearheads found on site date either from a Roman siege at that point or the suppression of a last local rising in about 90 BC. Entremont was fairly quickly abandoned in favour of a settlement on the plain founded, near some hot springs, by the victor of 125, Caius Sextius Calvinus, and therefore called Aquae Sextiae, contracted eventually as Aix.

At first Aquae Sextiae was mainly a garrison town. Near here in 102 BC Caius Marius conclusively defeated the invading Teutones. (It was long thought that this was why Marius became a popular first name in the area in later times, but it was more often simply a male form of Marie, designed to honour the Virgin.) But it soon became an administrative centre, promoted to the rank of *colonia latina* by Caesar and *colonia romana* by Augustus. Later, however, it was eclipsed by Arles and battered by Barbarian incursions. Further destruction and quarrying followed in the early Middle Ages. Mainly because of this, until recently there were almost no visible ancient remains in Aix. There was therefore great excitement in 2004 when, following a geophysical survey, local archaeologists uncovered the well-preserved remains of the town's Roman theatre.

Le Bon Roi René

Aix did not really recover its Roman importance until the days of King René (1409-80), who lived in Aix mainly at the end of his life and initiated, as Donna Bohanan puts it in *Old and New Nobility in Aix-en-Provence* (1992), "a renaissance that lasted until the Revolution".

René was more famous for his titles than for the lands he actually ruled. Inheritance made him Duke of Bar, Duke of Anjou, Count of Provence, and King of Naples, Sicily and even, theoretically, Jerusalem. Marriage made him Duke of Lorraine. But the fight for his rights in Lorraine made him a prisoner of the Duke of Burgundy from 1431 to 1436; and subsequent attempts to pursue his Italian titles led to his expulsion and supplanting by Alfonso the Magnanimous, of the house of Aragon, in 1442. Thereafter he divided most of his time between the possessions he did manage to hold on to, Anjou and Provence. Retaining even these was difficult in a period when the King of France was becoming increasingly powerful. In 1481, on the death of René's nephew and brief successor Charles III, Provence passed to Louis XI, of whom René had said, "the King of France can do all that he wills, and has a habit of doing so."

Given his lack of real power, it was fortunate for René that his interests were far from only political or dynastic. He was a keen patron of music, painting and poetry, a great organizer of elaborate and courtly tournaments and shows. (See p.189) As well as a treatise on jousting, he wrote *Le Livre du cuers d'amours espris* (translated recently as *The Book of the Love-Smitten Heart*). In this dream-vision, dated 1477 but probably composed up to twenty years earlier, René's lovesick heart is removed, as he sleeps, by Love—portrayed, in the best-known illustration of the manuscript now in Vienna, with long golden hair, deep blue tunic and boots, and bow and arrows in a gilded quiver at his side. Love hands the heart over to Desire, a courtier-figure clad in white. The Heart becomes a knight—heart between wings atop his helm— who, with Desire, experiences many allegorical adventures in quest of the lady Mercy. The heart was seen as the seat of imagination and understanding and the work is more psychological exploration than love-story or literal quest.

Such interests, together with his apparently well-endured misfortunes, helped develop him into the semi-legendary figure always called "le bon Roi René". He was said not only to have written verse and prose but to have painted the triptych at Villeneuve-lès-Avignon now known to be the work of Enguerrand Quaranton. He was supposed to have introduced to Aix the popular annual Fête-Dieu procession—really flourishing since the 1360s. And he was known to later ages more simply for his ability to relax; he forgot his political losses, it was said, by working as a gardener or a shepherd or just by availing himself of the good Provençal sun. In oral tradition this habit gave rise to the expression "warming yourself at King René's fireplace"—in the sun. He was a good fellow, one who studied, says Sir Walter Scott in *Anne of Geierstein* (1829), "to promote, as far as possible, the immediate mirth and good-humour of his subjects, if he could not materially enlarge their more permanent prosperity." Happy himself, he hops and skips with the joy of poetic, musical or pictorial composition. "Le beau climat!" enthuses René as he comes out of his castle, easel at the ready, in *Le Roi René*, an *opéra-comique* of 1824 with music by Hérold: "le bon soleil! quelle végétation!... heureuse Provence!"

Aix and Provence felt both nostalgia for the days of an independent ruler and fellow-feeling for a man who, it was sometimes felt, actually wielded rather little power. Elsewhere people were more likely to be amused or irritated by a ruler who allegedly spent so much time dancing and sunbathing. In Scott's novel René's daughter Margaret, ex-queen of England, explodes at the mention of this "weak old man, who, in sonnets and in music, in mummery and folly, in harping and rhyming, finds a comfort for all that poverty has that is distressing; and, what is still worse, even a solace in all that is ridiculous and contemptible." Margaret of Anjou—derived from the "she-wolf of France" or "tiger's heart wrapped in a woman's hide" of *Henry VI* Part Three—is not likely to be very tolerant of "the idiot gaiety of my father". But Scott's own verdict, while a little kinder, does not contradict his character's opinion:

> René was a prince of very moderate parts, endowed with a love of the fine arts, which he carried to extremity, and a degree of good humour, which never permitted him to repine at fortune, but rendered its possessor happy, when a prince of keener feelings would have died of despair. This insouciant, light-tempered, gay and thoughtless

disposition, conducted René, free from all the passions which embitter life, and often shorten it, to a hale and mirthful old age.

When father and daughter are together in Aix he annoys her so much, miscalculates so badly but so blithely, that it becomes funny. She arrives deep in misfortune and depression and so he tries to cheer her up. He tells her to make ready for a solemn procession to the cathedral of St.-Sauveur and then, as she emerges gravely from the palace, ambushes her with "more than a hundred masks, dressed up like Turks, Jews, Saracens, Moors, and I know not whom besides." They crowd round the furious woman "to offer her their homage, in the character of the Queen of Sheba." Up bounces her father, "grotesquely dressed in the character of King Solomon", a wiser monarch than himself, "with such capers and gesticulations of welcome to the Queen of Sheba as would," reports a witness, " ... have brought a dead man alive again, or killed a living man with laughing." Striking the "truncheon, somewhat formed like a fool's bauble", out of the old fool's hand, she breaks through the festive crowd and rides in a frenzy to the convent on Mont Sainte-Victoire. Later she becomes calm enough to praise his good intentions and gentle nature—their temperaments are different. But when she comes back to Aix the reader may wince as, undaunted, René prepares to greet her "at the head of an Arcadian procession of nymphs and swains" with their pipes and tambourines. His seneschal, however, persuades him, with some difficulty, that this is no way to meet someone arriving full of religious thoughts from the convent.

This René, a ruler who even wants to put off discussing the serious business of the future of Provence until "some dull rainy day", is of course a travesty of the fifteenth-century original. Scott confesses, in his introduction of 1831, that he wrote *Anne of Geierstein* without benefit of his usual access "to a library tolerably rich in historical works, and especially the memoirs of the middle ages." "Capers and gesticulations" are a pale nineteenth-century equivalent for sophisticated courtly shows, and to some extent the king is introduced to the novel for the sake of comic relief. The truth no doubt lies between this "merry monarch" and the noble, firm but benevolent figure sculpted by David d'Angers (1823) on the fountain in the Cours Mirabeau, who, says the Latin inscription beneath, "deemed himself contented only among the Provençaux". He holds muscat grapes, another useful gift which, tradition says, he gave Provence.

Saint-Sauveur

There are few physical traces of René in Aix. His palace, and the Roman mausoleum and towers it incorporated, was demolished in 1786; the Palais de Justice, completed in 1832 and extended upwards in 1957, occupies the site. But an older Aix and a contemporary representation of the good king survive at Saint-Sauveur's cathedral.

Saint-Sauveur includes work of many different periods. It is the sort of church which at first sight seems disconcertingly difficult to perceive as any kind of whole. Charles de Brosses, visiting in 1739, declared it "ugly and irregular". Ruskin in 1840 found "the outside... ugly enough" and "interior corrupt Roman, with heavy arches". Saint-Sauveur joins together a baptistery and two churches—Notre-Dame, begun in the eleventh century, and Corpus Domini, begun in the twelfth—together with later chapels and other accretions. There is both a restored Flamboyant façade and a simpler restored Romanesque one; fine walnut west doors carved by Jean Guiramand in 1508-10 with sibyls and prophets; some fifteenth-century stained glass; recent furniture in light-coloured bronze by Jean Mégard, including the bishop's throne and lectern.

The baptistery and the cloister work more coherently. Eight marble columns, most of them probably taken from the town's Roman basilica, surround the sunken baptismal area and support a sixteenth-century cupola. The cloister was built in the late twelfth century, in lighter stone and often lighter style than the one at St. Trophime in Arles. In April 1601 someone took advantage of the seclusion of the cloister to do to death the unfortunate Provost Gilbert-Charles Desbiès, head of the cathedral Chapter. No wound was apparent until the corpse was undressed, when it was found, François Roux-Alphéran informs us, that "his chest had been crushed by blows with bags filled with earth or with lead, which in Provençal is called *saquettar*." The principal suspect was another member of Chapter, *capiscol* (head of the cathedral school) Bernardin Delphin-Gonzard, a known enemy of the deceased. The Archbishop had him arrested and he remained a prisoner in the archiepiscopal palace (now the Tapestry Museum) for several years but, no proof of his guilt having been forthcoming, he was eventually released. Roux-Alphéran's *Les Rues d'Aix* (1846-8) is full of similar stories, possible openings for historical detective novelists or makers of historical investigative programmes: "So who really hated the Provost so much that he—or she?—was prepared, that spring day in 1601... And why did they think they could get away with it?"

The Burning Bush

Also at Saint-Sauveur is the Burning Bush triptych, completed for King René by Nicolas Froment in 1476. Originally it stood in the Carmelite church where the king's entrails were buried in 1480. (His main tomb was in the cathedral at Angers, the capital of Anjou.) The triptych came to the cathedral in 1804. In the upper half of the central panel the Virgin and Child sit on the bush itself—here more like a copse. The flames dance mainly at its edges. This is because, in iconographic tradition, the bush stands not only for the power of God as revealed to Moses but, in a New Testament context, for Mary's virginity: the bush in *Exodus* burns but is not consumed and, by a similar paradox, Mary is both mother and virgin. Below, the angel, who in *Exodus* appears in the bush, speaks to Moses but again reminds us of the story of the Virgin Birth by adopting the usual posture of the Angel Gabriel in Annunciation pictures, with one hand raised, palm outstretched; reasonably enough, the amazed Moses looks more up at the bush or heaven than at the explaining angel, but in so doing is also directing his and the viewer's awe towards the Virgin and the miracle of her virginity. What modern viewers may see as the extravagance of the conceit is mitigated—or the paradoxes made more striking—by such realistic elements as the gnarled Moses, the sheep, goats and slightly disdainful dog between him and the angel, the details of leaf and trunk, and the gushing spring (symbol of new life). Moses removing his shoes to stand on holy ground comes, like the flock he is keeping for his father-in-law, from the biblical account.

This realistic tendency probably indicates that Froment originated from an area subject to Flemish or Netherlandish influences. Although he is first recorded in the south, in Uzès, he may have come from Artois or Picardy. Northern interests are all the more apparent when one looks at the wings of the triptych, which provide the best known portraits of René and his second wife, Jeanne de Laval. Their attention is focused on the divine mysteries of the central panel and they are accompanied by their patron saints. He is with St. Mary Magdalene for Provence, St. Antony for Anjou and St. Maurice for the chivalric Order of the Crescent he founded. The queen has connections with Saints John the Evangelist, Catherine and Nicholas. But it is the royal couple, portrayed with what seems to many an unflattering directness, who take most of the attention. For Prosper Mérimée, who draws on some of the same traditions as Scott and indeed probably read *Anne of Geierstein*, "you can read the king's whole history from his physiognomy." He is "un bonhomme blasé", one

> full of fine feeling but lazy; one who asks himself, before undertaking any action, the question which suffices to put one off anything: *Cui bono?* The eyes are lively and all the features are so carefully rendered that one feels that this must be a perfect likeness. [It is] as truthful as the best Holbeins, as finely realized and executed, what's more, with as much spirit. Jeanne de Laval is, if I may say so, extraordinarily ugly and her ugliness isn't relieved, as the king's is, by an intelligent expression.

At the church of La Madeleine is another painting associated with René, an Annunciation believed to have been painted in about 1443-5 by his court painter, known in French as Barthélemy d'Eyck and possibly a relation of the Netherlandish master Jan van Eyck. Here a nobly certain Gabriel hails a composed but somewhat more meditative Virgin, in glowing gold, against a perspective architectural background. In the side panels of the triptych (later copies of the dispersed originals) the prophets Isaiah and Jeremiah attest the importance of the divine event, as do carved figures at the top of columns near the angel. A bat and a malignant winged devil suggest the evil which the Incarnation will overcome, or with which it must contend. The Madeleine more generally is a church full of art: "vaste, blande, encombrée de peintures" in the opinion of Paul Mariéton; a "museum" of all the allegorical and religious painters of Aix.

The Musée des Tapisseries and the Musée du Vieil Aix

The tapestry museum has, since 1909, occupied the baroque former palace of the archbishops, close to the cathedral. There are three series of tapestries, once archiepiscopal property, made in Beauvais: six "grotesques" (c.1689) with musicians and dancers, four "Russian Games" from designs by Jean-Baptiste Leprince (1769), and the surviving nine out of ten *Don Quixote* scenes from designs by Charles Natoire (1735-44).

In the *Revue des deux mondes* in 1932 Louis Gillet compared these romantic scenes of a *galante* Russia and Spain to some creation of Diaghilev's *ballets russes*. After Gillet's time this theatrical spirit became a direct interest of the museum, whose upstairs rooms display a selection of costumes, pictures, models and equipment connected with the annual Festival d'Art Lyrique which takes place in the palace courtyard. For some years after the beginning of the festival in 1948 it concentrated on operas by Mozart. These have remained a speciality but the range has widened considerably. There are costumes and designs from productions of Mozart, Lully and Britten; Osman's splendid orange robe for Rameau's *Les Indes galantes*; Elizabeth I's broad, lion-decorated wood and fibre-glass throne for Donizetti's *Roberto Devereux*; white furs for the Marschallin in Richard Strauss' *Der Rosenkavalier*.

Near the cathedral and the tapestry museum, in Rue Gaston de Saporta, are two seventeenth-century mansions, the monumental Hôtel d'Estienne de St. Jean, which contains the Musée du Vieil Aix, and the Hôtel de Châteaurenard. The museum shows furniture, faïence, the Roman urns found when the palace of the Counts was demolished, prints, marionettes, an eighteenth-century screen painted on both sides with scenes from the procession and games of the Fête-Dieu. The surviving decoration of the building includes a painted cupola by Jean Daret (1613-68), who was also responsible for the *trompe-l'oeil* staircase paintings at the Hôtel de Châteaurenard. In the seventeenth century this was also the home of the "cabinet de raretés" of the notary Borrilly. The catalogue of the collection, Paul Mariéton reports in *La Terre provençale* (1890), lists such treasures as "an embalmed Cyclops which had lived nine months."

"The houses very high and the streets ample"

Although Provence lost its independence in 1481, Aix continued to gain in regional importance. Its university had been established in 1409. In 1501 the city became the seat of the *Parlement*, or high court and administrative headquarters, of Provence. There were a number of other courts, fiscal organizations, and a mint. Aix was largely rebuilt in order to accommodate its centres of power, its students and its impressed visitors. John Evelyn summed up what he saw in 1644:

> Aix is the chief city of Provence, being a Parliament and Presidential town, with other royal courts and metropolitan jurisdiction. It is well built, the houses very high and the streets ample. The Cathedral, St Saviour's, is a noble pile adorned with innumerable figures especially that of St Michael; the Baptistery, the Palace, the Court, built in a most spacious piazza, are very fair... The Jesuits have here a Royal College, and the city is an university.

Visitors also took the spa water, which satisfied even the medically qualified and hard-to-please Tobias Smollett: it is "perfectly transparent, sparkling in the glass, light and agreeable to the taste, and may be drank without any preparation, to the quantity of three or four pints at a time." Outsiders and natives alike delighted in the broad thoroughfare built in 1649 and re-named Cours Mirabeau in 1876 after Honoré-Gabriel Riqueti, Comte de Mirabeau (1749-91), the versatile orator and politician who spent some of his career in Aix. Lady Blessington felt, even in a period of relative decline for Aix in the early nineteenth century, that the Cours conveyed "more the idea of a quarter in some large capital than the principal street in a provincial town".

One effect of the concentration of élite organizations was that there was an unusually high percentage of aristocrats in the population. Detailed figures from a census taken in 1695, as interpreted by Donna Bohanan in *Old and New Nobility in Aix-en-Provence*, show that 12.75 per cent can be reasonably classed as noble. Aix "had become," says Bohanan, "a town of the wealthy and the poor and very little else. Entrepreneurial elements accounted for only 9.1 percent of the population and were sandwiched between the nobility and those who served the nobility." Numbers were unlikely to decline: successful bourgeois were often ennobled, joining the order of "new" but increasingly powerful nobility. About nine per cent of inhabitants, some of them noblemen, were ecclesiastics. The lords made their presence felt by building, especially in the seventeenth and eighteenth centuries, their

town mansions or *hôtels particuliers*. The *hotels*—rather than country châteaux, as often in northern France—were usually their owner's main home.

There are many such residences in the Quartier Mazarin, begun in 1646 on the initiative of Archbishop Michel Mazarin (1607-48), brother of the famous Cardinal and himself briefly a Cardinal at the end of his life. This "quartier des nobles" inspires the "quartier Saint-Marc" in Zola's *La Fortune des Rougon* (1870-1): "a little Versailles with straight streets... whose broad square houses conceal immense gardens". Rue du Quatre-Septembre, which runs south from Cours Mirabeau, includes two of the more notable buildings: Hôtel de Villeneuve d'Ansouis, at no. 9, has a mid-eighteenth-century façade with grotesques, garlands and arabesques; the vast Hôtel de Boisgelin, at no.11, was built in 1650. Jean-Claude Rambot, who worked here, was also responsible for the Fontaine des Quatre Dauphins. For Louis Gillet, in the *Revue des Deux Mondes* in 1932, this is a fountain "like a musical toy that sends the idle hours to sleep and charms the silence of this quiet, provincial place." On either side of Place des Dauphins extends Gillet's "prude et patricienne" Rue Cardinale.

The Hôtel de Forbin: Royal Views

There are also some interesting noble hôtels on the south side of Cours Mirabeau—the northern edge of the Quartier Mazarin. The balcony of the classical Hôtel de Forbin (1656) at no. 20 has often been used as a vantage-point for important people. In 1701 the Dukes of Burgundy and Berri, grandsons of Louis XIV, came to watch a "combat d'oranges" in the Cours below. The account by Pierre de Galaup, Seigneur de Chasteuil, records that the balcony had been ornamented with a dais covered in gold-fringed crimson velvet, and closed in with a trellis to protect the princes—and the velvet—from stray flying fruit. There were 300 combatants, 150 reds commanded by the Chevalier de Saint-Marc, 150 blues under Monsieur de Saint-Louis Duranti. The two sides had agreed to try to make the princely entertainment last a decent time, but so fierce was the onslaught of Saint-Marc's men that the blues were rapidly driven off the Cours. The princes, who were, we are assured, delighted nonetheless, presented the two commanders with gold swords and gave 200 gold *louis* to their followers to recompense them for any "bumps, contusions and bruises" sustained in the battle. The Seigneur's account is too well-mannered to dwell on details of the fighting: the exploding citrus, the sticky morass.

In the spring and summer of 1807 the royal visitor staying at the Hôtel de Forbin was Princess Pauline Borghese, Napoleon's sister. In Aix she was carried about "in a sort of palanquin carried by men", notes Roux-Alphéran (*Les Rues d'Aix*, 1846-8) with some disapproval. At her expense—since her brother had refused the city permission to spend money in this way—the revived Fête-Dieu was celebrated with much pageantry, some of which she watched from the balcony. Inside the hôtel and other residences made available to her, she received guests mainly from the old nobility. This was, it seems, on imperial instructions: Napoleon wanted to win the nobles over and had the measure of his "good town of Aix, where people, and especially the fair sex, do not like the classes to mix." Apparently the aristocrats were quite willing to be won. Roux-Alphéran says it was amusing to see, at the hôtel and elsewhere, great ladies falling over each other, fighting to be the one to cover or uncover "the shoulders of the goddess" when the temperature went up or down a quarter of a degree, or "straightening her hair when it was ruffled by the slightest breeze." One lady proudly bore the parasol which stopped the sun from blotching her beautiful complexion, another was delighted to do up her shoe, "and all of them bombarded the beautiful Pauline with bland compliments on her charms, her kindness, and above all on the great and invincible emperor," her brother—without whom, charms or no charms, nobody would have taken much notice of her.

"Her Imperial and Royal Highness", as Pauline was known in spite of the fact that she was supposed, unconvincingly, to be incognito, was "capricious and self-willed", says the not entirely neutral Alphéran. Once she expressed surprise at the bareness of the courtyard at the Hôtel de Forbin and so it had to be transformed, within a few hours, into a garden. An immense quantity of vases of flowers was brought in and bushes and shrubs were rapidly planted—to wither after a few days. More natural surroundings still had to be controlled: at her country residence near Aix, the Château de la Mignarde, servants with long poles were hired to silence such frogs in pools and cicadas in trees as "might otherwise have troubled a sleep so precious for France."

Aix-la-Somnolente

Not all aristocrats relished their *ville aristocratique*. Cissie Fairchilds (*Poverty and Charity in Aix-en-Provence, 1640-1789*) quotes a poem by the Comte de Villeneuve de Vence on how in Aix boredom carries you through from Monday to Saturday. Having endured the "languors of Tuesday"—and Wednesday, and Thursday—"you cry on Sunday, without having laughed on Friday." More serious social problems also developed. A town with so little trade and industry offered few employment opportunities for the poor, who were therefore especially reliant on charity. Fairchilds studies the many charities which helped them and, in effect, mediated between them and the rich. But from 1760 the system was in crisis—a result, Fairchilds points out, of factors including financial mismanagement and centralizing royal government. Aix was left with "a splintered society of mutually antagonistic social groups on the eve of... the French Revolution."

The Revolution attacked the nobility and ended the Parlement.

Fairly rapid recovery might have been expected once the era of revolution and war was over, but Aix still did little to foster commerce and industry, unlike its rapidly developing neighbour, Marseille. And now Aix had been deprived of the political power it once exercised. It remained a legal and university centre; in the nineteenth century it was perceived on the whole as a quiet, provincial place, close to the countryside. When the right-wing writer Louis Bertrand first saw it in 1888 he dismissed it, at least initially, as "a dead town oozing with boredom, reeking of latrines and damp" (*Sur les routes du Sud*, 1936). Still in the early twentieth century, Darius Milhaud's widow Madeleine remembered, "Aix... was a town of silence, a kind of Sleeping Beauty." (Milhaud's *Le Carnaval d'Aix* for piano and orchestra and *Suite provençale* suggest some livelier aspects.) The Sleeping Beauty reference was a commonplace; Bertrand, more bluntly, once called the city "Aix-la-Somnolente".

Aix is less sleepy today. "You only have to move a little away from the Cours Mirabeau and especially from the marvellous Quartier Mazarin, and disaster begins," declares the novelist Renaud Camus in his journal for 1993: "disaster" in the form of the area "ravaged by suburban ugliness, dirt, vandalism, money-grubbing, indifference or stupid pretentiousness" he comes upon when trying to find his way to Salon-de-Provence.

Zola's Plassans

When Emile Zola moved to Paris at the age of eighteen in 1858 he wrote to Paul Cézanne, with a youthful taste for the epigrammatic but also probably with genuine feeling, that "Paris is big, full of amusements, of monuments, of charming women. Aix is small, monotonous, paltry, full of ... women (God forbid that I should slander the women of Aix). And in spite of it all, I prefer Aix." True, the home-sickness soon diminished and he did not, like Cézanne, find himself drawn inescapably back to the town where they had grown up together. Zola needed, in order to fight for the causes he believed in, to be based in or near the capital. But he and his mother cared passionately that Aix should publicly honour his father, the engineer François Zola (originally Francesco Zolla of Venice), who designed and began to build the dam across the Infernets Gorge near Aix before dying when his son was seven. The father had fought long and hard against bureaucracy, rival planners, and xenophobia, to have the project accepted. After his death his widow was effectively cheated out of large sums of money by his former business-partner; she engaged in lengthy legal struggles in the attempt to obtain repayment or redress. For mother and son it was a signal but belated victory over ungrateful Aix when a street was named after François Zola in 1868 and his canal officially named the Canal Zola in 1871. And although Paris features in a number of the great series of Rougon-Macquart novels, the roots of the Rougon and Macquart families—and the setting of several of the novels—are in Aix, or at least the semi-fictitious Plassans.

Plassans is smaller than Aix and the topography is not always identical, but there are many equivalences. Most obviously Saint-Saturnin corresponds to Saint-Sauveur, Cours Sauvaire to Cours Mirabeau, the Rue de la Banne to the Rue Thiers. But the moral and political equivalences are more important. In the second chapter of the first novel of the series, *La Fortune des Rougon* (1870-1), we are given an overview of the Plassans of 1851. It is an old-fashioned place, full of churches, monasteries and convents, and clearly divided by district and by social class. There are three districts, each "forming as it were a small town—distinct, complete, with its own churches, walks, customs, horizons." In the Quartier Saint-Marc the nobles have, since the fall of Charles X in 1830, lived a deathly life in their "grands hôtels silencieux". In the neat pale yellow houses of the New Town—as yet only five or six streets of them—the bourgeoisie "try to give some life to Plassans." They want to be popular with the lower classes but dream of being received by the nobility; since this dream will never come true, they proclaim themselves to be "free-thinkers", but "free-thinkers who are all words— great friends of Authority who throw themselves into the arms of the first saviour to come along" at any sign of discontent from the lower orders. The narrow, twisting alleys and hovels of the Old Town are occupied mainly by workers, unemployed people, shopkeepers and the few industries Plassans can boast: a few tanneries, hat makers (the source of Cézanne's father's wealth), a soap factory.

Only on Sunday evenings do the three areas directly encounter each other. The bourgeois pass through the Cours, leaving the nobles to walk on the south side ("grands hotels") and the people to walk on the north side ("cafés, hotels, tobacconists' shops"). They go up and down their separate plane-tree-shaded walks and neither class so much as thinks of crossing over. Similarly ossified is the custom of carefully double-locking the town gates at eleven in summer and ten in winter:

> The whole spirit of the town—cowardice, egotism, routine, hatred of the outside world and the fervent desire to lead a cloistered life—was apparent in this nightly locking of the gates. When it had padlocked itself in securely, Plassans would say to itself "I'm home" with the same satisfaction as a devout bourgeois who, knowing his cash-box is safe, certain that nobody will wake him with their noise, says his prayers and takes himself off contentedly to bed. No other city, I think, could be so obstinately determined, at so late a date, to shut itself away like a nun.

Such a conservative society is unlikely to rock the political or religious boat. Under Napoleon III's Second Empire (1852-70) Aix regularly returned to the Legislative Assembly the candidates the government supported. In Plassans the situation is slightly more complicated but the candidate agreeable to the government still wins. Self-interest usually dictates the choice. Zola writes from an anti-Bonapartist perspective, but even the Bonapartist authorities in Paris felt, according to an official report of July 1855, that Aix was "of all provincial centres incontrovertibly the one where petty local passions are the strongest and where people are most indifferent to the general interests of the nation." In 1851 there was an attempted republican rising in Aix in response to the *coup d'état* led by the future emperor. The rising was quickly suppressed. In *La Fortune des Rougon* the young Silvère and Miette discover love and revolutionary politics at the same time. They perish while opportunists like Silvère's uncle, Pierre Rougon, who expediently becomes leader of the Bonapartists in Plassans, prosper.

The Aix-like town is again the setting for the fourth *Rougon-Macquart* novel, *La Conquête de Plassans* (1874). Much of the action takes place in the house of the Mouret family. The way in which Abbé Ovide Faujas gradually takes over the house and its occupants is a parallel to, and necessary step in, his domination of the whole town on behalf of the Bonapartists. At first the unprepossessing clerical lodger in the Mourets' house is regarded with general contempt, suspicion or indifference. But he bides his time and comes to acquire a reputation, especially among middle-class women, for piety. He is seen to be actively combatting vice (after a local sex-scandal) by his involvement with the setting-up of a "maison pieuse" to look after girls while their parents are at work and, later, a "Cercle de Jeunesse" for young men; he makes himself popular with the influential women whose committee runs the house and with the influential parents of the young men. Marthe Mouret, in the mean time, abandons her initial scepticism and, obsessed with Faujas, is drawn ever further into masochistic, hysterical religious devotion. Her husband, once acerbically cynical, is steadily crushed and marginalized by members of Faujas' family and his own Faujas-admiring wife and servant; his earlier unreasonableness, the reclusiveness and silence with which he reacts to maltreatment, and Marthe's self-inflicted injuries, combine to fuel the general belief that he is insane and savagely beats his innocent wife.

There is a slow, inexorable logic to the action of the novel: for instance Faujas consents gradually to make use of the Mourets' garden and gradually to acknowledge the presence of important members of rival political factions who gather in the two adjoining gardens; as a priest he seems, slowly, unostentatiously, to be mediating between them, while his real political agenda is known only to a few allies like Marthe's mother, Félicité Rougon. Step by step he insinuates himself into the good graces of the bishop of Plassans, who wants a counter-weight to his dominant vicar-general and so appoints Faujas as curé of Saint-Saturnin and, later, vicar-general. (The church, as much as the political authorities with whom it is entwined, is a major target of Zola's satire.) And because everything he achieves comes from small beginnings and incremental, almost unnoticed daily efforts, his conquest—and *La Conquête* as a whole—does not seem implausibly schematic. The characters live in a dense domestic world of tables and chairs, fruit-growing and preserving, spying on neighbours from windows, who talks to whom in public and who in private, lodgers who do or don't dine with the family, games of shuttlecock next to the house.

La Conquête de Plassans is a more emotionally intense novel than summary can easily suggest. Gustave Flaubert told Zola, in his enthusiastic letter of 3 June, 1874, that he was particularly struck by the tone of the book, its "férocité de passion sous une surface bonhomme".

It explores deep psychological and psychosomatic disturbance, most obviously in Marthe's religious mania centred on unfulfillable dreams of being lifted always one stage higher, bringing in the end hatred out of disappointed love. The mental fragility of the Mourets is counterpointed with the coarse, get-what-you-can hedonism of Faujas' sister and brother-in-law, the Trouches, and the toughness of his loyal, redoubtable mother. It is difficult to overstate the ruthless self-centredness of those who succeed: even Faujas, having delivered Plassans to his masters, is dispensable.

The focus of the next *Rougon-Macquart* novel, *La Faute de l'abbé Mouret* (1875), is on another priest, the Mourets' son, Serge. He is a man of much purer intentions than his early mentor Faujas; his real "fault" is not that he gives way to the sensual pleasures that prove stronger than his religion, but that he abandons them and the girl he loves and has made pregnant. He is brought back to the holy straight and narrow by Brother Archangias, a misogynist like Faujas and many of the churchmen Zola opposed. Serge finds his personal and briefly sexual fulfilment with Albine—an innocent "Eve without any social sense, without learnt morality, the *bête humaine amoureuse*" as Zola puts it in his sketch for the novel. They come together in the wild walled gardens of a vast, abandoned country estate aptly called Le Paradou—Paradise—which derives from a place where Zola and his friends Cézanne and Jean-Baptistin Baille had wandered, the Domaine de la Gallice. There are glades, streams, herbs, wild roses, creepers; powerful nature, growing luxuriant and unchecked. Archangias, the "gendarme" of a jealous, angry God, shuts the lovers out of this Paradise and again small-mindedness prevails.

Cézanne and the Montagne Sainte-Victoire

Paul Cézanne, later known for his painted bathers, swam whenever possible in the Arc, the stream which, as the Viorne in Zola's *L'Oeuvre* (1886), "waters the low meadows of Plassans." With his close friends Zola and Jean-Baptistin Baille, pupils with him at the Collège Bourbon (now Lycée Mignet), he sought to escape the proverbial sleepiness and monotonous routines of Aix. The three "inseparables" walked miles into the country along roads white with dust, swam, read, debated together. A passage in *L'Oeuvre* looks back to the days when, full of "romantic frenzy", they would, beneath the willows at some spring, "act out plays they knew by heart, their voices declamatory for the heroes, piping for the *ingénues* and queens." At first Hugo's mighty antitheses appealed to them most, then Musset's more human passion, but in their "fine youthful gluttony" they were also happy to swallow less distinguished fare.

At home in Aix, Cézanne's father, a successful hatmaker turned banker, expected rather more conventional behaviour from his son, who studied law at his insistence. Nevertheless Cézanne did much of his painting in the prosperous bourgeois surroundings of the Jas de Bouffan or House of the Winds, west of Aix, which his father bought in 1859 and he inherited in 1886. In 1861 the artist and his mother prevailed upon his father to let him paint and study painting in Paris, but there he felt provincial, an outsider, and either underestimated or a failure as an artist. Zola, who had no such qualms, gave Lantier, the perfectionist failed painter of *L'Oeuvre*, some similar characteristics; when the novel was published Cézanne broke off communication with Zola. Throughout his career he spent long periods back in the south, which provided him with some of his most famous *motifs*, including the 37-acre grounds of the Jas de Bouffan; the quarry at Bibémus whose orange-red rocks and "gouged and eerily cubic topography" he exploited in the 1890s "to create a landscape of peculiar geometric character" (Mary Tompkins-Lewis, *Cézanne*, 2000); and the Montagne Sainte-Victoire, the subject of about thirty oil-paintings and forty-five watercolours.

The mountain often features in Cézanne's work of the 1880s, but it is in the 1890s that he begins to concentrate on it more intensely. He painted it in pinks, in ochres, in his light early impressionist manner and his firmly structured almost cubist later manner; and from Gardanne, from his brother-in-law's estate at Bellevue, from the Le Tholonet road, from Bibémus where (Tompkins-Lewis) "the vertical planes of the chiselled cliff walls serve as a stratified pedestal for the looming drama" of the Sainte-Victoire. The Austrian writer Peter Handke, visiting the Cézanne sites in his meditative account *The Lesson of Mont Sainte-Victoire* (1980, translated by Ralf Manheim 1985), describes one of the relevant viewpoints:

The mountain comes into sight before you even get to Le Tholonet. It is bare and monochrome, more radiance than colour... At first sight, the shimmering mountain looks like something in the sky, an impression favoured by what would seem to be the just congealed falling movement of the parallel rock faces, extended horizontally by the stratified fold at the base of the mountain. One feels that the mountain has flowed from above, out of the almost like-coloured atmosphere, and condensed in mid-air.

Having been forced to sell the Jas de Bouffan in 1899, following the death of his mother, Cézanne had used a studio in Aix but found it cramped and unsatisfying. In 1902 he moved into a purpose-built studio on the hill of Les Lauves, now Avenue Paul-Cézanne. Here he not only produced some of his most extraordinary views of Mont Sainte-Victoire—works in which paint as much as place is the "subject"—but worked on the three versions of his *Grandes Baigneuses*. In both groups of paintings the emphasis on underlying structure combines the classical and modern, realizing his declared ambition to "do Poussin from nature."

On 15 October 1906 Cézanne collapsed during a storm while he was out painting near the Lauves studio. He was found several hours later and taken home to Aix in a laundry-cart. The following day he determinedly walked back to the studio, painted in the garden and wrote a peremptory letter to his supplier demanding to know why the paints he had ordered had not arrived. But he soon succumbed to pneumonia, dying a week later. The studio (the Atelier Paul Cézanne) is preserved as it was in 1906, with the painter's furniture, stove, easel and still-life objects: bottles, pots, skulls, the plaster Cupid.

The Musée Granet

In the late thirteenth century the church of St.-Jean-de-Malte, often described as "austere" or "sober", was built as a chapel for the Priory or commander's residence of the Knights of Malta. In the seventeenth-century building of the Priory itself was installed, in 1838, the Musée Granet, recently refurbished at a cost of roughly 25 million euros.

The museum contains both "fine art", including eight Cézannes, and archaeology. Finds from pre-Roman Entremont include a group of four stone heads—two men, two hooded women—and a god's or hero's limestone torso and upper legs. Once his hands probably held, or rested on, his enemies' heads, "as if reflective", suggests Miranda Green in *The Celtic World*, "of the divine dominance over humans in life and death", perhaps even "in an attitude of benediction".

François-Marius Granet (1775-1849) left the museum three hundred of his paintings and 1,500 drawings and other works. Some of his work remains attractive to modern viewers, perhaps especially his watercolours of the palace of Versailles and its surroundings. The museum holds a portrait of Granet by his better known friend Jean-Auguste-Dominique Ingres: starched white collar, elegantly contrasting black coat and cape, big engaging eyes. This was painted in about 1807 in Rome, where Ingres and Granet shared a studio for a time; there is a (disputed) tradition that Granet painted the background to the portrait including the Palazzo del Quirinale.

One of the most famous paintings in the collection is Ingres' substantial (nearly eleven feet high and more than eight wide) *Jupiter and Thetis* (1811). The father of the gods, face framed with dark hair and beard, sits on his throne among the clouds of Olympus, admired by a similarly royal eagle. The sea-nymph Thetis has come to persuade him, on behalf of her aggrieved son Achilles, that the Trojans must be allowed to defeat Achilles' fellow-Greeks. Thetis pleads much in the manner specified by Homer—her right arm round his knees, her left hand lifted to his chin. At left Juno (Hera in *The Iliad*) looks on balefully. Jupiter sits still in long consideration. The throne, the clouds and the costumes seem to owe more to theatre design than to visionary classicism; and if this is theatre it is more tableau than conversation-piece. Yet the very stillness, and the strangeness of the petitioner's uncomfortable-looking pose, force viewers to look and puzzle.

"The figure of Thetis," Edward Lucie-Smith points out in *A Concise History of French Painting* (1971), "has a wilful elegance... [I]t is compressed in space, so that it forms a kind of shallow bas-relief rather than a fully-rounded three-dimensional form, and the head is forced back at an exaggerated angle... The figure of Jupiter is huge in proportion to that of his suppliant." Kenneth Clark, in *The Romantic Rebellion* (1973), also lingers over this "strange hieroglyphic of the female body, the neck like an amorous swan, the elongated arms, boneless, distorted, and yet disturbingly physical". None of the preliminary sketches survives; Clark "would give a lot to see the genesis of the marvellous hand, half octopus, half tropical flower, which caresses so insinuatingly the impassive Jupiter."

Saint-Maximin and La Sainte Baume

St-Maximin-la-Ste-Baume is, Prosper Mérimée told Sophie Duvaucel on 25 September 1834, "a wretched hole between Aix and Draguignan". The great (but unfinished) fourteenth- to sixteenth-century pilgrimage-basilica raised above the tomb of St. Mary Magdalene is "a large church where nothing is missing but a façade, towers, a steeple and other minor details." In the less flippant, more public *Notes d'un voyage dans le Midi de la France* (1835) he is more complimentary about the church, "the size and height of its three naves and the elegance of its apse", and full of praise for the Curé who had gone to extraordinary lengths—including locking the church and absenting himself with the key—to protect the interior from the familiar nineteenth-century scourge of "the whitewashers".

The Magdalene had been living a life of pious eremitical solitude, says tradition, some miles south of St.-Maximin in a cave called the Ste.-Baume (from the Provençal *baumo*, "cave"). The surroundings were, according to Caxton's 1483 translation of *The Golden Legend*, "a ryght sharp deserte". Rev. Sabine Baring-Gould, in *The Lives of the Saints* (1897-8) gives more detail:

> This cave is situated in a huge rock, 2,800 feet high, reached by a narrow stair in the rock; from it a path leads upwards to the chapel called St-Pilon, built on the top of the rock. The rock rises to a point, from the top is seen a terrific precipice, out of which grow wild pinks, and a few shrubs, and where falcons make their nests. At the foot are piles of stones, which have fallen from the basaltic crag. The plain at its base is covered with ancient forests of oaks, pines, and yew.

It was such hard work getting up to the cave that, declared the late seventeenth-century travellers Bachaumont and Chapelle, it must surely have been constructed by divine means. On the other hand, the "wily and subtle" Devil knows that pilgrims will consign themselves to Hell with their continual swearing by him as they battle up to the Baume. On went the travellers, nevertheless, in the pouring rain and, "by the grace of God, without so much as a murmur". But they did not linger long. At the hostelry (subsequently destroyed during the Revolution) "hideous-looking" monks served visitors no meat, only barley-bread and over-priced eggs. "Hunger, thirst and fear" soon drove them away.

Bachaumont and Chapelle were clearly not—at least as they project themselves in their jovial *Voyage*—men to be moved to devotion by stories of the saint's penitence and visionary piety. Had they been, they could have seen, at the chapel (called St.-Pilon because once there had been a column here), the very spot where according to the Breviary, "every day she was elevated in the air by angels, to hear celestial concerts." Baring-Gould cannot help wondering how, if she was living in solitude for thirty years, we know that she was lifted into the air.

Chapter Seven
Marcel Pagnol's Provence: Marseille

"Damned picturesque place"

Dickens' *Little Dorrit* opens with a hypnotic vision:

> Thirty years ago, Marseilles lay burning in the sun, one day. A blazing
> sun upon a fierce August day was no greater rarity in southern France
> then, than at any other time, before or since. Everything in Marseilles,
> and about Marseilles, had stared at the fervid sky, and been stared at
> in return, until a staring habit had become universal there. Strangers
> were stared out of countenance by staring white houses, staring white
> walls, staring white streets, staring tracts of arid road, staring hills from
> which verdure was burnt away. The only things to be seen not fixedly
> glaring and staring were the vines drooping under their load of grapes.
> These did occasionally wink a little, as the hot air barely moved their
> faint leaves.

The foul water in the harbour does not stir, "the ships blistered at their
moorings." Even when the August sun does not blaze like "one great
flaming jewel of fire", Marseille is often characterized in extreme terms.

History, besides, has visited extreme happenings on the city: its
capture and pillage in 1423 by Aragonese forces, for example, or the
plague of 1720 and the later outbreaks of cholera and smallpox, or the
rapid growth, in the nineteenth century, of what the popular poet Victor
Gelu rejected as "noxious foundries, unhealthy factories, sordid alleys
with wretched huts full of hooligans." There was much bloodshed
during the Revolution, when, Mr Meagles observes in *Little Dorrit*,
Marseille sent "the most insurrectionary tune into the world that ever
was composed": Claude Joseph Rouget de Lisle's "Battlesong for the
Army of the Rhine" became known as "La Marseillaise" once it was taken
up by revolutionary Marseillais soldiers on their way to help defend Paris
in the summer of 1792. The city "couldn't exist", claims Meagles, good-

humoured, but bored of being in quarantine there, "without allonging and marshonging to something or other—victory or death, or blazes, or something." (*Allons... marchons*, the battle-song enjoins.) In seemingly more stable times there was gang warfare, gun-running to Spain in its various periods of civil war, and drug-related violence. The Corsican and other mafias became powerful.

Gradually there grew the myth of a Marseille violent and sordid beyond any observable reality. Individual incidents appeared to confirm the myth: it seemed typical, to outsiders, that the assassination of the King of Yugoslavia and the French foreign minister in 1934 should have occurred in Marseille—in the most famous street, the Canebière. The 1930s gangster, brothel-owner and Fascist supporter Paul Carbone, "Emperor of Marseille", became as well-known a character as his Chicago equivalents. (He was eventually blown up by the Resistance in 1944.) Eugène Saccomare's account of the activities of Carbone and his assistant François Spirito in *Gangsters de Marseille* inspired Jacques Deray's film *Borsalino* (1970), with Jean-Paul Belmondo and Alain Delon. Earlier dramatically criminal versions of Marseille appeared in such films as *Justin de Marseille* (1935) and *Mémoire d'un flic* (1955) and many followed, most famously William Friedkin's *The French Connection* (1971) and John Frankenheimer's *The French Connection II* (1975). The Fabio Montale crime novels written by Jean-Claude Izzo in the 1990s were also set in the area.

Robert Guédiguian's film *La Ville est tranquille* (2000) looks more seriously and compassionately at a modern Marseille—side by side with the warm stone of the city's landmarks and the blue sea beyond—riddled with gun-crime, prostitution, drugs, racism, and the aftermath of unemployment. The picture is less uniformly depressing than it might be because Guédiguian concentrates so strongly on individuals—a large cast of them, whose difficult lives meet or simply overlap, but especially Michèle (Ariane Ascaride), who works at night in a fish market. She is soon driven to much more desperate measures in the attempt to cope with, then to pay for, her daughter's drug habit and to look after her baby granddaughter. There are few solutions for the characters' problems. Great human potential is being lost through social deprivation, addiction, and racist violence; what can happen when the potential is realized is shown when, in the film's partly optimistic ending, a grand piano, bought with donations, arrives for a brilliant Georgian boy-musician. He, an outsider who would not be accepted as "French" by many people, plays in the street and draws together a whole wondering group of neighbours and passers-by, their differences and pain, exclusion or exclusiveness, for a moment forgotten. (For many people it is football which transcends all the difficulties. "OM"—Olympique de Marseille—is the biggest and one of the most successful clubs in France, famous for the passion of its fans. Players and supporters come from many different ethnic backgrounds.)

Marseille, like many big cities, has had big problems. But partly because it has been as famous for humour as for violence, outsiders have not always taken the place seriously. Within France in particular, Marseille has often been viewed through a Parisian lorgnette. The historian Richard Cobb has explored this prejudice in *Promenades* (1980):

> In the 1930s and, I think, quite recently, Marseille has been good for a laugh, at least with Parisians; indeed, one might even say this was part of the city's export industry, along with soap and cooking oil, via Marcel Pagnol and his creations—Marius, Fanny and César... I am sometimes tempted to think that the joke was actually on the Parisians: the inhabitants of Marseille especially thriving under the convenient disguise of levity, loquacity, and mendacity, 'talking big', exaggerating, telling what the locals call *la galéjade*—the tall story.

An awareness of corruption and inefficiency in the city were "also a comfortable way of discrediting... a place that, throughout its immensely rich history, had shown itself again and again quite capable of prospering in the *absence* of Paris and *without* Paris." Taken on its own terms rather than those of the capital, Cobb's "cascading, steep-terraced, ochre-coloured" city has much to recommend it. In fact, as Frances Spalding reports Colonel Teed, resident of Cassis in the 1920s, as being wont to say, "Damned picturesque place, Marseilles. When you get the hang of it."

Massalia: "turning towards the Greeks"

The Musée d'Histoire de Marseille displays a poster for the celebration, in 1899, of the presumed twenty-fifth centenary of the foundation of the city. A girl in exotic costume, with robe, sash, and an extraordinary headdress with coiled yellow attachments like large rosettes, is offering a drinking-vessel to a responsive, clean-shaven young man who wears a fillet around his neat black hair. In the background men with huge, droopy blond moustaches look much less happy. An older man puts his hand thoughtfully to his great white Druid's beard; he looks a little puzzled, a little wary, but appears also to divine that the contact between the young people may be all to the good, may be what the gods desire.

The foundation myth which the poster alludes to runs as follows: it so happened that Nann or Nannos, king of a Celtic tribe called the Segobrigii, was preparing for his daughter's marriage when he was visited by some Greeks from Phocaea (now Foça in Turkey). According to the custom of his people, says the Gallic historian Pompeius Trogus, he would give his Gyptis to a husband who would be chosen during the feast. Hospitably, he invited the visitors to attend. All Gyptis' suitors were there. "And when her father commanded her to offer the water to the man she had chosen to be her husband, ignoring all the others and turning towards the Greeks she offered the water to Protis" [one of the leaders of the Phocaean party]. Nannos gave him the land on which to found the town which, established around 600 BC, became the Greeks' Massalia and the Romans' Massilia.

With or without such picturesque help, the Phocaeans, looking for new commercial bases, were attracted by the site: a deep *calanque* or creek made an ideal harbour (the "Vieux-Port"), and the rocky promontory was easy to defend. Massalia gave the colonists privileged access to western Mediterranean trade-routes. (They defeated their most dangerous rivals, the Carthaginians, in sea-battles of the sixth and fifth centuries BC.) The Rhône took them deep into the interior of Gaul. The Massaliotes traded principally in tin, amber, oil and wine; they are supposed to have introduced the olive and the vine to Provence. They established their own colonies at what would later become Nice and Antibes. Financial and military success, and continuing connection with the wider Greek world, were signalled by the dedication of the Massalian treasury at Delphi in about 530 BC. And the voyages of the explorers Euthymenes and Pytheas in the fourth century BC suggest an interest even in the little known world beyond the Mediterranean: Euthymenes is said to have investigated the west coast of Africa as far as Senegal and

Pytheas to have reached Britain and found beyond it "Thule"—Iceland or Norway.

The city itself was governed by a constitution which was held up as an example by several ancient writers. The city-state was ruled by an assembly of 600 *timoukhoi* or "honour-holders", headed by an executive committee of fifteen men, three of whom alternated as holders of supreme power. Strabo's *Geography* concludes that this is "the best ordered" of all aristocracies. It merited some brief approving comments from Aristotle in his *Politics*. Individual laws, too, were admired by the connoisseurs: women, who as usual played no part in running the state, were forbidden to drink wine and could be killed by their husbands if they did; mimes and acrobats were banned because the young might be corrupted by them; euthanasia (by hemlock) was available to anyone who could give good enough reasons to the 600—you might have known bad luck and feared it would go on for ever, or you might have known good fortune and want to depart before it could change. Another way to die was as the scapegoat who would take on the sins of the city: having been fed on ritually correct dishes for a year, he was led through the streets, attired in sacrificial robes, to his death. As he passed by, citizens shouted curses at him. We do not know whether the victim was a convicted criminal (perhaps unlikely if he was to be a pleasing sacrifice), drawn by lot, or a religiously or masochistically minded volunteer.

Perhaps Massalia placated the gods. More importantly for their survival, it placated, or did good business with, Rome. A loose alliance against the Carthaginians existed long before Massaliote ships helped the Romans against Hannibal in the third century BC; the favour was returned when, in the mid-120s BC, the city could no longer hold out alone against attacks by the Saluvii. A Roman army destroyed Entremont, and southern France—"the Province", "Provence"—soon came under Roman control. Massalia retained a fair degree of autonomy and the advantages of closer Roman protection. Only in 49 BC did the usually canny city fathers miscalculate. They backed Pompey against Caesar in the Civil War. The siege went on for six months until food shortages, disease and naval defeat forced the city to surrender. Humbled at last after 550 years, the Massaliotes were forced to hand over their ships, their weapons, and the contents of their treasury. They were also deprived of much of their territory. But Caesar spared the city itself: "more," he says, "on account of the name and antiquity of their state than for anything they had deserved of him."

Massalia's disgrace was to the advantage of Arles—Roman Arelate— which became politically dominant. But Massalia remained a considerable commercial centre. And it also kept its "name and antiquity", its reputation for that Greek culture which mattered so much to educated Romans. Strabo says that there were Romans who came here, instead of Athens, to study. Tacitus implies that this was a sensible choice, since this is "a place where Greek refinement and provincial puritanism are happily blended." Tacitus' father-in-law Gnaeus Julius Agricola, subsequently governor of Britain, came to live and study here "from his very early years". Agricola used to tell Tacitus that he had been "tempted to drink deeper of philosophy than was allowable for a Roman and a future senator" but that his wise mother "damped the fire of his passion." Presumably the "provincial puritanism" also played its part.

Vestiges: the Musée d'Histoire de Marseille, Musée des Docks Romains and Centre de la Vieille Charité

A passage in Blaise Cendrars' *L'Homme foudroyé* (1945) celebrates the fact that Marseille "today is the only one of the ancient capitals which doesn't crush us with monuments of its past." Generally the city remains mysterious, "difficult to decode... Everything has gone back underground, everything is secret." But some Greek and Roman remains have now, in fact, re-emerged. There was great excitement when part of the ancient city-wall was found in 1913, but most of the discoveries were made only after the building of the Bourse shopping-centre began in 1967. The resulting "Jardin des Vestiges", reached through the History Museum, includes part of the docks (the harbour extended much further inland than now), the foundations of towers, a fifth-century BC well, part of a Roman road running through the east gate of the city, and a first-century AD tank for fresh water. Rather more excitingly—the "vestiges" can seem rather forlorn—the remains of a Roman trading ship were found and are displayed, with a replica, in the museum.

The History Museum has much else on ancient Marseille, but a more immediate impression of daily life is available at the Musée des Docks Romains. This has been built around the excavation of a group of large *dolia*—ceramic containers in which oil or wine was stored, called *pithoi* in Greek. They were sunk into the ground in order to keep them airtight and the temperature even. Each container had a capacity of about 2,000 litres. A few are complete or put back together, but most look like the abandoned halves of egg-shells. Skilfully lit, the browns and slightly pinkish grey of the containers and their surroundings are as aesthetically pleasing as archaeologically informative. They look more like the aftermath of an explosion than something "Cool'd a long age in the deep-delved earth."

Further antiquities, from Egyptian to Amerindian, can be seen at the Centre de la Vieille Charité, a grandly restored late seventeenth- and eighteenth-century poorhouse, with domed Baroque chapel, by Pierre Puget. The north and east wings house museums of Egyptian, Mesopotamian and Mediterranean antiquities and of African, Oceanic and Amerindian arts. The collection includes material from the Celto-Ligurian settlement at Roquepertuse, most famously its reddish limestone portico with niches ready to receive human heads. The cult of the severed head, for which there is also archaeological evidence at Entremont and Glanum, is mentioned in Diodorus Siculus' *History*; the Gauls, he says, nail up their enemies' heads or, in the case of important enemies, embalm the heads in cedar-oil and show them off to visitors. (Such customs are also attested in much later Irish and Welsh sources.) It is an aspect of the culture which people still find it difficult to comprehend or assimilate—like the Romans, who probably sacked Roquepertuse in about 123 BC. It is conceivable that the heads displayed were sometimes those of tribal worthies rather than enemies. More clearly, there must have been an intention to control, display or propitiate the head—home, to the Celts, of the soul, the identity—or the forces it embodied or symbolized.

A number of sculptures are associated with the portico. There are two cross-legged figures of gods, heroes or princes, one with lozenge-patterned robe, the other with torc and arm-band. These statues have, as Ian Finlay suggests (*Celtic Art: an Introduction*, 1973), "a rigid, hieratic quality reminiscent of Egypt." And there is a two-headed "Janus" where, for Ruth and Vincent Megaw (*Celtic Art*, 1989), "the conventional rendering attains a curious distinction, almost the inscrutable beauty of a Gandhara Buddha, if without the compassion."

Passing Through

Marseille was a point of arrival and departure for Barbarian invaders and those fleeing them, for merchants, crusaders and the Foreign Legion, poets and colonial officials going to Africa or the east, tourists going to Italy, and migrant workers from Corsica, Genoa, the French colonies and Greece. The calendars of events in the *Almanach historique, biographique et littéraire de la Provence* for the late 1850s and early 1860s list the almost routine arrivals of princes and Grand Duchesses as well as a battalion back from China, ten Arab horses (a gift to Napoleon III from the new Bey of Tunis) and a black crocodile from Senegal, nearly two metres long and bound for the Zoological Garden. Biographies of nineteenth-century poets and novelists often feature Marseille as a brief stage in the journey, a halt imposed by illness or poverty or the need to organize one's affairs. George Sand and Frédéric Chopin arrived after a thirty-six-hour voyage which ended their difficult stay in Mallorca. Chopin was too ill—they stayed a month on doctor's orders—to take much notice of Marseille. Sand was writing too hard, in need of cash, to do more than dismiss the place as a town of "merchants and shopkeepers, where the life of the mind is completely unknown."

Arthur Rimbaud fell ill on arrival from Livorno in 1875, lived in Marseille in poverty for a while in 1877 and was admitted to the Hôpital de la Conception in May 1891 on his return to France from his years in Africa. He was suffering from bone cancer and had a leg amputated before leaving hospital in July. A month later he returned to the city and the hospital, still hoping to embark once more for Ethiopia, but died on 10 November aged thirty-seven. A day earlier he had dictated, in delirium, a letter organizing an imaginary ivory caravan and a last sailing on the imaginary but poetic-sounding "Aphinar" line.

Marseille itself, the beginning and end of adventures like Rimbaud's, could seem fairly exotic to northerners. Gustave Flaubert had rarely ventured out of Normandy when, at the age of eighteen, he toured Corsica with a colleague of his father. On the journey there and back he also saw the south of France for the first time; he admired Marseille as "a pretty town" with great houses like palaces and long streets full of Midi sun and air where one senses "je ne sais quoi d'oriental"; "one walks and breathes at one's ease." Ancient Persia and medieval Alexandria must have been like this: "a babel of all the nations, where one sees blond hair... black beards... blue eyes, black looks... the turned-down collars of the English, the turban and wide trousers of the Turks. You hear a hundred unknown languages spoken," including "those which are spoken in snowy countries and those which are sighed in southern climes." And here, insists the young man temporarily away from his sometimes suffocating relationship with his parents, people are enjoying themselves so much that it would chagrin the virtuous. "People are taking in pleasure through every pore, in every form, as much as they can; sailors—Jews, Armenians, Greeks... crowding into the *cabarets*, laughing with the girls, turning over jugs of wine, singing, dancing, love-making at their ease."

Flaubert had private reasons for delighting in Marseille. (Dickens, who did not, shared his delight in the nationalities and varying headgear, the "great beards, and no beards", of the port, but also registered "vile smells" in the harbour and "crowds of fierce-looking people, of the lower sort, blocking up the way.") In February 1860 Flaubert told the Goncourt brothers about his encounters with Eulalie Foucaud. He had found himself in "a little hotel in Marseille", the Goncourts report: Hôtel de Richelieu, which was run by three women who had recently returned from South America. In their full-length silk dressing-gowns they were "very temptingly exotic" for the "young Norman". One day when he came back from swimming, he told the fascinated brothers, he was beckoned into a bedroom by one of the three, "a woman of thirty-five, *magnifique*". Ecstatic sex followed. Later there were tears, letters for a while after he left, "then nothing more". Several times when he went back to Marseille he looked for Eulalie but found no trace. On his last visit, when he was on his way to Tunis to research his Carthaginian novel *Salammbô* in April 1858, he discovered that the ground floor of Hôtel de Richelieu had become a toyshop. Upstairs was a barber's, where he had himself shaved. He recognized the wallpaper. By this time he was deeply versed in the exoticism which nourished—or, some feel, killed—*Salammbô*; and in its inevitable disappointments, whether for an inexperienced young man or for Emma Bovary.

There has always been business for prostitutes, like those Flaubert saw with the sailors, in a port. James Boswell visited Mademoiselle Susette on his return from Corsica in December 1765. She had been recommended by a fellow-Scot in Genoa; Boswell had "determined", on reaching the age of twenty-five nearly two months earlier, "never again to risk my constitution with women," but was easily persuaded that this specimen was "honest, safe, and disinterested." Their encounter seems to have been little to his taste: he confides in his Journal, with a mixture of arrogance, honesty and self-castigation, that "she was so little that I had an idea as if she was a child, and had not much inclination for her. I recalled my charming Signora at Siena, and was disgusted at all women but her, and angry at myself for being in the arms of another. Susette chatted neatly and diverted me. I sacrificed to the graces. I think I did no harm."

The much more innocent Paul Pennyfeather, hapless hero of Evelyn Waugh's *Decline and Fall,* wonders why the driver who takes him to the old town warns him to hold on to his hat. Soon "a young lady snatched his hat from his head; he caught a glimpse of her bare leg in a lighted doorway; then she appeared at a window, beckoning him to come in and retrieve it." He hesitates briefly before fleeing, "forsaking, in a moment of panic, both his black hat and his self-possession."

Royal Arrivals

In November 1600 Maria de' Medici, the twenty-seven-year-old niece of the Grand Duke of Tuscany, stepped ashore in Marseille from her lavishly appointed galley. She had already married King Henri IV by proxy in the Duomo in Florence and was now welcomed, amid cannon salvoes, trumpeting and bowing, as the Queen known in France as Marie de Médicis. She was met by the Cardinals of France and the Consuls of Marseille in their scarlet robes. The senior Consul presented her with weighty golden keys to the city and fireworks were launched from ships and shore.

But a "most distressing incident" somewhat marred the welcome—as tends to happen, Maria's accompanying aunt the Grand Duchess observed, "in all the affairs of this world." The Knights of Malta had agreed that their ships, escorting the Tuscan ones, would take precedence—the position on the right—during the voyage from Livorno, but would cede it to the Tuscans when they neared their destination. In the event, however, the Knights made sure they maintained their position and this implied snub to the Grand Duke caused grave offence among the Italians. Things would have been distinctly easier if Henri IV had, as planned, been there to greet his bride and impose his authority. But he had been unavoidably detained by the need to finish his siege of Montmélian, an important stage in his war with Savoy; "Only the law of duty," he wrote to her, "can compel the law of love." But the delay in meeting the Beloved also gave him longer, it has been pointed out, to savour his liaison with Henriette d' Entragues. To his wife he sent "a hundred thousand kisses", to Henriette "a million".

On shore over the next ten days there were other problems. Accommodation for the 500 Tuscans was poor, provisions so inadequate that they had to be supplied from their ships. Some townspeople were unwelcoming, mindful perhaps of recent history: Tuscan soldiers had held the Château d'If and neighbouring islands against the Governor of Provence in the closing stages of the Wars of Religion, withdrawing only in 1598. There were some scuffles, and the Tuscan minister Belisario Vinta wrote to the Grand Duke that he found the Marseillais to be *travaglioso* [troublesome], *fastidioso, imperioso, e difficile.* Vinta's irritation was increased by the fact that he felt obliged to hand over Maria's dowry (350,000 gold crowns, much needed by Henri after years of civil and other wars) with due ceremony to the King himself. He was therefore forced, when most of his compatriots had set off for home—to their and their hosts' mutual relief—to go on with the Queen on her laborious winter journey to Lyon.

Twenty-two years later Peter Paul Rubens was commissioned by Marie, by this time the unhappy Queen Dowager, to paint the series of scenes from her life now in the Louvre. Whereas in reality she had dressed with simple elegance, Ronald Millen has pointed out that in the bravura "Disembarkation at Marseille" Rubens loaded her with "gold and pearl-embroidered cloth, encrusted the bodice and sleeves with precious stones, hung a heavy jewelled chain from her shoulders" and crowned her with a pearl and ruby diadem. Hefty nereids in the foreground help to draw the boat to shore—specimens of Rubens' usual predilection for ample flesh. (One witness had noticed with approval Marie's *fort bon embonpoint*, but she does not look particularly plump in the picture.) Instead of the actual cardinals and consuls, personifications of Provence and Marseille greet her. It all looks aptly celebratory, but there may be some hints that the difficulties and chagrins of the first days in France have not been forgotten—indeed have been carefully stored by the woman who has so often been at loggerheads with her adopted countrypeople, not least with her son King Louis XIII. The absence of the consuls and cardinals may be a deliberate slight, and Millen suggests that the Knight of Malta on the boat with the Queen may be intended to look arrogant rather than merely proud. The Knights' discourtesy may still have rankled.

Marie's grandson Louis XIV made sure that there was no discourtesy when he entered the city in 1660. Independent-minded or *fastidioso* as ever, many Marseillais had been agitating against the centralized rule increasingly being imposed on them. In January royal troops occupied the city. To make their point more clearly, they breached the old defensive walls. Through the breach, as conqueror rather than smiling royal visitor, Louis made his solemn entry on 7 March. Having arrived, he summarily revised the city administration. He abolished the title "consul", with its proud republican associations. Chief magistrates or "échevins" would henceforth be royal appointees, and other traditional liberties were lost. The King, more efficient than his grandfather, moved on towards the Spanish border to collect his new queen, but an unambiguous sign of his authority remained in the Fort St.-Nicolas, built in the mid-1660s to dominate the entrance to the Vieux-Port. The medieval tower opposite had already, in 1644, been expanded as the Fort St.-Jean. Both were intended more to police the town than to resist invaders from the sea.

Plague

Ports attract trade, royal visits, invaders, prostitutes—and disease. There were many outbreaks of plague and later of cholera. The last major plague, of 1720, was remembered longest. In 1805 Anne Plumptre, the English translator of an account of the epidemic by Dr. Jean-Baptiste Bertrand, found people in Marseille who were still acutely aware of its "ravages and desolation" in spite of the more recent horrors of the Revolution. Modern interest was stimulated by a popular documentary study first published in 1968, *Marseille ville morte*, by Charles Carrière and his collaborators; partly under its influence several novelists turned their attention to the plague, including Raymond Jean in *L'Or et la soie* (*Gold and Silk*, 1983).

The plague came on the merchant ship *Le Grand Saint-Antoine*, which returned from the Middle East on 25 May 1720. Several crew-members died on the way or soon after their arrival. Because quarantine was not strictly enough applied, infection soon spread ashore, whether from the people aboard or the cargo. Only much later did it become clear that the city's chief magistrate, Jean-Baptiste Estelle, wanted the ship unloaded as soon as possible so that its load of cotton, which he owned, could be ready for the fair at Beaucaire in July. Matters were made worse by the civic authorities' reluctance to accept the seriousness of the outbreak. The magistrates alleged that the doctors were diagnosing plague simply in order to frighten people into sickness and so to make money from them.

But as the casualties mounted—fifty a day and then, at the height of the outbreak in July and August, a hundred—it became all too obvious that plague it was. By the time it subsided in the autumn about 50,000 Marseillais, about half the population, had died. There were the usual terrible scenes of rotting corpses, of people left to die because even relations dared not help them, of doomed attempts to impose a *cordon sanitaire* on the city. (Plague killed 37 per cent of the population of Provence between 1720 and 1722.) Chevalier Nicolas Roze raised a force of 150 convicts and soldiers to remove and bury the dead. Only three of this force, apparently, survived. The needs of the dying and the living were addressed by the Bishop of Marseille, Henri-François-Xavier de Belsunce. While many of his clergy had fled or died, he went about distributing alms, encouraging the physicians, attending daily meetings at the Town Hall, leading prayers—the plague was, of course, widely interpreted as a manifestation of divine wrath. (Belsunce was sufficiently a man of his time and church to blame it especially on heresy.) Dr. Bertrand reports that most of Belsunce's household perished and the street outside his palace was so blocked with corpses that he had to move elsewhere. He went round with the only canon of the cathedral who had not fled, and with his almoners. "The generous pastor had soon the affliction to see the zealous canon... expire by his side; but for himself, he remained to the last unassailed by the dreadful foe." In the Musée d'Histoire de Marseille, beneath a radiant memorial painting of the bishop, a display of surgical instruments for dealing with plague gives some sense of the grim realities. There are probes, scissors, lancets, forceps. The long forceps or tongs used to give communion to plague victims must have been particularly familiar to Belsunce and his staff.

Early accounts stressed the individual heroism of Belsunce as one way of coping with the horrors of plague, one way of imposing order as the bishop had attempted to do as Marseille threatened to descend into anarchy. Later the emphasis often shifted to the more erringly human attitude of the city magistrates at the beginning of the summer. The origins of the plague, says Raymond Jean, "were attributed to fate, providence, the wrath of God. In reality they were of a completely human nature." Meanwhile the immediate bringer of disease, the *Grand Saint-Antoine*, was burnt as a sensible precaution. Its remains were found by divers off the Ile de Jarre, south of Marseille, in 1978.

Pagnol's Vieux-Port

Paul Pennyfeather, during his brief trip to Marseille in Waugh's *Decline and Fall*, enters the old town along a "cobbled alley" where "the houses overhung perilously on each side, gaily alight from cellar to garret; between them swung lanterns; a shallow gutter ran down the centre of the path. The scene could scarcely have been more sinister had it been built at Hollywood itself for some orgiastic incident in the Reign of Terror."

Cinema was indeed soon making the most of old Marseille, but more often for its colour, noise and camaraderie than for its sinister associations. Marcel Pagnol's films of the 1930s fixed the life of the Vieux-Port—or at least his dramatic version of it—in the French imagination. Pagnol himself grew up in a very different part of the city. In 1900, when he was five, his father was appointed to a teaching post in central Marseille. From then on the family lived in various streets in the quiet Quartier de la Plaine. Pagnol attended the prestigious Lycée Thiers, named after a former pupil, Adolphe Thiers (1797-1877), historian and first President of the Third Republic. (Edmond Rostand, author of *Cyrano de Bergerac*, was another notable student.) Pagnol later filmed his Christmas story *Merlusse* (1935) in the school's large main building: a seemingly unfriendly teacher manages to rise to the needs of children left behind for the holidays.

The grimier, louder, warmer Marseille of the Vieux-Port, where people speak their loves and usually temporary hates more openly than at the lycée or in the Quartier de la Plaine, had impinged little on the young Pagnol. "The charm of the little streets choked up with rubbish," he remembers in his 1962 preface to *Marius*, "had always escaped me." But four years away in Paris revealed the charm of deep shops with coils of rope in corners, folded sails, and "big brass lanterns hanging from the ceiling", of the small shaded bars along the *quais*, and the *fraîches Marseillaises*, like Fanny in *Marius*, at their shellfish stalls. And so, says Pagnol, he wrote the original play *Marius*. The opening stage directions set the scene firmly in the Vieux-Port: a little bar (the Bar de la Marine), its pavement tables, the back of Fanny's shellfish-stall, packing-cases bound for Bangkok and Sydney, barrels, a huge heap of nuts, and masts bobbing in the distance. Everywhere there is hammering and the clanking of cranes until, as the action begins, the ear-splitting midday siren at the docks sounds. (He feared that it would be all too Marseillais for Paris audiences, but the play ran for 800 performances after its first night in Paris in 1929. The popular film version by Alexander Korda for Paramount (1931) used Pagnol's adaptation. Pagnol then formed his own company, Les Films Marcel-Pagnol, which made the sequels *Fanny* (1932) and *César* (1936).)

Marius is a young man who works, not very efficiently, in the bar owned by his father, César, the "grande brute sympathique" created on stage, and later played on screen, by the great southern actor Raimu. Fanny wants Marius to marry her; he is reluctant, he explains in Act Two, because of his longing to go to sea. When he was about seventeen "there, in front of the bar, a great sailing-ship moored... It was a three-master, carrying wood from the West Indies—wood that's black on the outside and golden on the inside, which smelled of camphor and pepper." He chatted with the crew when they came to the bar; "they talked about their country, they gave me some of their rum—very smooth, very spicy." And as he watched the three-master sail away he was completely hooked. He knows that their exotic destinations could not live up to his imaginings, but he needs "elsewhere". Fanny understands this, and wants him even so.

Life centres on the bar, where there is a long card-playing scene between César, master sail-maker Panisse, customs officer Brun, and Escartefigue, "captain" of the "ferryboat" (they pronounce it "fériboîte"; a modern equivalent still runs) which carries foot-passengers from one side of the harbour to the other twenty-four times a day. Escartefigue and his driver take their jobs very seriously, to the incredulity of Marius, the would-be ocean sailor. In the second sequel, *César*, Panisse dies but the other three, not without tears, set out the cards at his empty place and play the game through. "Elsewhere", exciting for the young man, is suspect to his elders; César never misses a chance to insult the evidently long-established Brun for the *lyonnaiseries* characteristic of someone who originated from Lyon, and he points out that the Eiffel Tower is, "where width is concerned, half the size" of the transporter bridge or Pont Transbordeur in the Vieux-Port. (Erected in 1905, the bridge was partly blown up by the Germans in 1944 and the rest demolished in 1945.)

In the finely melodramatic ending of the first play, Marius has one last chance to join a ship's crew sailing for Rangoon and beyond. He has by now agreed to marry Fanny, but she realizes that he must go and suggests that they marry only after his three-year voyage. César is coming; she tells Marius to get out through the window and herself delays César by keeping him talking, giving the impression that everything is arranged for the marriage. Finally she faints as "the harbour sirens sound one after another in honour of the great sailing-ship as it goes out."

The respectful salute to the sailing-ship may remind us that the days of such romantic craft were already numbered and hint that Marius' dream is not really susceptible of fulfilment. Things are not to turn out as planned. Fanny and the audience learn, in the second piece, that she is pregnant by Marius and has no option but to accept Panisse's offer of marriage. Marius will spend much of his career not on the high seas but as a mechanic in Toulon. But by the end of *César* he has met his and Fanny's son Césariot, who thought he was Panisse's son until after the latter's death, and begun to recover his relationship both with Fanny and with his mostly unchanged, but now more reasonable, father.

The Holocaust and the Destruction of the Vieux-Port

In 1941 the anthropologist Claude Lévi-Strauss departed from Marseille, after many difficulties, on a boat bound for Martinique. The passengers were seen off by ranks of helmeted, machine-gun-wielding *gardes mobiles*; they went, he recalled in *Tristes Tropiques* (1955), like convicts. All 350 of them, mostly fellow Jews, foreigners, or suspected anarchists, were crammed into a small steamship with two cabins. A friend somehow got Lévi-Strauss into one of them. Other passengers piled into the hold, where bunks had been rigged up. These unfortunates included André Breton, whose friendship with Lévi-Strauss began with an exchange of letters, during the long and uncomfortable voyage, on "the relations between aesthetic beauty and absolute originality."

Breton and his family had been helped to leave France by the Emergency Rescue Committee, whose remit was to rescue artists and intellectuals. Heinrich Mann (novelist, brother of Thomas) and the historian and philosopher Hannah Arendt were also among those helped by this organization. Various other agencies gave more general assistance to people trying to leave, mainly in 1940-2. But thousands were less lucky; and many Jews who were long established in Marseille did not even try to leave, under the sadly mistaken impression that only more recent arrivals would be attacked.

Persecution began in earnest when the Germans took control of Vichy France in 1942. Memoirs and modern research have made it very clear that the Vichy authorities in the city were of considerable assistance to the Germans in their campaign against the Jews and other "undesirables". Jews were detained and deported in increasing numbers; 20,000 people were sent to an internment camp at Fréjus. Hitler ordered the destruction of the Vieux-Port, perceived as a den of Jews, Resistance, deserters, and prostitutes; Karl Oberg, head of the French Gestapo, declared that "Marseille is the cancer of Europe. And Europe cannot live until Marseille is purified." "Cleaning" would, accordingly, commence. In February 1943 the French police evacuated the inhabitants and arrested many of them. Two hundred Jews were rounded up, together with 600 others, mostly young men. (Only a hundred of this group, deported to Oranienburg-Sachsenhausen, survived the war.) German soldiers then dynamited nearly two hundred buildings in the Vieux-Port. With their usual concern for culture over people, the aggressors preserved a few historic buildings: the Town Hall with its Baroque façade, the sixteenth-century Hôtel de Cabre, the Maison Diamantée— named for its diamond-point stonework—which now houses the Musée du Vieux Marseille. Persecution continued until the liberation of Marseille in August 1944. The story of the Jews of Marseille and of the destruction of the old town is told in words and often harrowing pictures at the Mémorial des Camps de la Mort, a small museum just outside the walls of the Fort St.-Jean in Quai de la Tourette.

Galleys and Prisons; the Château d'If

John Evelyn, like many other travellers, was fascinated and a little shocked to come upon the galley-slaves of Marseille. After "the captain of the Galley Royal" had entertained him and his companions to the accompaniment of "both loud and soft music" played "very rarely" by his oarsmen,

> he showed us how he commanded their motions with a nod and his whistle, making them row out. This spectacle was to me new and strange, to see so many hundreds of miserably naked persons, having their heads shaven close and having only high red bonnets, a pair of coarse canvas drawers, their whole backs and legs naked, doubly chained about their middle and legs, in couples, and made fast to their seats, and all commanded in a trice by an imperious and cruel seaman... Their rising forward and falling back at their oar is a miserable spectacle, and the noise of their chains with the roaring of the beaten waters has something of strange and fearful to one unaccustomed to it.

Most witnesses took a measure of comfort in the fact that, as Evelyn puts it, "there was hardly one" of the rowers "but had some occupation by which, as leisure and calms permitted, they got some little money, insomuch as some of them have, after many years of cruel servitude, been able to purchase their liberty." Apparently some even had wives in the port and some were not criminals or captives but volunteers (desperate for work, presumably). But most were persecuted Protestants, captured Turks, smugglers, or minor fraudsters.

The city possessed its share of more conventional places of confinement. In *Pictures from Italy* Dickens describes, for example, "the common madhouse, a low, contracted, miserable building" whose chattering inmates "were peeping out, through rusty bars, at the staring faces below, while the sun, darting fiercely aslant into their little cells, seemed to dry up their brains, and worry them, as if they were baited by a pack of dogs." In the first chapter of *Little Dorrit* light penetrates a cell

The Château d'If: the "black, steep rock", and fortress like some "superfluity of flint", of Edmond Dantès' long imprisonment in *Le Comte de Monte-Cristo*.

in the Marseille prison to somewhat different, if no less despairing effect: "it came languishing down a square funnel that blinded a window in the staircase wall, through which the sky was never seen—nor anything else." In the cell the villainous Rigaud, who plays out the "game" of being a "gentleman" with the help of much "swagger and challenge", manifests his sense of superiority to the "sunburnt, quick, lithe, little" Genoese John Baptist Cavalletto while waiting to hear whether he is to be released or to face an appointment with the "national razor".

At times Edmond Dantès, the hero of Dumas' *Le Comte de Monte-Cristo* (1844-6), would rather have kept such an appointment than suffer as he does during his imprisonment in the offshore Château d'If. Fourteen years elapse between his dawning realization that he is being taken out, in the dark, to that notorious "black, steep rock" crowned by the fortress like some "superfluity of flint", and his arduous eventual escape. The fortress was built by François I in 1524-8 and served as a prison, especially for people deemed a danger to the state, for much of its history. Dantès is a young Marseille seaman falsely denounced as a Bonapartist agent by his personal enemies, and put away with no prospect of release as a result of a high official's self-interest. Solitary confinement very nearly drives him insane. Even galley-slaves, he reflects, have company, breathe the air and see the sky. On nights of "despair and fury" he counts 3,000 circuits of his cell—30,000 paces, nearly ten leagues. He can be saved only by the contact finally achieved with the inmate of a neighbouring cell, the learned but supposedly mad Abbé Faria. Faria educates and inspirits him and points his way to the vast treasure concealed on the island of Monte Cristo. Both the treasure and the training will do much to enable, many hundreds of pages later, the count's final revenge on his enemies. He visits the Château d'If, no longer a prison but a tourist attraction, and is told part of his own famous story and shown his and Faria's cells, as many a real visitor later would be. He sees the mark worn into the wall by his shoulders, the inscription in which he prayed not to lose his memory, and the remains of the bed in which Faria died. And the count no longer doubts, as for a time he had, the justice of his vengeance.

"Black Docker": Claude McKay and Ousmane Sembène

Many people in Marseille, or their ancestors, originate from the former French colonies in North and West Africa and the Caribbean. Claude

McKay (1890-1948) was from Jamaica and lived in America before and after his travels in Europe in the 1920s—but felt that he had much in common with the mixture of Africans, West Indians and African Americans he met in the city. His novel *Banjo* (1929) explores the life and the frustrated aspirations of black seamen in the "ditch" of Marseille. Any consolation is temporary and hedonistic; white power remains apparently unassailable.

McKay worked as an occasional docker. (He did light work but noticed that usually it was the heavier and more difficult jobs that the blacks were expected to do.) Ousmane Sembène (born 1923), the Senegalese novelist and film-maker, came as a docker and stayed much longer, becoming a communist trade-union official. *Docker noir* (1956; translated by Ros Schwartz, 1986) is a novel about racial injustice and hypocrisy set in a Marseille where conditions are still bad for black dockers. As well as hard work, they face uncertain employment prospects, harsh treatment by employers, illness and injury:

> The expressions on their faces reflected their inner discontent. Their skins were branded by the searing sun and dulled by the harsh weather which made deep furrows in their faces. Their hair was eaten away by bugs in the cereals. After years of this work, a man became a wreck, drained inside, nothing but an outer shell. Living in this hell, each year the docker takes another great stride towards his end. There were countless accidents. Mechanization had superseded their physical capacity, only a quarter of them toiled away maintaining the pace of the machines, replacing the output of the unemployed workers. It was the rivalry of bone against steel, a question of which was the stronger.

Churches and Cathedrals

The abbey of St.-Victor grew up around the traditional rock tomb of the saint, a Roman army officer who is supposed to have stirred up resistance to the emperor Maximian's persecution of Christians in Marseille. In prison he converted his guards, enraged the emperor by kicking a statue of Jupiter instead of offering incense, and endured terrible tortures including crushing by the grindstone of a mill, before eventually achieving his martyr's crown. In the eleventh century the early medieval church was adapted as the crypt or lower church; the upper church was rebuilt in the thirteenth century. The crypt and church are all that remain of the once-flourishing abbey complex.

The Romanesque former cathedral of Notre-Dame La Major also survives in reduced form: it was partly demolished to make way for the vast new Major, built between 1852 and 1893. From far out at sea, Richard Cobb notes, the new building looks "mosque-like"; it is "a place apparently of Eastern worship and rite." Elsie Whitlock Rose, in *Cathedrals and Cloisters of the South of France* (1906), agrees that the green and white exterior, in a style "variously called French Romanesque, Byzantine, and Neo-Byzantine, is very oriental in its general effect." The interior, too, is "entirely oriental in the luxury of ornamentation... and without that sober majesty which is an inherent characteristic of the most elaborate styles native to western Christianity." The greys, pinks and whites here "would seem almost too delicate, too effeminate for so large a building" (it is 141 metres long) but the combination is "made rich and effective by their very mass, the gigantic sizes which the plan exacts."

The construction of another large church, Notre-Dame de la Garde, overlapped with that of the cathedral. High on its limestone peak, the domed and towered neo-Byzantine church of 1853-74 is a distinguishing feature of Marseille, much photographed, included in many films, and traditionally venerated by sailors. The ex-votos dedicated by sailors, their families and others are the most noticeable feature of the interior: "countless votive pictures and tablets and medals and miraculously useless crutches" in the crypt; representations also of craft from rowing-boats to battleships, tanks and planes, in the "heartwarmingly, generously vulgar church" (M. F. K. Fisher, *A Considerable Town*, 1978). Like its smaller thirteenth-century predecessor—part of the fort which once commanded the city—Notre-Dame de la Garde is a centre of Marian pilgrimage and devotion. In 1644, however, John Evelyn felt moved to record only "In the chapel hung up divers crocodile skins."

Madeleine de Scudéry also came here in 1644, when her brother Georges took up his appointment as governor of the fort. She mentions no crocodiles, but does describe the panoramic view. She looked down, she wrote to a friend, at the harbour and city on one side, so close that she could hear the oboes playing on twenty-five galleys; in another

direction were "more than 12,000 *bastides*" (1,500 was Evelyn's more conservative estimate of the number of these country houses); a third way, islands and endless sea; and a fourth, wasteland all bristling with rocks, "whose barrenness and loneliness are as horrifying as the abundance of all the other places is delightful."

The royal minister de Brienne had expressed doubts about granting the post of governor to a poet. But the Marquise de Rambouillet, using her influence on Georges' behalf, replied, suitably poetically, that it was no use giving such a man a command in a valley; she could imagine him high on his castle keep, "head in the clouds, looking down with disdain at everything which is beneath him." In fact, residence at the fort was not even required of Georges, and if he felt disdainful it was mainly because it proved unexpectedly difficult to make any money out of the post. He appointed a lieutenant, who entertained the brother and sister to a feast and cannon salute on the hill. They lived down in the city, where Madeleine de Scudéry enjoyed the mild winters but suffered the "ennui" of exile; especially tedious were her women visitors, only a few of whom, she told friends in distressingly distant Paris, could speak French. She did admit, however, that there was something notable about the beautiful, young and learned Mlle Françoise Diodé. Perhaps the learning was a little ostentatiously paraded—Mlle Diodé had a habit of citing, in ordinary conversation, "Hermes Trismegistus, Zoroaster and other such gentlemen with whom," Scudéry alleges, "I am not acquainted." Nevertheless the two women were friends for a time.

In 1647 the Scudérys returned, without regret, to Paris and their familiar circle. Notre-Dame de la Garde made its way into the eighth part of her vast novel *Artamène, ou le Grand Cyrus* as a high tower with barren rocks on one side, fertile gardens and meadows on the other. Diodé finds a place in the third volume as the beautiful, intelligent but "a little strange" Philiste.

Le Corbusier's Unité d'Habitation

One building in Marseille has attracted more attention than any other. Le Corbusier's massive block of flats was built mainly between 1947 and 1949 and opened officially in 1952. Its "brutalist" architecture excited protests in the press, from architects' organizations, from the society for "L'Esthéthique de France". The fortunes of the project varied as ten different governments briefly held office; seven Ministers of Reconstruction came and went. A major health body decided that people living in the building would suffer from mental problems, and for years it was known popularly as the *maison du fada*—"the crackpot's house" or "the nuthouse".

The Marseille Unité d'Habitation has always had its champions, however. For Vincent Scully (*Modern Architecture: the Architecture of Democracy*, 1961) it

> stands upon its muscular legs as an image of human uprightness and dignifies all its individual units within a single embodiment of the monumental human force which makes them possible. The high space of each apartment looks out towards the mountains or the sea, and it is in relation to the mountains and the sea that the building as a whole should be seen... So perceived it is a Humanist building, as we emphatically associate ourselves with it, in the contrasting landscape, as a standing body analogous to our own.

And here, according to Charles Jencks' book about Le Corbusier (1973),

> the feeling of protection and individuality is so strong that it is comparable to standing in a cave. Yet the overall feeling is not cave-like or even monastic but more of being on a gigantic ocean liner ploughing through the choppy seas of verdure and haphazard suburban sprawl.

Marseille has two important galleries for indoor modern art: the Musée Cantini for pre-1960 work including Matisse, Derain, Picasso, Max Ernst and Kandinsky, and the Musée d'art contemporain (MAC) for the post-1960 Jean Tinguely, Jean-Pierre Raynaud, César, Arte Povera and much else.

Aubagne and La Treille

Marcel Pagnol was born at 16 cours Barthélemy, Aubagne, on 28 February 1895. The street is named after an earlier native of Aubagne, Abbé Jean-Jacques Barthélemy, author of the classical *Voyage du jeune Anacharsis en Grèce* (1788); according to Pagnol, the abbé developed some rather surprising political credentials in later centuries since locally his little-read book was remembered as an account of "Le Jeune Anarchiste". Such a title would perhaps not have appealed to the Foreign Legion, one-time defenders of French imperial power and based in Aubagne since withdrawal from Algeria in 1962.

The town was already closely connected with Marseille in Pagnol's childhood, but was less industrialized than now and seemed quite countrified to him. The family moved into Marseille when he was eighteen months old, but Aubagne remained, after the excitement of a tram-ride from the city, the starting-point for their holiday journeys into the hills. These hills are the main setting for Pagnol's autobiographical writings and for his film *Manon des sources* (1953). Subsequently he revised the story of the film—developing material which precedes the action there—as a novel, *L'Eau des collines* (1963); the two parts of this, *Jean de Florette* and *Manon des Sources*, were in turn filmed by Claude Berri in 1986.

The Pagnols' destination was a small *cabanon* or cottage near the village of La Treille, which becomes Les Bastides Blanches in the *Manon* sequence. (Pagnol filmed near La Treille, Berri further into the hills.) Les Bastides is a village of five or six unmade streets, "streets narrow because of the sun, tortuous because of the mistral." The lives of the villagers revolve around work, boules, gossip, and intense suspicion of outsiders. Above Les Bastides live the Soubeyrans. César Soubeyran, known as Le Papet (Grandpa), prides himself on belonging to an old and once flourishing family and is driven both by greed and by the desire to see the family continued by his nephew, the rather witless Ugolin. The Soubeyrans' lack of human generosity is shown mainly through their treatment of Jean Cadoret, a hugely enthusiastic and idealistic town-dweller who brings his wife and daughter to live in the country. Hoping to drive him out and buy his land cheap, they conceal the existence of the spring which could have made farming much easier for him, emphasize to the villagers that Jean comes from the hated rival settlement of Crespin, and neglect to mention that his mother, Florette, was Florette Camoins, originally of the Bastides. Jean (known less politely as *le Bossu*—"the Hunchback") toils ceaselessly to make a success of his new life, clearing land, breeding rabbits, growing crops, excitedly lecturing his family and his seeming friend Ugolin from suitable self-help books. But lack of water dooms him, for all his efforts, to failure.

The Soubeyrans achieve their aim, but in the long term they have conspired against themselves. Ugolin's nemesis is to fall in love with Jean Cadoret's daughter, the goatherd Manon, who has instinctively disliked him since childhood. His case is not helped when Manon, ferociously loyal to her father's memory, discovers the Soubeyrans' guilt and others' complicity—they knew about the spring but would not "interfere". She determines to take revenge on the whole village, blocking the water supply to the fountain. Eventually the love of the village schoolteacher, an outsider untouched by the collective guilt, helps her to resolve the situation; the curé, however, is convinced that the return of the water results from communal prayer, repentance and procession.

Manon often plays her father's harmonica in memory of him. This, together with the strong Provençal accents rarely indicated in the novel, is a memorable feature of the soundscape of the Claude Berri films. There the tune she plays becomes the overture to Verdi's *La forza del destino*, suitably in a work so aware of fate and with such consciously mythic dimensions. When Manon dances naked to the sun she is, even the spying Ugolin can sense, "the divinity of the hills, the pinewood and the season of Spring." Also familiar from Greek myth or tragedy is the shocking revelation, late in the novel, that means all Le Papet's efforts have been in his own and his family's worst interests.

Souvenirs d'enfance

Beyond the Bastides Blanches, says the opening paragraph of *Jean de Florette*, only a mule-track goes up into the hills. From the track issue "a few paths, leading to the sky." Up in the hills Manon herds her goats and Ugolin spies on her and here too, amid thyme and rosemary and kermes oak and beneath Garlaban and other peaks, takes place much of the action of Pagnol's autobiographical trilogy *Souvenirs d'enfance* (1957-60).

The trilogy, and especially the first two parts, *La Gloire de mon père* and *Le Château de ma mère*, is concerned above all with Pagnol's father Joseph and the way in which the young Marcel perceives and relates to him and to the adult world more generally. (The adult narrator shows the youthful perceptions; Pagnol, who studied English at the University of Aix, was a Dickens enthusiast and *Great Expectations* is possibly one influence on this dual perspective.) Joseph belonged to a generation of French schoolteachers most of whom were resolutely anticlerical, fierce opponents of alcohol, and upholders of the Revolution—Pagnol professes himself uncertain as to quite how they ignored the violence of the "lay angels" of their "golden age of high-mindedness and brotherhood." Sometimes, however, he can be helped to depart a little from his principles.

When Joseph decides to start hunting with his brother-in-law Jules, Marcel is worried that his hitherto apparently all-knowing father—teacher, examiner, invincible boules player—will fail humiliatingly while the confident and experienced Uncle Jules will end up "decked out with partridges and hares like a shop window." Marcel follows them secretly and witnesses the scene in which both men fire at some partridges, Jules successfully, but a hare then escapes through Joseph's legs because he had failed to re-load. Jules' resulting outburst gives Pagnol one of many opportunities to enjoy the distinctive rolled "r"s of a man who originates from Narbonne: "Malheureux! il fallait recharrger tout de suite! Dès qu'on a tirré, on rrecharrge!!!"

After this Marcel loses his way, going on bravely across stony plateaux and ravines thick with rosemary and thyme, but sustained, in spite of thorns and minimal provisions, by his memories of *Robinson Crusoe* and tales of the Comanche. Eventually he hears gunshot. Two large birds come down in the bushes, one hitting him on the head. He realizes, to his astonishment, that they are rare *bartavelles*—the much sought-after rock partridge. Perhaps Uncle Jules brought them down with his usual skill. But no: Marcel hears his uncle reprimanding Joseph for having scared them off by firing too soon when they were obviously heading his—Jules'—way. He is, to say the least, sceptical about Joseph's belief that he "clipped" one of the *bartavelles*. Joseph begins to sink. But then, restoring his beloved father's credibility at a blow, Marcel leaps up onto some rocks and yells out "He killed them! Both of them! He killed them!" Joseph receives his glory, the book its title: "And in my blood-stained little fists, from which hung four golden wings, I lifted my father's glory to the sky, before the setting sun."

The father proceeds to show the *bartavelles* to anyone he possibly can; even the curé suddenly gains his goodwill by photographing him and his trophies. Through his uncle as well as his father Marcel learns that adults are very human, and not necessarily less loveable therefore. Jules is as fervently Catholic as Joseph is convincedly atheist. Whenever an argument about religion seems likely to blow up between them, their wives, Aunt Rose and Marcel's mother Augustine, expertly cause distractions. On one occasion Jules is profoundly shocked at a remark which suggests just how irreligious has been young Marcel's education; as metaphorical daggers are drawn, Rose the quick-thinking peacemaker seizes a basket and a cape, shouts "Jules! The rain has nearly stopped! Quick—get us some snails!", and rams the cape over his head before bundling him out of the door into the heavy rain. On his way out "he tried", encumbered as he was, "to roll some rs, and we heard 'Vvraiment ttrop ttriste et ttrop affrreux'… Ce pauvre enfant." By the time Jules comes back with his snails the incipient argument is apparently forgotten: Joseph is playing the flute, Augustine is listening as she hems some towels, and the children are playing dominoes.

How and whether such incidents actually happened is uncertain. Pagnol saw himself as essentially a *conteur*, a story-teller: he strives to reach the essence of his parents—their truth at least in relation to him—rather than to reconstruct their lives. He continues to think about both parents in *Le Château de ma mère*, where one of the main stories is about the family's short-cut along a canal, to save themselves five kilometres' hard walking. This involves trespassing on the land of several châteaux, with the help of a key given them by a canal worker, Joseph's ex-pupil Bouzigue. At first Joseph stoutly refuses to take advantage of his offer. To accept would be particularly improper for an employee of the state. ("Oyayaïe! … Les principes, oyayaïe!" cries the less fastidious Bouzigue.) But he is persuaded that, since he has some knowledge of building (his father was a stonecutter), he can keep an eye on the state of repair of the canal and so will be "serving the community, albeit in a slightly irregular way."

One château owner, a friendly colonel, offers them hospitality, but at another property they are confronted by an angry, drunken guard and his dog. Joseph's original scruples look to have been justified. With the help of Bouzigue and two colleagues, the crisis is soon resolved, but Augustine's reactions—the nervousness she struggles to control when crossing the private land, her shock and fainting when the guard berates them—remain poignantly present to Pagnol at the end of the book; she died when he was fifteen. Years later, he says, when he became a film-maker, he was searching for a place in which to establish a "Cité du Cinéma". Having bought a promising-sounding château without having seen it, on going there he recognized the octagonal towers, the canal, the hawthorn and wild roses of the place of his mother's terror and his father's humiliation. (It was the Château de Buzine, near Les Camoins; its cinematic life was brief, but Joseph Pagnol later lived and, in 1951, died there.) There by the door, beneath the white roses "and on the other side of time, for years there had been a very young, dark woman, still clasping the colonel's red roses against her fragile heart. She heard the guard's shout and the dog's rough breathing. Pale, trembling, and for ever inconsolable, she did not know that she was at her son's house."

In *Le Temps des secrets* Pagnol goes on to recount his school experiences and some further hunting stories, but *Le Château*, with its sudden final sadness (movingly captured in Yves Robert's film of 1990), was his favourite book. A copy was buried with him in the cemetery at La Treille in 1974.

Cassis: "brilliant yellow and ink black"

The eponymous hero of Frédéric Mistral's *Calendal* (1867) hymns his native Cassis for its adventurous fishing-fleet (out catching crayfish, mullet, anchovies, John Dory and *L'Auriòu damasquina*—damascened mackerel); its skilled and industrious women who polish red coral and weave baskets while the men fish; and its wine sweeter than honey which *brihol Coume un linde diamant* ("shines like a limpid diamond") and is scented with the rosemary, heather and myrtle of the surrounding hills.

Cassis retained its ideal status, especially for visitors from the dark, damp north. Virginia Woolf, back in England, remembered, in a letter to Roger Fry of September 1925, a place of "heat and light and colour and real sea and real sky and real food instead of the wishywashy watery brash we get here". She had stayed at the Hôtel Cendrillon, on the waterfront, that spring. She stayed there again in 1927 but spent most of the time with her sister Vanessa Bell, Duncan Grant, and Clive Bell, at the Villa Corsica. "I am writing, with difficulty, on a balcony in the shade," she told Vita Sackville-West on 5 April. "Everything is divided into brilliant yellow and ink black." Woolf and Clive Bell write while underneath, on the next balcony, Vanessa and Duncan are painting the loveliest pictures of rolls of bread, oranges, wine bottles. In the garden, which is sprinkled with saucers of daisies, red and white, and pansies, the gardener is hoeing the completely dry earth. There is also the Mediterranean—and some bare bald grey mountains.

Such irritations as there were in this apparently perfect place were minor. In April 1928, when Leonard and Virginia Woolf were staying at the Château de Fontcreuse and the others were installed at a house called La Bergère, Woolf wrote to her nephew, Quentin Bell, about the vociferous frogs which bark whenever Clive (Quentin's father) is about to say something inspiring. "Thus Clive's words are never heard, and the truth is lost—which is a great pity, but after all, why should not frogs have their will now and then?"

The eccentric English colony were only slightly more irritating than the frogs, and often just as amusing: on 6 May 1929 Woolf wrote to a friend about "leading a delicious life, with a great deal of wine, cheap cigars, conversation, and the society of curious derelict English people, who have no money, and live like lizards in crannies, sometimes keeping a few fowls or breeding spaniels."

L'Estaque: "masterful smears and smudges"
"Unfortunately what they call progress," Paul Cézanne told his niece Paule Conil in 1902, "is only invasion by bipeds who will not stop until they have transformed everything into odious *quais* with gaslamps and—even worse—with electric lighting. What a time we live in!" As a result L'Estaque, the fishing-village by Marseille which he had often painted in the 1870s and 1880s, was no longer a picturesque place. It was being steadily industrialized, its population rising from 800 in 1850 to 10,000 in 1920. Change continued until it became the unrecognizably different setting for the films of the L'Estaque-born Robert Guédiguian in the 1980s and 1990s: not just painterly pines and the blue Mediterranean but unemployment, racism, crime, and industry now in decay like the closed cement-factory in *Marius et Jeannette* (1997). Guédiguian, however, modifies the bleakness with his sympathy for his characters and human involvement in local issues: "Demonstrations and petitions by intellectuals are no use... I must speak to my neighbour, who lives and

goes shopping in the same place as me: I'm not going to tell him lies."

There are already a few factory chimneys in some of Cézanne's paintings, and clay-extraction has left huge holes in the shoreline in Zola's "Naïs Micoulin", a story of love and unexpected revenge written at L'Estaque when he stayed there in 1877. But it was still somewhere for contemplating sunsets from cliffs, as the lovers do in "Naïs"; a place where Zola could write on in peace, in spite of the wonders of the view, temperatures sometimes of 40 degrees, and bouts of illness which he felt were brought on by excessive indulgence in *bouillabaisse* and shellfish. It was still sufficiently out of the way for Cézanne to come here in 1870-1 to avoid both conscription and his father discovering that he was living there with Hortense Fiquet. With personal difficulties and in a country convulsed by the Franco-Prussian War and its aftermath, Cézanne painted *Melting Snow at L'Estaque* (now in a private collection in Switzerland), a work very different from those he would produce here only a few years later. Lawrence Gowing sees *Melting Snow* as presenting

the fearful image of a world dissolved, sliding downhill in a sickeningly precipitous diagonal between the curling pines which are themselves almost threateningly unstable and Baroque, painted with a wholly appropriate slippery wetness and a soiled non-colour unique in his work.

The later Cézanne views at L'Estaque are to be seen in galleries including the Fitzwilliam in Cambridge, the Musée Picasso in Paris and the Museum of Modern Art in New York. Their significance in the development of his distinctive style is suggested by the letter he sent Camille Pissarro in July 1876:

I have begun two little motifs showing the sea... – It's like a playing-card. Red roofs over the blue sea... The sun is so tremendous that it seems to me that the objects are silhouetted not only in black or white, but in blue, in red, in brown, in violet. I may be mistaken, but it seems to me that this is the opposite of modelling.

It took most observers some time to appreciate Cézanne's method. When the view of L'Estaque now in the Fitzwilliam was shown in New

York in 1916, Frank J. Mather, Jr., writing in *The Nation*, showed a degree of understanding which had been rare in the painter's lifetime: "There are, from the ordinary point of view, no surfaces, just masterful smears and smudges which fix the position and indicate the direction of the planes." Braque, Dufy and others who painted at L'Estaque in the early twentieth century were strongly aware of Cézanne's work here, and perhaps achieved a more intimate grasp of what he was trying to do. Braque moved on from it in *Houses at L'Estaque* (1908), which Matisse regarded as the original Cubist painting.

Chapter Eight
The Provence of Jean Giono and Henri Bosco

This chapter is concerned mainly with the hilly and mountainous areas north and north-east of Aix-en-Provence, places often written about by the novelists Henri Bosco and Jean Giono. Bosco knew especially the southern flank of the Montagne du Luberon (sometimes written "Lubéron"), Giono its eastern edge and the Montagne de Lure. Giono contrasted his landscape of high mountains and high plateaux, "hard, dry stone... olive and almond-trees" with Bosco's "undulating hills" and rich, fertile plains. If sometimes the characters in their books seem to be alike, that is because they are "deep-rooted" in the earth, "but *chez lui* there is plenty of water. My characters are looking for it, or conserving it."

The distinctive shape of the Luberon has prompted many a simile and metaphor. Bosco sees, near Lourmarin, "the silhouette of a sleeping beast". For John and Pat Underwood (*Landscapes of Western Provence and Languedoc-Roussillon*, 2004) it is more specifically "a giant cat in slumber". Maurice Lever, in his biography of the Marquis de Sade, goes to extravagant lengths: seen from La Coste the mountain looks like an eagle with "an enormous wingspan", the wings hiding its head—or perhaps the village of Oppède is its stone beak. Only one of its eyes is closed and it could fly off at any moment. For Albert Camus, when he lived at Lourmarin, the Luberon was, perhaps more interestingly, "an enormous block of silence that I listen to endlessly." The more remote Montagne de Lure has attracted less literary attention, but Giono once called it "the monstrous backbone of Dionysos' bull."

In the mid-sixteenth century a number of villages on and near the Luberon fell victim to brute, unmetaphorical fact. In 1540 nineteen Vaudois or Waldensians from Mérindol, members of a mainly peasant sect whose origins went back to the twelfth century, were condemned

to be burnt at the stake in Aix. Their village was also to be destroyed. Appeals to the crown continually delayed the sentence from being carried out, but fighting between Catholic and Vaudois villages began to flare up in 1543. The bishop of Cavaillon launched an attack on Cabrières d'Aigues. Vaudois raiders sacked the Abbey of Sénanque and hanged twelve monks. And then Jean Meynier, Baron d'Oppède, took on the task of rooting the heresy out. He and his associates were also eager to seize some land. During a few bloody days in April 1545 his army killed about 3,000 people, committed many rapes, and took about 600 prisoners who were sent to the galleys. They fired Mérindol, most of whose inhabitants had fled; its ruins remain near the modern village. There were terrible massacres at Cabrières d'Aigues, Cabrières d'Avignon, and Lourmarin. Having smashed up Cabrières d'Avignon, the persecutors inscribed on what was left of the main gate: "Cabrières, for having dared to resist God, has been punished." Meynier d'Oppède was eventually brought to trial in 1549 but was swiftly acquitted. Many Vaudois fought on, using the mountain terrain to advantage as would the Resistance 400 years later. The Vaudois struggle fed into the wider Wars of Religion of the 1560s onwards—the Vaudois leaders were in close contact with the Calvinists from the 1530s and later, at least in France, tended to merge with them. And there was a legacy of distrust between Catholic and Protestant villages in the Luberon which diminished only in quite recent times.

Roussillon

The village of Roussillon takes its name from its cliffs and quarries of red ochre; locally the industry produces about 3,000 tonnes a year. Seventeen shades of red have been observed. Such a landscape was, not surprisingly, simply "trop déclamatoire" for Samuel Beckett. (His remark is reported in James Knowlson's *Damned to Fame: the Life of Samuel Beckett*, 1996.)

Beckett and Suzanne Deschevaux-Dumesnil (later his wife) lived in Roussillon, in a house on the road to Apt, between 1942 and 1944. They had narrowly escaped to Vichy France, with the help of friends, when the Germans uncovered the Resistance cell they belonged to in Paris. During his time in the village Beckett did heavy work on farms and vineyards in exchange for food and drink, and wrote much of *Watt*

(1953), "partly," as Knowlson says in his article on Beckett in the *Dictionary of National Biography*, "as a stylistic exercise and partly in order to stay sane in a place where he was cut off from most intellectual pursuits." The novel is, appropriately to this period in the life of Beckett and of France, full of uncertainties. He also helped the local Resistance, who remained unaware of his previous experience in Paris. He was involved mainly in transporting weapons and radio components dropped by the RAF and hiding explosives in his house; he received training in the use of rifle and grenades but was glad he never had the opportunity to use them. He intensely disliked violence and claimed to his friend Lawrence Harvey that he was "lily-livered". But his fellow *maquisards* or Resistamce fighters respected him enough to have him lead the liberation procession into the village, vigorously waving the French flag and singing the *Marseillaise*: a somewhat unfamiliar image of the playwright. Obviously he was relieved that the long years of isolation, of waiting, were over—almost that he was moving out of the world of *Waiting for Godot*, in whose original French version (1952) Vladimir mentions grape-picking in Roussillon, down there where "everything's red"; but if they were there at all Estragon "noticed nothing."

The village soon returned to its less flag-waving everyday life. Laurence Wylie, the American sociologist who studied Roussillon in 1950-1 for *Village in the Vaucluse* (1957), found people "haunted by despair". There was much "nostalgic yearning" for an earlier communal life; Roussillonnais who were "traditionally inclined to accept the worst with a fatalistic shrug... found little to hope for in the gloomy future. "'On est foutu! (We're done for!)... Why should I plant fruit trees?' said Jacques Baudot. 'So the Russians and the Americans can use my orchard for a battleground? No thanks'." But when he came back ten years later Wylie encountered less emphasis on the past and a greater optimism about the future: "Baudot took me to see the apple and apricot trees he had planted... There was no more talk about being 'done for'."

Lourmarin

At the end of his life Albert Camus (1913-60) lived mostly in the Grand'rue de l'Eglise, Lourmarin. In his unfinished novel *Le Premier homme* he wrote about the heat and light of his native Algeria and—at least as much of a contrast with the hills of Provence—"that cramped, flat country full of ugly villages and houses which extends from Paris to the Channel" through which Jacques Cormery travels one pale spring afternoon on the way to visit the grave of his father. Camus himself is buried in the cemetery at Lourmarin; he died in a car-crash on the way to Paris on 4 January 1960 with the manuscript of the novel in his briefcase. In 1967 a bas-relief of Camus' head was added to the village fountain, with an aptly existential inscription from his *Myth of Sisyphus*: "The struggle towards the summit, in itself, is enough to fill a man's heart."

The novelist Henri Bosco (1886-1975), who was connected with the Luberon for much longer, is also buried here. His first novel *Pierre Lampédouze* (1924) ends with the troubled hero's consoling vision of the landscape from the terrace of the château. (Bosco knew Robert Laurent-Vibert, who restored the fifteenth- and sixteenth-century château before his death in 1925, and became one of the trustees of the subsequent Laurent-Vibert arts foundation, which is still based there.) In the more famous *Le Mas Théotime* (1945) the setting, although the place-names are changed, is recognizably the countryside around Lourmarin. And it is the land which plays as great a part as the characters in this and much of Bosco's work.

The narrator Pascal and his tenant farmers the Alibert family are engaged, season by season, in a long struggle with the soil they nevertheless love. If, as Bosco said in an interview reported by Robert Ytier (*Henri Bosco ou l'amour de la vie*, 1997), you let yourself be taken over by the *sauvagerie* of the land—stop loving it—you "go mad, lose all sense of proportion and destroy yourself," like Pascal's hostile, misanthropic cousin and neighbour Clodius. But even Clodius feels a bond to the land: he neglects but fiercely defends his farm, and wills it to the hated Pascal rather than letting it pass out of the family.

Pascal is aware that he shares something of Clodius' *sauvagerie*. His frequent desire to be alone, to preserve some private space in the *mas*, both complicates and helps him survive his relationship with another, more sympathetic cousin, Geneviève. He loves her yet—she is wild in her own way and still married to another man—cannot move into a full or permanent relationship with her. Her intuition and unpredictability make her, often, a woman very much as we might expect a man of Bosco's generation to see her. "Perhaps she realized," we are told, "that a

Lourmarin, where Albert Camus would "listen" to the
Luberon, "an enormous block of silence."

woman can never achieve" complete control over herself; to find herself she needed "the love of a man".

Hard work on the land and an almost mystical devotion to the *mas* heals Pascal, prevents him giving way to his feelings when Geneviève leaves. As he comes back to Théotime in the half-light on one occasion he perceives it as a moral and religious entity as much as a physical: "It was an old house of goodness and of honour, a house of bread and of prayer." Although the name Théotime comes directly from Pascal's uncle, it also means, he points out, "you will honour me as a god." Later he explains the mutuality of his relationship with the place: in him "it is naturally Théotime which thinks, loves, wants," and he will undertake nothing contrary to its laws, however difficult the violence of his desires sometimes makes this. And so the many descriptions of the place—this is a slow-moving, ruminative novel—seem often to take us beyond the purely physical; at dawn the light seems not to be reflected from the tiles but "to emanate mysteriously from their porous clay."

Pascal's destiny is not with the fascinating, troubled Geneviève but with the Aliberts and their daughter Françoise, who are silent by preference and completely dedicated to the land and the work. In the end "the land saved me."

Lacoste: "making a spectacle of oneself"

In 1765 Donatien Alphonse François, Marquis de Sade (1740-1814) ,arrived at one of his main ancestral residences, the medieval and Renaissance château of La Coste (now usually written Lacoste). Defiant, as ever, of public opinion, he came not with his wife but with his current lover, the actress Mlle Beauvoisin. His vassals turned out to welcome their lord and, they assumed, their new lady, in song.

Sade finally brought his Marquise to La Coste in 1771; perhaps one fine lady looked much like another to the villagers. A few years earlier he had begun to fit out a theatre in the château and his main aim now was to organize an ambitious season of productions. The theatre could seat an audience of sixty people and had standing-room for sixty more. The scene showed a salon, as convention dictated, but could be altered with backdrops to become a public square or a prison. (Nobody can resist remarking on the prison. Sade had already been arrested for involvement in one sexual scandal and would spend twenty-nine of his remaining

years in prisons and mental institutions.) The theatre was well lit with candles and lamps and the blue stage curtain could be operated—a great sophistication for the time—from the foyer.

The season, with Sade as director and often as one of the actors, was to last six months, beginning in May 1772. Twenty-four plays were to be performed in pairs first at La Coste and then a few days later at Mazan, another family property where he had installed a theatre. The repertory was mostly modern, including pieces by Diderot and Voltaire which were not, in the event, performed. Without care for the cost, Sade hired professional actors from Marseille and repeatedly moved them, and a considerable retinue, between the two venues. He, the Marquise and her sister Anne-Prospère de Launay also took part in at least some of the plays. As often—frequently in more controversial circumstances—Sade pressed hard at the boundaries between performance and reality. He cast his sister-in-law as the heroine of his own play *Le Mariage du siècle* with himself as her husband and his wife as her confidante. At the same time he embarked on an affair with his co-star—perversely attracted off-stage, no doubt, by her nun's habit (she was in minor orders) and the element of incest, but also by the theatrical and erotic thrill of performing with her.

Sade's fellow aristocrats seem to have been reluctant to come to his productions at La Coste and Mazan. He therefore found himself welcoming a less socially exalted audience, made up of more or less anyone he could persuade to come. This tended to confirm the view of his wife's mother, Mme de Montreuil, who lamented to his uncle the Abbé de Sade that such spectacles are all very well at home among equals but that it is quite ridiculous "when someone makes a spectacle of himself in front of a whole province." Actors are paid to entertain people of the Marquis' rank in society, not to perform on an equal footing. Up to a point, she says, he can do as he likes, but he must not go on compromising her daughters by involving them. (She did not, of course, know quite how involved was her daughter Anne-Prospère. There is some debate as to when exactly the Marquise found out.) Moreover the whole enterprise is, she is aware, mountingly expensive. Money is needed for actors, costumes, scene-changers, food and drink for cast and audience, candles, transport, and Sade has already, she points out, "diminished his fortune by every possible extravagance."

By June 1772 it was apparent even to Sade that funds were running short and so he went to Marseille to raise money. But it was not finance that cut short his theatre festival. While in the city he decided to divert himself with some prostitutes. Allegedly—the full truth remains difficult to come at—he drugged them before using them in his customary scandalous way; they suffered after-effects and he was charged with poisoning them (and with sodomy). When he failed to give himself up, the Parlement in Aix condemned him to death and, in his absence, he was executed there in effigy in the Place des Prêcheurs. In September, after a period in hiding, he fled to Italy with his sister-in-law. She soon came back to La Coste while he moved on to Chambéry, then in the Kingdom of Sardinia. There in October he was arrested at the request of France. After five months in prison he escaped and went to La Coste in May 1773. An extraordinary cycle of arrest, escape and return had begun. In January 1774 a carefully organized police raid on the château seized some of Sade's papers but missed the man himself. According to his wife, the arrest party burst in after dark, smashed open desks, burnt documents, and admitted that they had orders to kill the Marquis. Again he returned, fled, returned and further fortified the château, hired some new women who made fresh accusations against him. He escaped another raid and departed for Italy once again in the summer of 1775 but was soon back at La Coste.

In January 1777 Sade's strange career almost came to an abrupt end. A certain Treillet appeared at the great gate of the château; he was the father of a girl the Marquis was suspected of seducing or trying to seduce, having hired her as a domestic. According to Treillet's account Sade refused to let the girl leave and bundled him out of the door. The aggrieved father pulled out a pistol and tried to shoot him point-blank but the gun failed to go off. He came back later after drinking freely in the village (say his enemies) and talked to the Marquis through the door. He tried to shoot him again, this time through the window, but missed. Finally people more influential than Treillet caught up with Sade: Mme de Montreuil had him arrested in Paris through a royal *lettre de cachet* the following month. Although the 1772 charges against him were dropped on appeal, the *lettre de cachet* prevented his release. There was one last escape: he had been brought down to Aix as a prisoner for the appeal hearing, and on the way back north managed to evade his guards near Valence and persuade a boatman to take him cheaply down the Rhône to Avignon in an old leaky boat. Yet again he came back to La Coste. There he was finally captured in a night raid in August 1777 and began thirteen years of captivity at Vincennes, the Bastille and Charenton.

After his release in 1790 "Citizen Sade" became for a time a revolutionary judge in Paris and—too moderate for the liking of his colleagues and superiors, in fact no sadist—himself came near to being guillotined. Meanwhile, in September 1792, a mob looted and burnt the château of La Coste, sending it well on the way to its present ruined state. The loss was "above expression", the Marquis told his lawyer Gaufridy in October: "There was enough in this one château to furnish six... The scoundrels smashed and broke what they could not carry. Apparently the *département* has given orders that everything [saved from the looters] should be taken to Marseille. And by what right? Am I not at my post?" Although the local authorities claimed that they had done everything they could to restore order, Sade remained angry that he—the former victim, at least as he saw it, of *ancien régime* "ministerial despotism", and now the friend of revolution—should have been targeted as if he were any other traitorous aristocrat. He sold what was left of the château in 1796-7.

Ménerbes: "the darling buds of Mayle"

This village is the main setting of Peter Mayle's *A Year in Provence* (1989) and *Toujours Provence* (1991). The eccentricities of the Provençal characters, the joys and perils of living abroad, truffle-hunting and the history of *pastis*, appealed to a wide audience, but there was condemnation of the books both by people who felt that this was an over-simplified, caricatured Provence and by those who blamed them for swamping the once-peaceful Ménerbes with visitors. A recent "caricature account of the region has proliferated to the author's profit, but little to its advantage," icily observes Ian Robertson's *Blue Guide: France*. *Private Eye* seized on the satirical opportunity presented by the fact that Mayle had worked in advertising: in "A Year in Advertising" Pierre Maille "is a peasant from Provence. A year ago he decided to sell up his farmhouse and join an advertising agency in London." His "warm and witty book" describes how well he adapts as—not quite the expected reversal—"the pace of life slows down." Maille writes, breaking into "Franglais", "of the glorious lunches:

> Le déjeuner est magnifique. Il commence à midi and lasts until le soir. Mon favourite petit restaurant is dans Charlotte Street, where nous mangeons *outside* sur le pavement... It's all here. Les meetings, les mobile phones, les bouteilles de champagne "on the client".

When *A Year in Provence* reached television in 1993 the satirists returned to the fray. Mayles (more often known as Miles) Kington gave over "Let's Parler Franglais" No.94 to an episode of "The Darling Buds of Mayle", introduced by "silly French accordion music". Inspector Morse—John Thaw starred in the dramatization—declares happily: "Ah, ici nous sommes en Provence. Ah, le food! Le vin! Le brandy! Et les tres amusant French locals, avec ses mosutaches [sic] et le fameux beret!" He faces the problem of "how can zees tres thin libre be strung out comme les oignons sur la bicyclette?" But somehow he gets to the end of the episode: "More silly accordion music. Loving shots of Provençal countryside." (The articles were reprinted in *A Gnome in Provence: the Best of Private Eye 1991-3*, the work apparently of one Peter Maylionaire.)

Ménerbes has reminders of more serious business. The citadel was rebuilt after a long siege in the 1570s. Protestant forces had seized the village in 1573 and held it for six years in spite of vigorous attempts by papal and royal troops to dislodge them. The Castellet, another rebuilt defensive structure, was lived in by the painter Nicolas de Staël in 1953-4. Ménerbes was also the birthplace of Clovis Hugues (1851-1907), the socialist poet and journalist who was imprisoned for four years for his involvement in the Marseille commune of 1870.

Céreste

René Char came here to convalesce after septicaemia in the summer of 1936. Having served in the army in 1939-40 he returned to his home in L'Isle-sur-la-Sorgue but had to flee, having been denounced for anti-Fascist sentiments (he was tipped off by a well-disposed Vichy policeman that he was about to be arrested). He came back to the mountains, to Céreste, where he worked for the Resistance. As "Capitaine Alexandre" he led sabotage and other missions, operating across a large area of southern France. During 1943-4 he wrote a sequence of short diary entries or meditations on his experiences, *Feuillets d'Hypnos*. Partly published in a review in 1945, it attracted Albert Camus' attention and he arranged for its publication by Gallimard.

In the *Feuillets* Char is able to talk about the stress that, as a commander, he had to hide from his men. It was essential to show even more courage, to eat and smoke evidently less, than those around him. He records a particularly harrowing instance of how strong and apparently unreasonable he had to be when, hidden only about 100 metres away, he was present at the execution of "B.":

> I had only to press the trigger of my Bren gun and he could have been saved. We were on the heights above Céreste, armed to the teeth and at least equal in numbers with the SS. They with no idea we were there. To the eyes all round imploring me to give the signal to open fire, I shook my head... The June sun chilled me to the bone... I didn't give the signal because this village had to be spared [from German reprisals] at *any cost*... Perhaps he knew this, himself, at that last moment?

Manosque and Jean Giono

Jean Giono was born at 1 rue Torte, Manosque, in 1895, lived as a child and young man in rue Grande, and from 1929 in a house on the Mont d'Or, Le Parais, which can be visited; there is a more extensive museum and library at the Centre Jean Giono, near the Porte Saunerie—a medieval gate but, in Giono's opinion, *tripatouillé*, "tampered with", by municipal restorers.

The Porte Soubeyran survives as well as the Porte Saunerie and there are two interesting churches: the tenth-century and later Notre-Dame de Romigier with its miracle-working statue of the Virgin, and its traditional rival the Romanesque and Gothic St.-Sauveur. But for Giono Manosque was truly beautiful only before 1914, when its streets were full of horses and carts and sheep, the elms were full of nightingales and, he claims, a hermit on St.-Pancrace hill rang a bell when dangerous storms approached from the west. Part of his novel *L'Hussard sur le toit* (1951), however, is set in a less blissful nineteenth-century Manosque. Angélo, the hussar of the title, takes to the roofs after escaping from the violent and panic-stricken inhabitants who, during a cholera outbreak, imagine all outsiders to be intent on infecting their water-supply. From here he surveys the tiles and towers, and watches the collapse of new victims, the murder of another suspected poisoner, the cart-loads of corpses going by. By 1963, when Giono wrote about his home-town for *Elle*, it was, he said, dominated by "arrogant, hideous and flimsy" council-flats and other "humorous" examples of modern architecture. "The only architecture of any quality" is that of the surrounding hills and plateaux and wild places—the places he explores in much of his work.

One of the best known early novels, *Regain* (1930) concerns the repopulation and revival—*regain*—of the village of Aubignane. (It is based partly on Redortiers, a ruined village in the foothills of the Montagne de Lure. When Marcel Pagnol filmed the book in 1937 he built his own Aubignane in the Massif d'Allauch, much nearer to Marseille.) The revival of the place relies on that of the characters, especially Panturle, who as a result of his love for Arsule abandons hunting, cultivates the land instead, and rediscovers simple, natural joys. *Que ma joie demeure* (1935) develops some of these ideas further. Bobi has worked as a travelling solo acrobat, a sign of his lack of ties and his transformative ability: he can transform and control his own body and can bring joy to the joyless. This he seeks actively to do when he arrives, seemingly from nowhere, on the semi-fictional Plateau of Grémone. He arrives in the night and first meets Jourdan, ploughing in the starlight in mysterious expectation of a stranger's coming. The context sounds messianic, but Bobi brings, at first, very simple joys: for instance he makes Jourdan see Orion as never before, shows how to perceive "Orion fleur de carotte". More generally he encourages openness to nature as the way to remove the boredom and anxieties of the small community. A stag (rather comically to later ears, perhaps, "il s'appelle Antoine") lives freely near the farms, spreading delight and representing other "great inner joys": for Bobi "today the 'stag' consisted of tasting the taste of winter, the bare forest, the low clouds, walking in the mud... feeling cold in his nose, warmth [from his pipe] in his mouth."

Does are brought in to give joy to the stag. Animals are respected, horses released from their stables to mate as they choose. Music, sex, the skilled handling of a scythe or a loom, can bring similarly intense pleasure. The new emphasis is on what will give joy rather than what is done out of dull habit or for unnecessary financial benefit only. After some discussion the people of the plateau—of whom there are idyllically few—agree to combine their arable land and to harvest it together. Their community is defined in opposition to the world of towns, heavy industry, war and money. (The small-scale, individual and country aspects differentiate Giono's ideal from Communist orthodoxy.) Obviously this is a utopia, but it is a very concrete one. And the second half of the novel makes clear the limits of the human capacity to hold on to joy. Sexual love complicates the communal harmony and the individual freedom and results in a death where Bobi thought he was bringing only life. Yet a strong sense of utopian possibility remains.

Le Contadour: "une expérience à la Bobi"

The ideal community of the plateau in *Que ma joie demeure* was soon to have its non-fictional parallel. In September 1935, soon after finishing the novel, Giono went up to the plateau of Le Contadour to lead the first of what became twice-yearly gatherings (Easter and late summer), mostly of young people. They chose the hamlet of Le Contadour as their centre, apparently, because Giono had to stop there having fallen and hurt his knee. Some people camped, others slept in barns. Soon Giono and two friends bought a building known as "the Mill".

The people who came to Le Contadour were united by a strong faith in pacifism. Later, somewhat embarrassed by the myth of the "mage" Giono which grew up, he said that "People have greatly exaggerated my 'teaching'. It amounted to no more than going for walks, camping and eating the odd slice of *saucisson* together." But he did have a considerable influence on those who walked and ate with him, many of whom might have been happy to call themselves his "followers". Usually they were enthusiastic readers of his novels as well as committed anti-militarists. At times Giono did function very much as a guru. Photographs show him sagely smoking his pipe surrounded by younger visitors to Le Contadour. "For us, a new life has begun," he wrote in his journal on 15 September 1935; they will have "une expérience à la Bobi". Clearly he will, he hopes, be central to that experience, will be Bobi the bringer of joy.

The camping and the talking went on as the European crisis came to a head. Giono rained telegrams, pamphlets and declarations on the

French, British and German governments. He was even involved, his friend and biographer Pierre Citron reports, in a wildly impractical plan to meet Hitler. Giono intended to put his point to him with the aid of an interpreter, who must, he would insist, be Jewish. One of his last desperate bids for peace, *Recherche de la pureté* (1939), emphasizes the horror and injustice of the First World War, in which he had fought; warriors are those "who do not have the courage to be pacifists." The last "Contadour" was interrupted by the Nazi-Soviet pact, the invasion of Poland and the declaration of war. Perhaps unsurprisingly, Giono was arrested on 14 September and imprisoned in the Fort St.-Nicolas in Marseille. (Citron concludes that Giono did not, as he claimed, destroy his call-up papers. That story is one more example of his romantic myth-making.)

Giono was released, partly through the intervention of André Gide, in November 1939. He was arrested again, unjustly accused of collaboration, after the Liberation in 1944, and spent five months in prison. His later novels take a rather more oblique, ambivalent look at life than the earlier, more utopian tales: a metaphorical look, with his Hussar, from the roofs of Manosque.

Chapter Nine

Alphonse Daudet's Provence: Nîmes

"I was born... in a town in Languedoc where there are to be found, as in every town in the Midi, plenty of sun, not a little dust, a Carmelite convent and two or three Roman monuments." So begins Alphonse Daudet's partly autobiographical novel *Le Petit Chose* (1866-7). Nîmes, where Daudet was born at what is now 20 Boulevard Gambetta in 1840, is the southern town in question. Its two or three best known Roman monuments are its amphitheatre, Maison Carrée and Tour Magne, but it has been for centuries—not merely ancient and dusty—a centre of textile manufacture. In 1787 Thomas Jefferson noted that "this is the cheapest place in France to buy silk stockings"; the father of Daniel Eyssette, the "Petit Chose" or "weak little thing" as his schoolfellows and various later persecutors call him, owns a factory where scarves are made.

The most famous substance once made in Nîmes is denim. The word is, as the *Oxford English Dictionary* explains, "shortened from *serge de Nim*, French *serge de Nîmes* ... A name originally given to a kind of serge" and subsequently to "a coloured twilled cotton material used largely for overalls and hangings, etc." The Musée du Vieux Nîmes, next to the cathedral, includes a display of the history of denim from practical aid to fashion icon. The city might, however, have become more strongly associated with a perhaps less useful substance: Murray's 1843 guide notes that it was the birthplace of Nicot, "a physician who first introduced from Portugal into France *tobacco* (called after him Nicotiana)."

Glimpses of the life of earlier Nîmois are to be had at the Archaeological Museum: Roman and pre-Roman ex-votos, a mosaic with Bellerophon on Pegasus found in what is now Boulevard Gambetta, a fifth- or sixth-century Christian sarcophagus carved with vines and grasses. One of the best-preserved items is the funerary monument of a powerful late first-century AD couple, Licinia Flavilla, priestess of the imperial cult, and Sextus Adgenus Macrinus, variously a

"The proportions of the building... so happily united"
(Tobias Smollett): the Maison Carrée and the Carré d'Art.

legionary tribune, justice, priest and "prefect of the workers". She wears the distinctive braided imperial hairstyle of her period and a fairly dignified expression. He, with large sun flaming vigorously on his breastplate, looks calm, responsible, lined with experience as much as age. Above the pair swim dolphins, symbols of regeneration or bearers of the soul to the Isles of the Blessed.

The Maison Carrée and the Carré d'Art

The Maison Carrée is all that remains above ground of the forum of ancient Nemausus. It was built at the end of the first century BC or the beginning of the first century AD and dedicated to the memory of Lucius and Gaius, Augustus' grandsons and adoptive sons. It was a temple of the Imperial Cult.

"The proportions of the building are so happily united," says Tobias Smollett in *Travels Through France and Italy* (1766), "as to give it an air of majesty and grandeur, which [even] the most indifferent spectator cannot behold without emotion." You need not be "a connoisseur in architecture, to enjoy these beauties. They are indeed so exquisite, that you may return to them every day with a fresh appetite for seven days together." Arthur Young, in 1787, concurs: it is absurd that modern architects who have seen such "chaste and elegant simplicity of taste" can "rear such piles of laboured foppery and heaviness as are to be met with in France."

A rare dissenter is Prosper Mérimée, whose job as inspector of ancient monuments made him of necessity "a connoisseur in architecture". For him the portico may be magnificent but the engaged columns have an unfortunate effect; their capitals are short and squashed-up, and the cornice is heavy and overloaded. On the other hand Stendhal, or his commercial-traveller narrator in *Mémoires d'un touriste* (1838), likes the building but not the familiar name: "Quel nom bourgeois pour ce charmant petit temple!" After all, it isn't square— "carré"; "it is shaped like a playing-card, like any self-respecting ancient temple." (Earlier generations were less geometrically precise than Stendhal's: "carré" could mean rectangular as well as square.)

The Maison Carrée was put to various later uses. It was a town hall, a stable, a church. Joseph Spence, accompanying young Lord Middlesex on his Grand Tour in 1733, thought "the inside... spoiled by making a modern church of it, though that's the way of making it sacred and preserving the outside." At the Revolution that protection was lost, the Augustinians expelled, the church closed. In the youth of Stendhal's traveller birds nested among the sculptures of the capitals and children threw pebbles at them or climbed up the columns. This was bad, but as far as he was concerned it was no more appropriate to put a museum in the place in 1823. At that time the museum displayed both archaeological finds and more recent paintings. It now houses a few statues and fragments; a mosaic found near the Maison and pre-dating it by a few years, with linked black swimmer and dolphin; and a first- or second-century AD mosaic in black and white with panthers flanking a crater or mixing-vessel.

Louis XIV's minister Colbert had more drastic plans for the temple. He considered removing it, stone by stone, to Paris. The idea was typical of the absolutist and centralizing nature of the régime; the Nîmois had less to fear from Thomas Jefferson and the Countess of Blessington. Even before Jefferson came and admired the original in 1787, he had based the State House in Richmond, Virginia, on drawings of the Maison Carrée—probably "the most beautiful and precious morsel of architecture left us by antiquity." Blessington, in *The Idler in France* (1841), expressed the desire "to have a small model of it executed in silver, as an ornament for the centre of a table."

Opposite the temple, echoing its name and its architecture, is the Carré d'Art (by Sir Norman Foster, 1993), which displays a permanent collection of art post-1960 and temporary exhibitions. The building is, says the architect, "a conscious exploration of Classical themes"; the pillars of the portico are the clearest classical reference. But the materials—steel, glass, concrete—and the atmosphere are modern. The walls are mostly see-through. From several levels there is a view of the street, a row of olive-trees in tubs, and the temple. People are part of the spectacle, whether using the various gallery and library facilities of the Carré d'Art, or in the street, or going in and out of the Maison Carrée. Sound-proofing helps make even the traffic aesthetically satisfying. But for some observers the juxtaposition of ancient and modern is too stark. The novelist Renaud Camus, according to his 1993 diary, could try only "méritoirement", dutifully, to admire Foster's "big white building".

The Arena and *Le Charroi de Nîmes*: "they will have bull fights"

The Roman amphitheatre, built in the late first century AD, could seat about 20,000 spectators. Like the one at Arles, it went through long periods as a settlement and a fortress before emerging as an archaeological site and bull-fighting arena. (The Musée des Cultures Taurines is near the Arena, in Rue Alexandre Ducros. Ezra Pound, in 1912, observed that in this town where at least "the water is brought you iced in a carafe" and "the ice-cream is passable", the people "are probably all right but they will have bull fights.")

In 1733 Joseph Spence noted that "the bottom has a little town built in it." John Addington Symonds in "Old Towns of Provence" looked back to less tranquil days, marvelling that "Charles Martel's conflagration, when he burnt the Saracen hornet's nest inside it, has only blackened the outer walls and arches venerably." Arabs or "Saracens" had captured the city from the Visigoths in 725. Charles Martel—just as much of a "hornet" as far as they were concerned—damaged the arena during his incursion into Muslim territory in 736, sixteen years before Nîmes finally came under Frankish control.

The wars between Arabs and Franks are the setting for *Le Charroi de Nîmes*, a twelfth-century *chanson de geste* about the legendary Guillaume d'Orange, a figure based distantly on Charlemagne's cousin, Guillaume, Count of Toulouse. The hero (also known as "Shortnose" as a result of a wound received, as he angrily reminds the insufficiently grateful King Louis, in royal service), uses a traditional and rather homely stratagem to take Nîmes from the Saracens. Having come upon a cart carrying barrels of salt, he requisitions all the carts and oxen he can find. *Charroi* here means a convoy of carts or waggon-train. He hides his knights and their weapons in barrels and disguises himself and some of his followers as peasants, drivers or merchants; his nephew Bertrand's inexperience as a driver provides a comic interlude in which he gets his cart stuck in the mud. Eventually they enter the city and Guillaume advertises his wares—rich cloth, spices and (more truthfully) arms and armour—to the interested Saracens. Meanwhile barrels are being placed strategically. After a time Guillaume, having got himself into an argument and killed the king's brother, sounds his horn and the knights emerge. They proceed to slaughter all the Saracens with that genocidal thoroughness which is casually accepted in such tales—as, often, in life.

The arena in Nîmes: "little town", fortress scorched by Charles Martel, and setting for ancient and modern games.

("*Tote la terre est couverte de sanc,*" we are told.) Their king would be spared if he converted to Christianity. He refuses and so Guillaume throws him to his death from an upper window. With equal but more commendable thoroughness, he returns the carts and oxen to the countryfolk and richly rewards them from the spoils of conquest.

"Seething with Heresy": Religion in Nîmes

The medieval town was concentrated on the narrow streets round the amphitheatre and the cathedral of Our Lady and St. Castor. The cathedral was consecrated in 1096, on the site of an earlier church, by Pope Urban II, who was in France to preach the First Crusade. Little of this Romanesque church remains, however, because it was mostly destroyed in the religious conflicts which beset the city in the sixteenth and seventeenth centuries or by subsequent re-building.

What does survive includes part of the frieze on the upper façade showing scenes from *Genesis* in high relief. In the first panel, beneath a border of lions' heads and acanthus, a large serpent with suitably diabolical eyes twists around the tree. He addresses Eve, whose missing hand probably took the missing apple, while Adam, naked like her, looks on. Further right we see the consequences of their forbidden knowledge. Each has a fig-tree. A large leaf covers Eve like a skirt and she clutches another leaf across her breasts. Adam too covers his genitals and becomes—so strong is the desire to cover and to hide—almost part of his tree. But it is no use hiding from God: in the next section the angel, holding an emphatically prominent sword (equivalent to the "flaming sword which turned every way" in *Genesis*) presides over their expulsion from the garden. The results of the Fall continue as, after a large divine hand has accepted Abel's sacrifice, his brother kills him. It is this scene which is much the most noticeable from below. The figures fill almost all the available space, as unavoidable as the hatred and ferocity with which the deed is done. Whereas the angel holds his sword upright, Cain drives his long curved knife straight down through Abel's neck. With his free hand he holds his victim by the hair. Abel's outstretched hand, open in prayer or to beg for mercy or perhaps just reaching towards his killer's leg, underlines his vulnerable humanity.

The rest of the frieze is less vigorous, more bunched, but often interesting, seventeenth-century work. The story continues with Noah's ark; the building of the tower of Babel (a crane lifting blocks, masons at work) and its spectacular collapse; and Abraham prevented from sacrificing the kneeling Isaac with an almighty sword-stroke when the angel seizes the end of the sword. In view of the violent history of the church and the town the prominence of weapons and of Cain's fratricide is unfortunately apt.

Local Protestants sacked the cathedral, and smashed the originals of these seventeenth-century replacements, in 1567. The Nîmes area was, King François I had proclaimed in 1541, "seething with heresy, error, new sects and false doctrines." He ordered the local magistrates to extirpate "this wretched Lutheran sect". But Nîmes was a long way from Paris, and Protestantism—mainly not Lutheran but Calvinist, with close links to Geneva—continued to grow apace, more often helped than hindered by persecution. By the late sixteenth century Protestants in Nîmes outnumbered Catholics about three or four to one. Artisans, especially the city's many textile-workers, were mostly Protestant. With the outbreak of the Wars of Religion through much of France in the 1560s, the reformers seized their chance to take control of the city. The sacking of the cathedral was accompanied by the killing of at least a hundred Catholics, including one of the city Consuls and the bishop's Vicar General. (This St. Michael's Day massacre was remembered as *la Michelade*.) The Protestants dominated the local administration almost without break until the 1630s. A Catholic revival then followed under Bishop Cohon, who rebuilt the cathedral (sacked once more in the 1620s). His main addition was the Chapel of the Immaculate Conception at the west end, where he was buried in 1670. Restoration has successfully maintained its baroque flavour, including "barley-sugar" pillars on either side of the altar. The bishop himself, portrayed here in the customary dark clothes and skull-cap, looks more sober.

Catholic hegemony was strongly assisted by Louis XIV's revocation of the Edict of Nantes in 1685; Protestant places of worship were demolished and the worshippers had to pay the demolition costs. Religious troubles were far from over, however. Troops set fire to a mill and murdered a hundred Protestants just outside the city in 1703, and by that time many of their co-religionists in the Cévennes, north-west of Nîmes, were in full-blooded rebellion. The insurrection had begun in 1702 with the murder of the hated Abbé du Chayla. Since then they had waged an extraordinarily successful guerrilla campaign. (The popular name for the rebels, *camisards*, derives either from the fact that they fought not in uniform but in their shirts—*camisa* is an Occitan equivalent of *chemise*—or from a word meaning "ambush".) Among their leaders was Jean Cavalier, a former baker's boy in his early twenties but gifted with a remarkable flair for military tactics. On one occasion he had routed seven hundred soldiers with a force of sixty. But in 1704 royal troops discovered and seized his arms depots and Cavalier decided to open negotiations with the enemy. Talks took place in Nîmes, at a convent garden near the Maison Carrée. Murray's *Handbook for Travellers in France* (1843) gives a colourful, if fairly accurate, account:

> Marshal Villars had an interview in 1704 with the celebrated chief of the Camisards Cavalier, who... at that time a mere youth, had raised himself by his talents for command, and by fanatic eloquence to be the head of the rebellion of the Cevennes. He appeared on that occasion magnificently mounted, and attired in lace coat, cocked hat, and plume of white feathers, escorted by a body-guard on horseback. The result of this memorable conference was to detach him from the insurgents by flattering promises of rank and reward... as the price of his defection, together with assurances of justice and tolerance in religion to the persecuted Protestants of the Cevennes. Neither one nor the other were destined to be kept or fulfilled. Villars, however, thus dealt a death-blow to the insurrection, by depriving it of one of its heads, and Cavalier, despised and deserted by his own party, and neglected by the court, was soon driven into exile.

Tolerance was indeed not delivered. Many *camisards*, accordingly, went on fighting. Many were hanged or broken on the wheel in Nîmes. Cavalier went on to serve with the British army, became Lieutenant Governor of Jersey in 1735, and died there in 1740.

Stability was achieved only after fresh sectarian violence—settling of old scores—during the Revolution and in 1815. Today the communities live in peace. Nîmes remains, however, a significant Protestant centre; for some, adherence to the reformed faith is a badge not only of belief but of regional identity.

The Tour Magne and the Temple of Diana

On 29 December 1914 Guillaume Apollinaire, in barracks at Nîmes with the 38th artillery, addressed a poem to his beloved "Lou"—Louise de Coligny-Châtillon—whose initial rejection of him was one reason for his enlisting. (Temporarily swayed, she came to stay in Nîmes for ten days. The enthusiastic sex which occurred whenever he could leave barracks fuelled the erotic letters and love-poems of the next few months.) As he returned to barracks, thinking of Lou, "The Tour Magne was turning on its laurelled hill", slowly dancing; "As the lovers descended the hill/The tower was dancing slowly like a Saracen woman."

Perhaps the tower does not dance for everyone; its original more practical function was probably as a watch-tower—or, as Dr. Edward Rigby persuaded his late eighteenth-century travelling companions, "an ancient gazebo". Other theories are that it was a triumphal monument or a mausoleum. The first tower on the site was built in about the third century BC and incorporated into the surviving Roman edifice—part of the extensive city walls—in 16-15 BC. It stands 33 metres high even without its original top storey, and looks altogether more substantial than most photographs suggest.

The Tour Magne is at the top of Mont Cavalier, the hill which Apollinaire's lovers come down. They would go first through the gardens planted in the nineteenth century with cypress, holm-oak and (as in the poem) laurel, then down to the Jardin de la Fontaine, the military engineer J.-P. Mareschal's eighteenth-century remodelling of the area around the ancient spring. For the author of *The Gentleman's Guide, in his Tour Through France* (1770) the canals, basins, cascades, the "walks form'd, trees planted, in the most uniform manner imaginable", made this "the most complete high finished work throughout the kingdom." The gardens also include the mainly second-century AD building known as the Temple of Diana, which was perhaps a library, certainly part of a complex associated with the imperial cult and the sacred spring of Nemausus. Here Philip Thicknesse (*A Year's Journey Through France and Spain*, 1777) found anything but "high finished work": the place was "covered with broken statues, busts, urns, vases, cornices, friezes, inscriptions... lying in the utmost disorder, one upon another, like the stripped dead in a field of battle." It would, says Thicknesse, do admirably to illustrate the melancholy of Milton's *Il Penseroso*. In 1787

Hubert Robert painted a grander, more romantic version of the scene as part of his series of ancient Provençal sites, now in the Louvre.

The contents of the Temple of Diana were removed long ago. It may still seem melancholy with its battered columns and empty plinths, open to the elements. There is free access from the park; especially at the weekend people tramp through, children cycle and climb about in spite of interdiction, balls bounce past. Nevertheless the building has something of the air of a Roman or Ptolemaic monument in Egypt as painted by David Roberts. The ground is sandy where the central paving once was, there is the odd palm-tree nearby, and there is a sense of a once mighty place abandoned, its tall arches and strong masonry still marking strength and power.

The Pont du Gard: "the measuring, contriving mind"

The aqueduct of which the Pont du Gard formed part ran from the Fontaine d'Eure, near Uzès, to the "Castellum" in Nîmes, where the delivery-tank survives. At least 30,000 cubic metres of water arrived here every day. J.G. Landels, in *Engineering in the Ancient World* (1978), gives some of the facts about the bridge: it

> has two tiers of arches, with an additional structure of much smaller arches on top, and the total height above the river bed is 180ft. (54.8m). The highest tier is made in the same material as the rest, and carries a water channel about $4\frac{1}{2}$ ft. (1.36m.) wide and $5\frac{1}{2}$ ft. (1.66m) deep. During the many centuries when water flowed through it, a thick incrustation of calcium carbonate has been deposited on the sides and bottom. Even at this great height, stone slabs were hoisted up and placed over the channel, to shield it from the sun and from pollution.

Sober measurement is not the only reaction available. Until recently—there now seems to be more policing—a few brave or foolhardy young tourists would leap the 22 metres into the river from the first tier. (The highest tier was, until its closure to the public, a favourite and dramatic launch-pad for suicides.) Less worryingly, you can inspect the aqueduct from a number of different angles, stroll across and back, or eat and drink while looking up from the rocky

The Pont du Gard: "the hugeness, the solidity, the unexpectedness, the monumental rectitude of the whole thing leaves you nothing to say" (Henry James).

white outcrops below. Having done all this, and wondered at its size, dramatic setting and completeness, visitors have frequently felt that it ought to stand for something, to make a point. For J. A. Symonds, "the human labour yet remains, the measuring, contriving mind of man, shrinking from no obstacles, spanning the air, and in one edifice combining gigantic strength and perfect beauty." Murray's *Handbook* of 1843 declares that "like Stonehenge, it is the monument of a people's greatness, a standard by which to measure their power and intellect." (Victorian Britons—and members of other imperially-minded nations—liked to compare their own "power and intellect" and "measuring, contriving mind" with those of the Romans.) For Stendhal, it tells us more about personal refinement or sensitivity than national greatness: it ought to operate like "sublime music", which can be appreciated only by the chosen. Meanwhile lesser mortals wonder only at the money it must have cost. (In modern times vast sums have been spent on visitor centres, shops, cafés and car-parks, all screened discreetly from the bridge itself.)

Henry James remains his ambivalent self when confronted by Roman grandeur: "the hugeness, the solidity, the unexpectedness, the monumental rectitude of the whole thing leaves you nothing to say." He "discovered in it a certain stupidity, a vague brutality", the rigidity of a race which could do nothing small. Nevertheless, the bridge speaks of the Romans "in a manner with which they might have been satisfied."

Tarascon: the Tarasque

Before St. Martha arrived, say several medieval accounts of her life, there was a barren wilderness between Arles and Avignon. The most ferocious of the various venomous creatures that inhabited this area was the Tarasque. Most sources say it was a dragon; or perhaps, suggests one nineteenth-century defender of the truth of the tale, it was simply a crocodile which had travelled up the Nile, across the Mediterranean and on up the Rhône. In one Latin version its breath was poisonous, its eyes shot out flames, and its teeth made a fearsome noise. Usually, like most such monsters, it ripped up people and animals. Even its odour was deadly. Jacobus de Voragine, in *The Golden Legend*, makes it part-fish and gives it wings. A French account (also known in Spanish translation) goes into rather more detail: "it was stouter than an ox and longer than a horse and had a mane and the mouth of a lion, and hair like a horse, and sharp teeth which cut like a sword, and legs like a horse... and lion's feet, and bear's nails, and a tail like a viper." Probably it would not have been difficult to persuade such commentators that the Tarasque was very like a whale.

The dragon ate shepherds and sheep and overturned boats. Local people asked Martha to do something about it and, having rebuked them for their lack of trust in God, she obliged by going off and binding the beast with her girdle. (Her faith and her virginity, symbolized by the girdle, made her strong.) They were then able to kill it; in some later traditions, she led it away captive or ordered it to submerge itself permanently in the depths of the Rhône. The place formerly called "Blackhearth" was renamed Tarascon after the monster, and the saint made her home in the wilderness, which she transformed into a much more agreeable place. Her house was decorated not with "useless ornaments" but with virtues. She lived an ascetic life, welcomed and fed the poor, and performed such miracles as resurrecting a boy who had drowned when trying to swim the Rhône in his eagerness to hear her preach. More miracles followed after her burial in the house, which now became St. Martha's church: the blind, the deaf, lepers and those possessed by demons were healed and Clovis, the first Christian king of the Franks, was cured of kidney disease when he touched the tomb.

The grateful Clovis, say the writers of Martha's life, endowed the church with lands on either side of the river. In fact, he cannot have done this since the area was not under his rule; his donation, like the whole story of the saint's adventures in Provence, was probably invented in order to justify St. Martha's church's claims for revenue against those of a rival church in Tarascon, St.-Nicolas. The church of Ste.-Marthe is first recorded in the tenth century but became considerably more prominent after the convenient discovery of her body on site in 1187. The third- or fourth-century sarcophagus is still to be seen in the small crypt. Her "recumbent effigy in white marble, not badly executed, but modern" (Sabine Baring-Gould, *The Lives of the Saints*, 1897-8)—seventeenth-century—has been moved into the church. The crypt was restored in the seventeenth century and the church is mainly fourteenth-century, restored after major bomb damage in 1944. The most interesting features are the Romanesque south portal (badly vandalized during the

EN PROVENCE. — *La Tarasque et ses Servants à Tarascon*

"A procession of mummers, attended by the clergy...
paraded the town escorting the figure of a dragon, made
of canvas, and wielding a heavy beam of wood for a tail,
to the imminent danger of the legs of all who
approached" (Rev. Sabine Baring-Gould).

Revolution) and, by the steps leading to the crypt, the Renaissance tomb-effigy of King René's loyal follower Jean de Cossa, Count of Troia and Seneschal of Provence, who died in 1467.

The Tarasque also continued to lead a vigorous legendary life in Tarascon. King René was credited with founding the *jeux de la Tarasque* in the 1460s but they must have had much earlier beginnings, ultimately as a fertility rite. Baring-Gould records how

> a procession of mummers, attended by the clergy... paraded the town escorting the figure of a dragon, made of canvas, and wielding a heavy beam of wood for a tail, to the imminent danger of the legs of all who approached. The dragon was conducted by a girl in white and blue, who led it by her girdle of blue silk, and when the dragon was especially unruly, dashed holy water over it. The ceremony was attended by numerous practical jokes, and led to acts of violence, in consequence of which it has been suppressed. The effigy of the dragon now reposes in the lumber room of the theatre.

Sometimes legs and arms *were* broken, at which, according to the 1787 account of Claude-François Achard, the crowd applauded and yelled at the top of their voices in praise of the Tarasque: "Well done, *ben fai!*" A rather less violent version of the festival has been re-established and expanded—fireworks and bulls as well as procession and practical jokes—and the Tarasque now usually "reposes" at the information centre.

Tartarin de Tarascon: "Prodigious Adventures"

Tarascon's other famous hunter of fierce beasts is Tartarin, the comic hero of Daudet's *Les Aventures prodigieuses de Tartarin de Tarascon* (1872) and its two sequels. But Tartarin does nothing comparable to killing or taming a Tarasque. His reputation as a big-game hunter follows on from the way he himself blurs the line between the tales of intrepid explorers and adventurers he reads and his real, timid, stay-at-home inclinations. There is also some evidence of his shooting-prowess—gained on the Sunday expeditions where, in the absence of game other than one persistently escaping hare, he and his friends throw their caps in the air and gun them down. (This is good for the hat-trade in Tarascon. Some shops even sell helpfully ready-holed and torn headgear for "les maladroits".) Tartarin seems also to be a weapons expert, for his study walls are covered with "carbines, rifles, blunderbusses, Corsican knives, Catalan knives... Malay krises, arrows from the Caribbean, flint arrows, knuckle-dusters... Hottentot clubs... and heaven knows what else!" And he has a reputation as a traveller: the fact that there was once a possibility of his accepting a job in Shanghai has elided, for him and for others, with the idea that he actually went and was accustomed to breaking off work to blaze away with his rifle at "the Tartars".

Tartarin further shows his firmness by standing his ground before the cage of a lion from the Atlas Mountains, part of a menagerie which visits Place du Château. "The lion of Atlas" roars at "the lion of Tarascon", who stands firm while others rush for the doors. He is, or seems to be, prepared for anything. Absorbed in some adventure-story, he will leap up (unadventurous long johns and headcloth forgotten) to brandish an axe or a tomahawk and shout "Now let them come!" Who "they" are he does not entirely know: they are everything "which attacks, which fights, which bites, which scratches, which scalps, which shouts, which roars." They might be Sioux or grizzlies, Malay pirates or Abruzzi bandits—"*them*! In other words war, expeditions, adventure, glory." Such aggressors are unlikely to visit the sleepy Tarascon of the book, but the hero takes his precautions, especially when he visits friends in the evening. Armed only with an iron-pointed knuckle-duster, a sword-stick, a truncheon in his left pocket, a revolver in the right, and a kris across his chest, he checks his property before leaving. Slowly ("à l'anglaise, messieurs, à l'anglaise! c'est le vrai courage") Tartarin walks round the garden and then suddenly throws open the heavy door. If *they* were there they would be pounded to a jelly, but "unluckily, *they* were not behind it." In the silent streets he meets not a dog, not a drunk, only, annoyingly, the pharmacist and his family. Without further incident he reaches a friend's house, where he spends the evening playing cards.

But greater undertakings are to come. Since the visit of the menagerie, rumour has had it that the famous huntsman will soon go to Africa in quest of lions that do not live in cages. Eventually the Tarasconnais begin to notice that he has not gone. His reputation is in danger. Two Tartarins struggle, one a romantic idealist, the other a plump, comfort-loving bourgeois: Don Quixote in the body of Sancho Panza. Chapter 7 includes a dialogue between them: the exalted "Tartarin-Quixote" cries "Cover yourself in glory, Tartarin" and the calm "Tartarin-Sancho" replies "Cover yourself in flannel"; the first calls for his axe, the second rings for the maid to bring his morning chocolate. Sancho has won so far; Jeannette brings such "excellent chocolate, warm, silky" and such succulent grilled meats that Tartarin-Sancho laughs for joy, stifling the cries of Tartarin-Quixote. But in the end the man who has never left Tarascon must go—after due time buying trunk-loads of equipment, and a huge send-off at the station—all the way to Marseille and from there to Algeria, whose colonization by France had begun in 1830. He insists, inevitably, on adopting Algerian dress before he even leaves Tarascon.

Abroad Tartarin's endeavours are more often farcical than heroic. Algiers, with its customs officers, cafés, hotels and military band playing polkas by Offenbach does not correspond with his "eastern, fairy-tale, mythological" expectations. Even in the countryside lions are hard to come by—they tend, of course, to live further south. He succeeds instead in shooting a donkey, whose owner, an old woman from Alsace, belabours him with her umbrella until her husband arrives and agrees to take massive over-payment for the animal. For a while Tartarin is distracted from his quest by Baïa, a woman he accepts (mistakenly) as the exotic eastern creature of his dreams. When at last he sets off again, after a month of searching he finds and shoots what turns out to be the tame, blind and holy lion he met once before with its keepers. In order to pay the large fine which the local authorities impose on him he has to sell all his equipment. He is left with only the lion's pelt and a loyal but melancholy and unsaleable camel which refuses to be left behind. But soon all is well again. The hero sent the lion-skin home, as promised, to his friend Bravida. As a result Tarascon and the whole of the Midi believes that he has killed not one but innumerable lions and he returns to a huge and triumphant reception. Even the camel, which he has persistently tried to shake off but which has followed him for so long, confirms his adventurous credentials. ("For a moment Tarascon thought its Tarasque had come back.") By the time he reaches his house he is beginning to tell the story of his great hunts "in the depths of the Sahara".

Daudet claimed that he received hate-mail from inhabitants of Tarascon who felt themselves dishonoured by this local "hero". He also irritated some of his fellow southerners by his insistence that everything they say is interspersed with redundant cries of "autrement"—"otherwise"—which they comically pronounce "autre*main*". And he endeared himself even less to many with his smiling, faux-naïf declaration, when talking about how Tartarin got his reputation, that "the man from the Midi does not lie, he is mistaken. He doesn't always tell the truth, but he thinks he is telling it... His particular lie isn't a lie, but a sort of mirage"—an effect of the southern sun which makes everything look bigger. But then, Daudet can say in his defence, he himself is exaggerating. In *Histoire de mes livres* he goes on, in part-apology, part-continued mockery, to exaggerate the reaction of the good people of Tarascon to his work: every morning, from every shop-entrance and every window, come the same angry fists, the same flashing of black eyes, the same shout of rage in the direction of Paris: "Oh, if ever that Daudet comes down this way..." But in fact, he says, the Tarasconnais should not feel singled out for unjust treatment: he chose Tarascon just because when he heard the name called at the station it rang out, more than any other, "like the cry of an Apache warrior". The place he was really talking about in *Tartarin* was, he maintains, his native Nîmes.

In one respect Daudet had evidently come too close to Provençal reality. Originally, when the book was published in parts in *Le Figaro*, Tartarin had been called Barbarin and there were vociferous complaints from a real Barbarin family. (Daudet clearly found this name, which replaced the even earlier Chapatin, suitably comic.) But the author did not capitulate completely. In *Le Figaro* the unreliable Grégory, allegedly prince of Montenegro, who later robs Barbarin, misremembers him at one point as "Tartarin". Therefore in the revised version he misremembers him as "Barbarin", drawing the reader's attention to the name, or the change of names, and perhaps cocking a final snook at the complainers.

Aptly for a character who thrives on his completely unjustified reputation, the fictional character has a real "Maison de Tartarin" in Tarascon. (It opened to the public in 1985.) Here are carefully realized his garden of exotic plants; his study full of weapons, with the marvellously absurd notice warning "Poisoned arrows, don't touch!"; the scene in which Mme Bézuquet, the pharmacist's mother, plays the "duet" from Meyerbeer's *Robert le Diable* where Tartarin's stirring contribution, "with arm stretched out, clenched fist, trembling nostril", is the repeatedly thundered word "Non!" (pronounced "*Nan*"). By the stairs and on the landing are "a real zebra skin", says the label, a python-skin, an eagle, and a crocodile. The house also displays illustrations, reviews of theatrical and cinematic versions of the *Tartarin* books, postcards and posters.

Tarascon: the Château du Roi René

For Henry James the outside of the castle is "severely feudal... bare and perpendicular ... It has, above all, an extreme steepness of aspect; I cannot express it otherwise. The walls are as sheer and inhospitable as precipices." As James Pope-Hennessy says, the exterior is "imposing and functional—a solid, yellow, square-built edifice with fat turrets at the four corners, castellations, machicolated galleries...; it seems a castle in some miniature illustration to the chronicles of Froissart." It does not feature much in *Tartarin de Tarascon*: it is too large and dominant to fit with the quintessentially small town Daudet creates.

As befits the unwelcoming outside, this has been a place of violence and constraint. Shells have pocked and pitted the stone towards the river-bridge. In 1794 Robespierre's local partisans were thrown from the broad high terrace at the top of the castle—where in more peaceful times can be enjoyed wide views of the Rhône, Beaucaire castle, wooded hills and more distant mountains. The castle was used as a prison from the seventeenth century to 1926 and in several rooms prisoners' graffiti survive: both written inscriptions and detailed pictures of sailed and oared ships, a chessboard, and a lover's heart. Some of the prisoners were English seamen, captured in war or lesser disputes in the eighteenth century. One inscription is by "John Wallters Taken in the Constantine Privateer of Bristol on the 19th Day of February. Landed on the Island of Minorca the 9th Day of March. Brought to Toulon the 28th. Brought to the Castel Tenth Day of April 1747."

The château was built, on the site of earlier fortresses, mainly by King René's father, Count Louis II of Provence, in the early fifteenth century. It was designed to police the Rhône, the western border of

Provence. René completed it, however, as a civilized setting—behind the exterior military might—for his court. Today little is left of the décor of his palace. There are busts of René and his wife Jeanne (lacking his face and half her head) and some painted decoration on the roof-beams of the Salon du Roi: gold stars and floral patterns, horses, lions, long-snouted dragons. The written records of the festivities which took place in René's Tarascon are much more detailed.

Over several days in June 1449 René presided over "The Joust of the Shepherdess". Knights fought for the fantasy heroine played by a young noblewoman, Isabeau de Lénoncourt, who first appeared with her sheep on the river-island of Jarnègues (now part of Tarascon). Louis de Beauvau, one of the knights, describes her appropriately pastoral but refined costume in his verse account of the proceedings: she wore "figured damask, a very fine grey, not too dark, well lined and fringed with fur" and a scarlet hood. She carried a crook, but a crook decorated with fine silver, and a small silver keg to drink from. Her knightly "shepherds", also bearing crooks, baskets and other shepherdly equipment when they first appeared, wore gold-embroidered grey. The king, other sources show, made his entry in a doublet of green damask with black breastplate.

After much ceremony the jousting began. Beauvau gives us some breaking of lances but, like René in his courtly treatise "on the form and the device of a tournament" (c. 1444), seems more particularly interested in the symbolic costumes and accoutrements of the jousters and their horses, for example the black, gold and blue ostrich feathers on the armoured frontlet of the charger of Tanneguy Duchastel, Grand Seneschal of Provence. After the last combats all assembled at the castle, where the Shepherdess, amid courteous speeches and trumpet fanfares, handed over the prize jewel to Ferri de Lorraine in the presence of his father-in-law, King René. The lady danced with the winner, food and wine were brought in, and eventually the lords and ladies took their elegant leave of the king and queen.

Beaucaire

Tartarin de Tarascon, brave though the Tarasconnais have long imagined him to be, is not keen on the idea of crossing the bridge to Beaucaire: that "devil of a bridge" is knocked about by the wind; "it is so long, so weak, and the Rhône at this point is so broad…Tartarin de Tarascon preferred terra ferma."

Some people have been more intrepid. Hannibal is said to have crossed the river at this point on a bridge of boats as he proceeded from Spain to Italy. Later visitors include the lords of Provence who gathered, in 1174, for a great festival at the castle (built in the eleventh century; it would be extended in the thirteenth). They were celebrating the reconciliation of the King of Aragon and the Duke of Narbonne, which had been brought about by Henry II of England. The kings and duke were not present, but, says the Latin account of Geoffrey of Vigeois, the lords found ways to honour them and to do it *inaniter*—inanely, foolishly. The inanity consisted in lavish largesse to knights, ploughing land near the castle and sowing money instead of corn, and some more inventive oddities: Guillelmus Gros of Martello is supposed to have cooked all the food in the kitchen by means only of wax and pitchpine torches. Raymond of Vernoul, Geoffrey assures us, burned thirty horses *causa jactantiae*—"because of a boast". The medievalist Linda Paterson points out that Geoffrey may be exaggerating—he was biased against Provence and all its ways—but if stunts like Raymond's did occur they were regarded as examples of "the spirit of *foudrat*, deliberate foolishness or whimsicality".

Beaucaire also had a less eccentric reputation as the home of a court which welcomed troubadours. Perhaps because of this association, it is one of the main settings for the early thirteenth-century French romance *Aucassin et Nicolette*. Aucassin, son of the Count of Beaucaire, is hopelessly in love with Nicolette, a slave who eventually turns out, unsurprisingly, to be the daughter of the king of Carthage. She returns his love and both suffer much woe. Despairing searches for each other are punctuated by frequent imprisonment and escape until at last Nicolette arrives back in Beaucaire, disguised as a minstrel, and announces a song to Aucassin, now Count, as he sits before the castle listening to the birdsong and thinking of his love. Her topic will be Nicolette's (her own) undying love for Aucassin—effectively the tale re-told, the listener directed to savour it again—and soon they are reunited.

The castle was also famous in the same period for its involvement in the double siege of 1216, during the Albigensian Crusade in which mainly northern French armies sought not only to extirpate the Cathar heresy but to subjugate the south more generally. When the townspeople of Beaucaire declared their loyalty to the Counts of Toulouse, the "young Count" Raymond (the future Raymond VII) moved into the town. The castle garrison, however, held out in support of the crusaders, whose leader Simon de Montfort was absent in the north. For three months Raymond's forces besieged the castle and Simon's forces (he soon returned to take charge), outside the town, tried to prise them out. In the end Simon, until then regarded as invincible, withdrew in exchange for the garrison's safe passage—but without their weapons and horses—out of Beaucaire. The siege is vigorously narrated, chiefly from the Toulousain point of view, in the second part (1227) of the Occitan *Canso de la crotzada.*

In later centuries Beaucaire castle remained a useful stronghold. In 1633 Cardinal Richelieu took the precaution of partly demolishing it following the defeat of the rebel who had seized it, the Duc de Montmorency. What was left remained a picturesque backdrop to the annual July fair which had flourished in Beaucaire since the Middle Ages. By the eighteenth century the fair was attracting possibly as many as 30,000 people and had spilled over from the fields between the castle and the river to dominate the town, increasing its population from 4,500 in 1651 to 7,400 in 1709 and hugely inflating the price of accommodation. The Chevalier Forton, whose history of the town was published in 1836, not long before the fair began at last to go into decline, points out some of the advantages of its position: "the Rhône provides easy access for merchandise from Burgundy, Switzerland and Germany" as does the Mediterranean, only seven leagues away, for goods from Italy, Spain and the Levant. The Canal du Midi brings people in from Bordeaux and down the Atlantic coast from Brittany—and sometimes Britain—and the newer canal between Beaucaire and Aigues-Mortes allows yet another approach. "The principal goods for sale," Forton says, are "groceries, hardware, haberdashery, silk and wool fabrics, ... drapery, cotton, every sort of leatherwork" and jewelry. Other accounts add wine and foodstuffs, perfume, horses, toys.

Doubtless the fair was also, as the anonymous "galante" novella *La Foire de Beaucaire* (1708) observes, an excellent place for finding lovers. And there was a fairly good chance, amid the milling crowds and multiple distractions, of being robbed. The commercial traveller who narrates Stendhal's *Mémoires d'un touriste* (1838) has been trying hard to understand what a fellow visitor is saying to him in Catalan when he discovers that the contents of his pocket have vanished. But with so much to see or, in a "street" whose walls are made up entirely of strong-smelling onions and garlic, to flee, he does not let the loss unduly distress him. Porters stagger under enormous burdens borne on their heads; there are people selling figs, plums, rosaries; singers "gesticulate and bawl" to the accompaniment of a horn and a double bass.

There is silence only where the waxwork figure of Napoleon on his death-bed at St. Helena is displayed, silence in the moments before the proprietor's assistant announces to his respectful (and gullible) audience that he can show them the very handkerchief which the emperor used to bind around his head. The living and as yet unvenerated Napoleon himself was in Beaucaire in 1793. The forceful young artillery officer's pamphlet, *Le Souper de Beaucaire* (1794), is set at the fair, where a transparently Napoleonic character, "Le Militaire", lays down the law to a Marseillais whom he meets there. Bonaparte was serving with the army which had just occupied Beaucaire and Tarascon, having driven the Marseillais forces, who were in rebellion against the Republic, out of Avignon. The unfortunate Marseille man in *Le Souper* is lectured by the soldier and two Languedociens; but any ill-feeling is dissipated when, after the "debate", they consume several bottles of champagne. The Marseillais, of course, pays.

Fontvieille and Daudet's *Lettres de mon moulin*

"A windmill for flour, situated in the Rhône Valley, in the very heart of Provence, on a hill wooded with pines and ilex; the said mill having been abandoned for over twenty years" and no longer able to function, overgrown as it is with wild vines, moss, rosemary, and other parasitical verdure which extend right to the end of the sails. "This notwithstanding," goes on the deed of sale which opens Alphonse Daudet's *Lettres de mon moulin* (1869), Monsieur Daudet "declares that he finds the said mill suitable for him" and for his "poetic labours".

Near Fontvieille the "Moulin de Daudet" can be visited. Daudet manuscripts, illustrations and mementoes are shown on the lower floor. But he composed the *Lettres* mainly in Paris and visited "his" mill—the deed of sale is of course fictional—while staying with his wife's cousins at the nearby Château de Montauban. And the mill he had in mind was the Moulin de Tissot, not the similar one his admirers later purchased, the Moulin de St.-Pierre. Some people, perhaps because they have taken the naïve tone of some of the tales at face value, find these facts disappointing. But the *Lettres* are not an account of life in a windmill. It, and various Provençal traditions and stereotypes, function more often as points of departure, motifs, ways of linking a series of largely unconnected stories. Frost around the mill makes Provence briefly a northern land where the pines are fringed with rime, and so the story-teller writes two "prose ballads" of appropriately "Germanic fancy". Unable to sleep as the mistral noisily shakes the damaged sails, he is reminded of the time when he lived in a lighthouse in Corsica.

The windmill does feature more directly in the introductory sections. In the "Installation" the narrator takes possession, meets his "silent lodger" (the owl that lives on the upper floor), enjoys the quiet of the pine-wood, and watches sheep being brought down from the mountains for the winter—all part of a world to be contrasted with a Paris of "newspapers, cabs and fog". "Master Cornille's Secret" is also set at the mill, back in its working days. Old Cornille has been a miller all his life, but when a Parisian company builds a large steam-mill on the road to Tarascon people desert him and the other traditional millers. For a week he rushes round madly, warning anyone he meets that "steam is an invention of the devil", whereas he, Cornille, works only with the winds—"the *tramontane* and the mistral, which are the breath of the good Lord." Then he locks himself up in his mill. Nobody brings him their corn. But soon everyone is surprised to see the sails turning and, in the evenings, the miller going along with his donkey loaded with what appear to be bulging sacks of flour. Eventually it is discovered that there is no corn or flour in the mill: nothing but a few bags of plaster and rubble. Cornille has proudly tried to keep up appearances. Discovered, he is in despair. But the local people take pity on him, abandon the steam-mill, and bring him their corn once more. Only at his death does the windmill stop production and decline gradually into its state in the *Lettres*.

Daudet includes a great variety of other stories, and narrative voices, in the rest of the volume. Frequently human follies are exposed, but it is lightly, genially done. As Zola noted, the jokes are good-humoured, there is no real bitterness, nothing too "crudely sarcastic". There are tales of simple human observation, almost like Maupassant if a little more sentimental. "L'Arlésienne" economically and movingly explores unhappy love. A young man cannot marry the woman of the title once he learns that she is involved with another man. After a time he seems cured of his love, happily joining in the celebrations for the feast of St. Eloi, to his parents' relief. But next morning at dawn he throws himself to his death from an upper window. We are left with a terrible, realistic *pietà*, where it is the mother, who ran after him from her bed, who is naked: "in front of the stone table covered with dew and with blood... the mother, completely naked, wailed with her dead child in her arms." "L'Arlésienne" is based quite closely on the events leading up to the suicide of Daudet's friend Mistral's nephew in 1862, as described to him by Mistral. (As Roger Ripoll points out in the authoritative Pléiade edition of Daudet's works, there is no truth in the tradition that Mistral objected to the material being used.) Daudet later turned this unusually intense piece into a play, for which Georges Bizet provided a now better known overture and incidental music.

There are Provençal landscapes—the powdery hot white road in "Les Deux auberges", the windmills in action in Cornille's time—and animals including the resident owl and rabbits, cranes and bittern in the Camargue, the Pope's mule (see pp.13-15) and the anthropomorphized but obstinately goatish goat in "La Chèvre de M. Seguin". There is a visit to Mistral, fast becoming a symbol of Provence. The diversity of the book reflects its origins as a sporadic series of newspaper pieces. Possibly the links would be even looser without the presumed editorial contribution of Paul Arène to some of the stories. Daudet first mentioned his involvement in 1883, and this gave rise to accusations of dishonesty, but Arène himself said that he provided only a few details of colour and style. Daudet's wife Julia was also involved in the editorial process.

It is difficult to typify such a various collection, but one tale which illustrates a fair number of its qualities is "Les Trois messes basses". A seventeenth-century chaplain is so gluttonously anxious to enjoy the grand Christmas meal to be served at the château that, with encouragement from a devil in the form of his young clerk, he rushes at extreme and irreverent speed through all of the three low masses he must say. He eats so much at the feast that he dies. He had no chance to repent of his ways. When he arrives at the gate of heaven God tells him that his punishment is that he must return to say his masses each Christmas for three hundred years. His flock, whom he led astray, must also attend. A local wine-grower witnesses the ghostly gathering in the ruined chapel, all that is left of the château. In the first part of the story especially, bright surfaces, rich tastes, succulent dishes, evidently point in the direction of excess but are not made disgusting. They are unspoilt by the coming moral. The morality, too, is palatable—tempered by the folkloric elements and atmosphere. Geniality is maintained; there is nothing very frightening about the ghostly masses, which are as much "a singular spectacle" for the wine-grower as a dire warning. The costumes of the congregation are old and faded but picturesque and even amusingly old-fashioned. The witness is particularly delighted to see one of the dignitaries in difficulty because one of the birds who usually lives in the ruins has become entangled in his high black wig.

St.-Michel-de-Frigolet

Monks first came here from Montmajour in the tenth century. The church and cloister of St.-Michel survive from the twelfth century, as does the domed chapel of Notre-Dame-du-Bon-Remède. Anne of Austria, Louis XIII's queen, was one of many pilgrims who sought the Marian remedy on offer. In her case the problem was her failure to provide a desperately needed male heir to the throne. When at last the future Louis XIV was born in 1638 (to be king only five years later) the grateful mother had the chapel embellished with gilded wooden panelling and pictures.

After the Revolution the abbey fulfilled various functions, including a hideout for smugglers and an illicit gambling-den. It housed the rather ramshackle boarding-school attended by Frédéric Mistral in 1839-41; the pupils spent much of the time, according to Mistral's memoirs, running wild among the rocks and thyme, stunted almond-trees and asphodels. They would roll in the thyme, pick mushrooms, set traps for small birds, search for the mythical treasure of the Golden Goat, and wear out their clothes sliding and climbing and tumbling about. In bad weather they charged about the cloisters, played hide-and-seek in the abandoned church of St.-Michel and even went into the open vaults full of monkish skulls and bones. This semi-scholastic interlude came to a rapid end when the only young woman in the establishment, a servant from Tarascon, became pregnant. The cook left when he was, rightly or wrongly, accused of responsibility. The woman left too and so did the underpaid teachers. The proprietor, M. Donnat, was, as usual, away looking for pupils or money; his old parents held the fort until the food ran out and then told the pupils they would have to go. The better-organized Premonstratensians or White Fathers moved in in 1858. But the fathers were expelled in 1880, provoking the comical siege in Daudet's *Port-Tarascon* (1890), where Tartarin and the Tarasconnais occupy the abbey of "Pampérigouste" in defence of the monks but are starved out by the army after a fortnight. Tartarin's longing for his morning cup of chocolate is a factor in their defeat.

The nineteenth-century monks incorporated Notre-Dame-du-Bon-Remède in the larger and more controversially decorated abbey church. This is not unfairly characterized, by the authors of *Provence: Art, Architecture, Landscape* (1999), as "a gothic fantasmagoria, overflowing with crenellations and turrets". The church is, for the more excitable Paul Mariéton (*La Terre provençale*, 1890), painted, illuminated, Byzantine, multicoloured, garish; inevitably contrasts with the simpler medieval survivals have continued to be made.

The smooth functioning of divine office in the fictional equivalent of the great abbey church is interrupted in Daudet's story "L'Elixir du Révérend Père Gaucher", in *Lettres de mon moulin*. Father Gaucher arrives late and is observed, to his colleagues' consternation, plunging his arms and sleeves deep into the holy water, bowing to the organ instead of the high altar, and wandering about for five minutes as he tries to locate his stall. He is, increasingly obviously and outrageously, drunk. He caps his performance by breaking, in the midst of the Ave Maria, into a rather different song beginning "In Paris there is a White Father,/Patatin, patatan, tarabin, taraban." But this is no neglectful sot of a monk, no whisky-priest, for what has made him drunk is the liqueur he distils, sales of which have redeemed the abbey from ruin; before the surprise brainwave of the then Brother Gaucher, the burly, seemingly slow-witted monastery cowman and figure of fun, the buildings were crumbling, the monks lived on water-melon, and the abbot's woollen mitre was embarrassingly moth-eaten.

The liqueur, wonderful stuff, "green, golden, warm, sparkling, exquisite", is the occasion for Daudet's story: the curé of Graveson begins by carefully, lovingly pouring the narrator a sample. It is so wonderful, of course, because it includes, following the recipe of mad old "aunt Bégon" who brought Gaucher up, fine local Provençal herbs, perfumed, sunned, and probably not rolled in by young Mistral and his friends. This is particularly apt in a place whose very name derives from *ferigoulo*, a Provençal word for thyme. (About thirty herbs, among other ingredients, go into the real liqueur now produced at Châteaurenard.) Herbs have long been used here for palliative as well as palate-pleasing ends. But Gaucher's problem with his "elixir" is that he needs to taste it in order to check that the finish is velvety enough, and cannot resist taking more. When he is inebriated he remembers, and cannot stop singing, Bégon's ribald songs. Worse, he thinks he will be damned for such irreligious behaviour. All this is seen as the punishment for the pride he takes in his potion, but the senior monks are very keen that he should go on distilling nonetheless. The Prior has an ingenious solution, but the dangers are still there, as the curé of Graveson becomes ruefully aware: bursting, in effect, out of the frame of the tale, he contemplates the awful prospect of his parishioners hearing the vigorous rendering of Gaucher's song he has just given—perhaps under the effects of the elixir as much as the requirements of the story. "Patatin, patatan": it is the sort of song which has little intention of ending.

Maillane: "Happy lizard, drink your sun"

Frédéric Mistral was born at the Mas du Juge, just outside Maillane, in 1830. The farm and the village remained central to his identity and imagination for the rest of his life. In 1851 Mistral came home to the Mas after completing his studies in Aix. His father told him that he was free to choose his course in life and, bolstered by that assurance, "there and then", he says in his memoirs,

> with my foot on the threshold of the paternal Mas, with my eyes turned towards the Alpilles, in myself and for myself, I made this resolution: first, to raise up and revive the sense of race which I saw being reduced to nothing at the hands of the false, unnatural education practised in every school; second, to instigate this revival by

> restoring the natural and traditional language of the land, against which all the schools were waging war unto the death; third, to make Provençal popular once again by the influx and the flame of divine poetry.

Mistral admits that he did not really formulate these idealistic sentiments so clearly at the time, but certainly he felt confident enough to begin his own metaphorical "war unto the death".

Full of love for his homeland, "one evening during sowing-time, as I watched the ploughmen following the ploughs along the furrows and singing as they went, I started, God's be the glory, the first canto of *Mireille.*" The tone may strike readers now as immodest, but Mistral was looking back after more than forty years at the genesis of a work widely regarded as the first great victory of, as emblematic of, the whole Provençal movement. He worked gradually at the long poem (*Mirèio* in Provençal), a story of doomed love set in the Crau, Les Baux and the Camargue and making extensive use of local customs and legends. At the same time he took over the running of the farm under the direction of his eighty-year-old father, who was now blind. The two activities went well together. "This poem of Provence" was all around him at the Mas du Juge; he saw Mireille go past every day, "not only in my young man's dreams, but also in person" in the girls who came to gather mulberry-leaves for the silkworms, hoed, made hay, picked grapes or olives. "From dawn to dusk the actors of my drama, my ploughmen, my reapers, my cowmen and my shepherds... were moving about."

In 1855, when Mistral's father died, an elder half-brother inherited the Mas and the poet and his mother moved into a smaller but substantial house in Maillane itself. It was known as the Maison du Lézard in honour of the lizard he had had carved on the front of the house, above a sundial and a verse inscription encouraging readers—and himself—to seize the day: "Happy lizard, drink your sun:/Time passes only too quickly/And perhaps tomorrow it will rain." Here he profited from this advice by finishing *Mirèio* (1859). At the time of the visit described by Daudet in "Le Poète Mistral" (in *Lettres de mon moulin*) he had nearly completed his next Provençal epic, *Calendau* (1867). Daudet's experience of the Maison du Lézard probably fuses several such visits in the early and mid-1860s and aims to promote *Calendau* and—

furthering the same aim—to show the Parisian reader the newly famous poet at home. For the man who had come "to show Paris to his Mireille"—a man in a tight collar and inconvenient high hat—was not really Mistral. Here, in his "little one-storey house with garden in front", he is to be found in his felt hat, afire with inspiration, as he paces about composing. Describing the poet's study, Daudet strikes the balance between the homely and the intellectual so often sought in accounts of the *félibres*: the yellow check sofa and straw chairs, casts of the Venus of Arles, a painting and a photograph of the poet, a small desk overflowing with old books and dictionaries. His old mother, who speaks only Provençal, works away in the kitchen and produces a fine traditional meal including roast goat, mountain cheese, muscatel grapes, and Châteauneuf du Pape. Daudet has the opportunity not only to hear and read and marvel at the new poem but to go to the Maillane fête with its processions, banners, wooden saints, bells, bulls, games of strength, and joyously danced *farandole*.

In 1876, when Mistral married a woman twenty-seven years younger than himself, the couple moved into a newly built house just across the road. This would become his monument, the Museon Mistral. The rooms remain as they were at his death in 1914. His tomb in the village cemetery, built several years before his death, is a copy of the small, highly decorated sixteenth-century structure near Les Baux known as the Pavillon de la reine Jeanne. The tomb is crowned by a cross but the Provençal associations of the pavilion were more interesting to Mistral than the religious: he believed that there "the princesses of Les Baux held their courts of love."

Uzès

Soon after his arrival in Uzès in the autumn of 1661 Jean Racine had his first encounter with olives on the tree. He picked some splendid looking specimens, put them in his mouth and, he told his friend the fabulist La Fontaine, could not rid himself of the bitter after-taste for four hours. It was a painful way to discover that only after much cleansing and processing do olives become edible. He was also, more pleasantly, surprised by the taste of olive oil; in northern France everything was cooked in butter. At first he liked much else about Uzès. Fine nights in January 1662 had him sending verses to his friend Vitart concluding "Et nous avons des nuits plus belles que vos jours." ("And we have nights more beautiful than your days.") He found the people courteous. He found the women attractive, but felt he must not dwell too much on such matters since he was living with his uncle, Antoine Sconin, Vicar-General of the diocese, who hoped to obtain a benefice for him.

For a time it seemed likely that Sconin would succeed, and although with hindsight it seems clear that Racine was much better qualified to write tragedy than he would have been to participate in the politics of southern churchmanship, he would have accepted a suitable position. (This would not, of course, have ruled out some kinds of literary career; his royal marriage ode "La Nymphe et la Seine" was well received in Uzès.) Sconin, however, had his enemies and turned out not to be as influential as he had imagined. The job did not materialize and the small town soon began to taste as bitter as the olives. The letter which praises winter nights in verse also, in prose, complains about "accursed" Uzès, a place full of faction where if you make one friend you make a hundred enemies. Here malice and self-interest are everywhere, declares Racine in a rather hyperbolical letter to his friend the Abbé Le Vasseur. (To some extent, all his remarks about Uzès, favourable or unfavourable, are epistolary or literary *jeux d'esprit* rather than considered opinions.)

In May 1662 Racine told Vitart about the case of a girl who had poisoned herself with arsenic after a quarrel with her father. Everyone assumed she must have been pregnant, but the autopsy revealed otherwise. In Racine's opinion, this suicide for some more trivial cause was typical of "the disposition of the people in this region", how they "portent les passions au dernier excès." But clearly his own nature was as much of a problem as that of the fiery Uzétiens: he told Le Vasseur in July that he would like to write a play but was in no spirits to do so with such cause to be melancholy in Uzès. Throughout his year there he remained eager to hear as much news as possible from the literary world of Paris—to which he returned, with relief, in the autumn of 1662.

In André Gide's childhood, in the 1870s and 1880s, Uzès seemed scarcely less remote than in Racine's day. "The progress of the century seemed to have forgotten the little town," says Gide in his autobiography *Si le grain ne meurt*. When he came on family visits from Paris the railway took them only as far as Nîmes; they completed the journey, he remembered, in some old boneshaker of a carriage, crossing the river

The Tour Fenestrelle. In Uzès Jean Racine encountered faction, passions taken to excess, and nights more beautiful than northern days.

Gardon into a different world, "Palestine, Judaea", where purple and white cistus and lavender grew in the "rough *garrigue*" and "enormous grasshoppers suddenly unfolded their blue, red or grey membranes— light butterflies for an instant" before blending, drab once more, back into the undergrowth and stones. Racine may have been happy to get back to Paris, but for Gide it is only unfamiliarity which keeps the northerners away: "if only you were in Umbria," he tells Uzès, "tourists would come running from Paris to see you." In modern times they have come running, mainly to see the Duché, the ducal residence with its partly-eleventh century keep and elegant 1550s facade designed by Philibert Delorme. And the chic Place aux Herbes, with its vaulted archways, became well known as one of the settings in Jean-Paul Rappeneau's 1990 film of *Cyrano de Bergerac*.

Gide mentions the "shaded gardens of the Duché" on the steep slope of the rock of Uzès, but his particular passion was for the surrounding *garrigue*. He wandered there whenever he could, turning stones to wonder at "hideous scorpions, millipedes and centipedes". But in Uzès too, early forms of life were still flourishing. Strict Protestants, linked with Gide's forebears, lived on, "formes... quasi paléontologiques de l'humanité" which still seemed normal in a place where the memory of past persecution remained fresh. Another sort of ancient survivor was his grandmother, unchangingly old, it seemed to him, from year to year, always knitting stockings but never finishing them. "She knitted all through the day, the way an insect would" and tucked her needles behind one ear. Although she herself hardly ate, she continually feared that her visitors were not getting enough food. She was not convinced that four courses were enough at a sitting and her daughter-in-law, Gide's mother, was for ever intervening to prevent the equally ancient servant from buying too much.

Grandmother would surely have been pleased, while hoping also for some stouter comestibles, at what Elizabeth David found in the market at Uzès, even on a cold February day, in 1984: "good creamy firm-fleshed potatoes", goat's cheeses and ewe's milk cheeses, "little round, crisp, bronze-flecked, frilly lettuces, baskets of *mesclun* or mixed salad greens, great floppy bunches of chard, leaf artichokes, trombone-shaped pumpkins... fat, fleshy red peppers, new laid eggs, eight or nine varieties of olives in basins and barrels, thick honey and clear honey."

Appendix:

Some Other Places of Interest

Aix-en-Provence. The collections of the poet St.-John Perse (1887-1975)—library, manuscripts, letters to Gide, Giraudoux, Breton and others—are in the Fondation St.-John-Perse, at the Cité du Livre. The Fondation Vasarely was designed, and houses work, by the kinetic artist Victor Vasarely (born 1908). The Pavillon de Vendôme was built in 1664-7 and extended in the eighteenth century; the Aix-born painter Jean-Baptiste van Loo (1684-1745) lived here in his last years after a successful career in Paris and London.

Ansouis. The medieval part of the château was the home of the fourteenth-century saints Elzéar de Sabran and his wife Delphine, who took a vow of chastity. The less saintly lovers Dido and Aeneas appear in the Flemish tapestries of the seventeenth-century banqueting-hall.

Apt. Even at Paris, the Abbé Boze was proud to note in his 1813 history of Apt, "on estime la finesse et la transparence" of the sweets and jams made here. Since much earlier times St. Anne, the Mother of the Virgin, has been venerated at Apt. Tradition says that when the future Emperor Charlemagne visited the cathedral on Easter Day 776 a deaf, blind and mute boy rolled about and scratched at the floor. Digging revealed a forgotten crypt where would be found, the miraculously cured boy declared, the long-lost body of the saint.

Avignon. John Stuart Mill (1806-73) and his wife Harriet (1807-58), formerly Harriet Taylor, are buried in St.-Véran cemetery. An inscription by Mill salutes "her great and loving heart, her noble soul, her, clear, powerful and original comprehensive intellect... Were there but a few hearts and intellects like hers this earth would already become the hoped-for heaven." Also buried here are Théodore Aubanel and the naturalist Esprit Requien.

The Chapelle des Pénitents Noirs, extensively restored in the eighteenth century, served the confraternity specializing in care for mental illness. On the façade the head of St. John the Baptist is borne heavenward by small angels. "The interior, in which white and gold predominate... seems at first sight more like a salon" than a church (*Provence and the Côte d'Azur*, edited by Marianne Mehling, 1984).

Ile de la Barthelasse (between Avignon and Villeneuve): "As you roll down its narrow willow-fringed roads you have the sudden illusion of being in Normandy... Cows graze peacefully in green fields. Yes, it is a landscape by Corot" (Lawrence Durrell, "Laura, a Portrait of Avignon", 1961).

Bagnols-sur-Cèze. Antoine Rivarol (1753-1801), satirist, wit, and author of *Discours sur l'universalité de la langue française* (1784), was born here. The museum is named after Albert André (1869-1954), friend and disciple of Renoir, and contains many of his paintings as well as work by Matisse and Bonnard.

Barbégal. "The Roman mill that once covered the hillside at Barbégal is the largest surviving powered industrial unit in the classical Mediterranean world" (James Bromwich). Partly surviving aqueducts brought water, from Eygalières and Maussane, to turn the sixteen mill-wheels. Bromwich notes that recent estimates point to daily production of two or three tonnes a day rather than the twenty-eight once accepted, feeding not 80,000 people but a still impressive 10,000. The model in the Musée de l'Arles Antique makes it all look a more practical proposition than is easy to imagine, now, among the ruins and rocks of this peaceful site.

Barbentane. The elegant late seventeenth-century château reminds Roland Pécout (*Itinéraires de Van Gogh en Provence*) of one of the mansions of Aix transferred to the country. The fourteenth-century keep of the earlier castle, the Tour Anglica, also survives.

Barjols. James Pope-Hennessy (*Aspects of Provence*) gave his impression in the early 1950s: "By trade Barjols is a town of tanneries, and it is partly the effect of the weather-board warehouses and little factories of these, partly the abandoned quality of the rocky but leaf-laden scenery, that reminds you, at first sight, of a town in southern Norway."

Boulbon has a castle of c.1400 and the Romanesque cemetery chapel of St.-Marcellin.

Brignoles. The thirteenth-century summer residence of the Counts of Provence houses the Musée du Pays Brignolais. John Locke observed in the 1670s that here are grown the best "Prunellas... or brignols": plums gathered when "thorough ripe", skinned, and stuck on "scuets about six inches long and very slender" to dry.

Calanque de Port-Pin, near Cassis, is one of the locations used in *The French Connection* (1971).

Cavaillon. The town possesses a small Roman arch, the mainly fourteenth- and seventeenth-century former cathedral of St.-Véran, and the Romanesque and sixteenth-century Chapelle St.-Jacques. The rococo synagogue of 1772-4 includes, on the ground floor, the Musée Juif Comtadin. Cavaillon is also famous for its melons; Dumas *père* recalls, in his *Grand dictionnaire de cuisine*, how he agreed to give the municipal council the many volumes of his complete works for their new library, on condition only that in exchange he must receive, annually, a dozen of the "frais, savoureux et sapides" Cavaillonnais melons.

Châteaurenard. The title-character of Mistral's *Nerto* (1886) is the daughter of Baron Pons, lord of the castle here. (Two prominent towers survive on the hill.) Pons has sold his daughter's soul to the devil; learning of this, she seeks a pardon from the (schismatic) Pope Benedict XIII, who is under siege in Avignon. Nerto enables his escape, and wins her reward, by telling him about the long, legendary tunnel connecting "your Trouillas tower/And the castle on the horizon."

Digne. The interior of the cathedral of St. Jérôme (1490-1500) is described by Elsie Whitlock Rose (*Cathedrals and Cloisters of the South of France*, 1906) as "large and sumptuous, with the munificence of a Veronese canvas, a singular and most curious contrast to the cold severity of its outer walls." Like many people, Rose prefers the simplicity of the basilica of Notre-Dame du Bourg, begun in the thirteenth century. The town is the setting for early scenes in Hugo's *Les Misérables* and for Pierre Magnan's detective novel *Le Sang des Atrides* (1977), the first of the Commissioner Laviolette series.

Fontaine-de-Vaucluse. The Musée d'Histoire 1939-1945 looks at resistance and collaboration.

Forcalquier has the ruins of a medieval citadel, a Romanesque and Gothic former cathedral, and a former Franciscan convent with vaulted scriptorium.

Ganagobie. The Benedictine priory church contains early twelfth-century mosaics with an inventive variety of winged, looped and clawed monsters.

Gordes. The mid-sixteenth-century château houses works by Victor Vasarely. A village of *bories* (stone huts) has been rebuilt outside Gordes; the examples here date from the sixteenth to eighteenth centuries, but the design has been in use since much earlier times.

Graveson. The museum, in a former mill, shows paintings by Auguste Chabaud (1882-1955).

Gréoux-les-Bains. If the lime-trees, green grasses and refreshing waters around Gréoux do not cure all the "frenzies" of modern life, Jean Giono will, "as the Englishman says, eat my hat" (*Reflets de Provence*, 1953).

Malemort-du-Comtat. The republican *félibre* Félix Gras (1844-1901) was born and is buried here, and part of his best known novel *Li Rouge dóu Miejour* (*Les Rouges du Midi*, 1896) is set here.

Manosque. Apocalypse murals by Jean Carzou (1907-2000) are at the Fondation Carzou.

Marseille. The Palais Longchamp is "a garishly wonderful palace that houses natural and manmade history [the natural history museum and the Beaux-Arts]... It is almost nightmarish at close hand, like being lost in a foetal Disneyland", but beautiful from afar (M. F. K. Fisher, *A Considerable Town*, 1978).

The church of St. Vincent de Paul, known as Les Réformés, is for Fisher "typically Marseillais, in its tongue-in-cheek bravura, for although it looks pure northern Gothic of about the thirteenth century, it was... dedicated in 1867. It still remains impressive: plainly an ecclesiastical joke, but not a shoddy one... [I]t is noble as well as subtly prankish, a fitting comment on the street it dominates," La Canebière.

The neoclassical 1770s Château Borély was the country house of one of the richest merchant families in Marseille. Between 1863 and 1989 it housed the archaeological museum now at La Vieille Charité.

Gordes

Mazan, near Carpentras. Sixty-two Gallo-Roman sarcophaguses are in the churchyard at Notre-Dame-de-Loup. The château, which is not open to the public, belonged to the Marquis de Sade (See p.161)

Montfavet, near Avignon. The fortified Gothic church, Notre-Dame-de-Bon-Remède, is all that remains of a fourteenth-century monastery. The sculptor Camille Claudel (1864-1943), sister of Paul Claudel and lover of Auguste Rodin, is buried in the cemetery at Montfavet. For nearly the last thirty years of her life she was incarcerated in a mental hospital nearby.

Nîmes. The Musée des Beaux-Arts includes works by Rubens and Fabritius, and Bassano's dramatic *Susannah and the Elders* (1585). Paul Delaroche's *Cromwell Viewing the Coffin of Charles I* (1831) was condemned by some contemporary critics for its lack of emotion, but the imaginative Heinrich Heine claimed almost to hear Cromwell's thoughts—harsh words, "peevishly snarled and hissed" in "that English dialect which is like the distant rumble of the sea and the shrill cries of the storm birds."

Oppède-le-Vieux. In *Oppède* (1945) the sculptor Consuelo de Saint-Exupéry, wife of Antoine de Saint-Exupéry, tells the story of the community of artists, students and refugees which occupied the deserted village during the Second World War.

Pernes-les-Fontaines. Late thirteenth-century frescoes at the Tour Ferrande show Charles I of Anjou invested as King of Sicily, the battle of Benevento which he won, and the legendary hero Guillaume d'Orange (see pp.36-7, 173-5) with the giant Isoré.

Pont Van Gogh is a reconstruction, on the canal 3 kilometres from Arles, of the Langlois bridge painted by van Gogh in 1888.

Port-St.-Louis-du-Rhône, on the Rhône and the Golfe de Fos, is no longer easily recognizable as Roy Campbell's "little shanty town with its air of having been built yesterday out of broken jam tins" (*Broken Record: Reminiscences*, 1934).

St.-Blaise has the remains of a settlement of the Avatici tribe, rebuilt on a grid pattern in the third century BC and captured by Roman forces probably in 125 BC. Hellenistic defence walls, some houses, and a Romanesque chapel can be seen.

St.-Chamas. Just south-east of St.-Chamas is the Pont Flavien, a one-arch limestone bridge over the river Touloubre built in the early first century AD and named after the man who paid for it, Flavos or Flavius, priest of the Imperial Cult. There are arches at either end— one an eighteenth-century replacement, as are three of the four lions which, as Roy Campbell puts it, "the mistral has by now eroded and sand-papered into the thin shapes of greyhounds" (*Light on a Dark Horse*, 1951).

St.-Pons, in woodland near Gémenos, was founded as a Cistercian convent in 1205 and abandoned in the early fifteenth century.

St.-Rémy. St. Martin is an imposing white neoclassical church, with dome and huge Ionic columns, built in 1821-5 to replace its collapsing medieval predecessor. Pope-Hennessy thinks it "a grandiose, unsuitable construction." Charles Gounod sometimes played the organ here during his visit of 1863, while he was working on the operatic version of Mistral's *Mireille*. In 1913 the fiftieth anniversary of the opera was commemorated by a bust of Gounod in the small garden (and *terrain de boules*) behind Notre-Dame-de-Pitié, and a plaque and flamboyant relief at the Hôtel d'Almeran-Maillane. More wittily, a painted Gounod leans on a painted rail in place of an upper window at the Hôtel Ville Verte, where he wrote much of the work.

St.-Roman, near Beaucaire, has the ruins of a partly troglodytic medieval abbey and sixteenth-century fortress.

Sanary. Aldous Huxley wrote *Brave New World* at a villa near here (the misspelt Villa Huley) between April and August 1931.

Saumane-de-Vaucluse. The Marquis de Sade spent part of his childhood in the fifteenth-century château (closed to the public) with his uncle, the Abbé de Sade. After the sale of La Coste he lived here again for a time in 1797.

Sénanque. The Cistercian abbey was founded on a remote site in 1148. The twelfth- and thirteenth-century cloister and church have survived mostly intact. In September 1976 James Lees-Milne observed here "strikingly pure Romanesque architecture, Benedictine rather. Empty church sad. The clean precision of architectural lines deeply impressive. Smell of mortality in the nave" (*Through Wood and Dale: Diaries 1975-1978*). After various expulsions and absences monks returned in 1989.

Sérignan-du-Comtat. The entomologist Jean-Henri Fabre (1823-1915)

Sénanque: 'strikingly pure Romanesque architecture...
The clean precision of architectural lines deeply
impressive' (James Lees-Milne).

lived and worked at the Harmas J.-H. Fabre from 1879. (*Harmas* is the local term for an area of rough fallow land.) Having managed to acquire an education in Avignon in spite of an unpropitious beginning selling fruit at Beaucaire fair, he taught in schools in Carpentras and Avignon. Later he taught in Corsica, where there were ample opportunities for him to develop his interest in flora and fauna. The first instalment of his *Souvenirs entomologiques* was published in 1878 and his keenness of observation was admired by Darwin. He was also accomplished as a *félibrigien* poet. At Sérignan are shown Fabre's collecting equipment and specimens, and editions of the works.

Silvacane. The abbey church and cloister, undecorated, as at Sénanque, in accordance with the Cistercian rule, were built in 1175-1230 and about 1250-1300. The fine rib-vaulted refectory dates mainly from the fifteenth century.

Simiane-la-Rotonde. The "Rotunda" is a domed Romanesque keep. What was once the upper storey may have been used as either a living area or an audience-chamber.

Sisteron. Paul Arène (1843-96) was born here, wrote his novel *Jean des Figues* (where Sisteron becomes "Canteperdrix"), and is buried in the cemetery. The town is dominated by its huge citadel, mainly of the sixteenth and seventeenth centuries but on a site used for defensive purposes since pre-Roman times.

Sivergues. In Henri Bosco's *L'Habitant de Sivergues* (1935) the narrator meets the last surviving descendant of local Huguenots.

La Tour d'Aigues. A twelfth-century castle was replaced, in 1566-77, by a Renaissance château which, according to a wondering contemporary (quoted by Jean-Paul Clébert, *Mémoires du Luberon*), was endowed with strength, wealth, "a sumptuous and spacious *jeu de paume* [real-tennis court], fine ponds, parks, gardens, warrens, meadows, dovecots, mills, mazes, walks, and a splendid *pallemart* alley." (*Pallemart*, more usually *paille maille*, was a game in which a wooden ball was knocked though an iron ring with a mallet— English "pall mall".) What remains after the fires of 1782 (accidental) and 1793 (revolutionary) includes the west front with its emphatically classical entrance portal.

Toulon. "Yesterday we went to Toulon [from Bandol] in the bus—a port, all sailors and cats and queer people—not unattractive," notes D. H. Lawrence. Earlier visitors commented mainly on the town as a port and naval centre and, as at Marseille, on the life of the galley-slaves. In *Les Misérables* Jean Valjean escapes from captivity here by diving under a boat. Toulon is still an important naval base.

Vacqueyras. The Festival des Crus de la Vallée du Rhône takes place here in July. The troubadour Raimbaut de Vaqueiras (flourished 1180-1205) was born here. He worked mainly in Italy and went on crusade with his friend and patron Boniface of Montferrat.

Valréas. This was the main town of the "Papal Enclave"—land owned by the Papacy from 1317 until 1791. The town hall was, as the Château de Simiane, a home of Mme de Sévigné's granddaughter, Pauline de Grignan, and her husband the Marquis de Simiane.

There are several memorials to the fifty-three people who were shot by German soldiers in Valréas on 12 June 1944.

Vauvenargues. Pablo Picasso bought the seventeenth-century château and its 2,000-acre estate (not open to the public) on the slopes of Mont Sainte-Victoire in 1958, worked here until 1961, and was buried here in 1973. "Its noble proportions and its rugged surroundings reminded him of a Spanish *castillo*, and its remoteness promised to make it the refuge he had dreamt of, far from the frivolities of Cannes" (Sir Roland Penrose, *Picasso: his Life and Work*, 3rd edition, 1981).

Venasque, which gave its name to the Comtat Venaissin, has an interesting twelfth-century building (re-using some ancient columns), of unknown function but traditionally described as a baptistery. The church is twelfth- and thirteenth-century with later additions.

Vernègues. There are remains, in the grounds of the Château-Bas estate, of a first-century BC Gallo-Roman temple and a twelfth-century chapel.

Further Reading

John Ardagh, *Writers' France: a Regional Panorama*. London: Hamish Hamilton, 1989

Donna Bohanan, *Old and New Nobility in Aix-en-Provence 1600-1695: Portrait of an Urban Elite*. Baton Rouge and London: Louisiana State University Press, 1992

James Bromwich, *The Roman Remains of Southern France: a Guidebook*. London and New York: Routledge, 1993

Pierre Citron, *Giono, 1895-1970*. Paris: Editions du Seuil, 1990

Jean-Paul Clébert, *Mémoires du Luberon* [1984]. Lyon: Aubanel, 1995

Jean-Paul Clébert (ed.), *Histoires et légendes de la Provence mystérieuse* [1968]. Paris: Sand, 1986

Dickens on France, ed. John Edmondson. Oxford: Signal Books, 2006

John Edmondson, *Traveller's Literary Companion to France*. London: In Print, 1997

A. Trevor Hodge, *Ancient Greek France*. Philadelphia: University of Pennsylvania Press, 1998

Prosper Mérimée, *Notes de voyages*, ed. Pierre-Marie Auzas. Paris: Hachette, 1971

Michelin Guide de Tourisme: Provence (1997); translated as *The Green Guide: Provence*. Michelin Travel Publications, 4th edition, 2000

Roland Pécout, *Itinéraires de Van Gogh en Provence*. Paris: Les Editions de Paris, 1994

Ronald Pickvance, *Van Gogh in Arles*. Metropolitan Museum of Art, New York, 1984

Ronald Pickvance, *Van Gogh in Saint-Rémy and Auvers*. Metropolitan Museum of Art, New York, 1986

Georges Poisson, *Guide des maisons d'hommes célèbres: écrivains, artistes, savants, hommes politiques, militaires, saints*. Paris: Pierre Horay, 1982. [Occasional women feature, in spite of the title.]

James Pope-Hennessy, *Aspects of Provence* [1952]. Harmondsworth: Penguin, 1988

Laura Raison (ed.), *The South of France: an Anthology*. London: Cadogan, 1985

Donna F. Ryan, *The Holocaust and the Jews of Marseille: the Enforcement of Anti-Semitic Policies in Vichy France.* Urbana: University of Illinois Press, 1996

Letters of Vincent van Gogh 1886-90: a Facsimile Edition, ed. Jean Leymarie. London: Scolar Press, 2 vols, 1977.

Index of Literary & Historical Names

Index of Places & Landmarks